Critical praise fo

'Marjorie Mayo has added anoth
tribution to her wide-ranging canon on the struggles for
ordinary people's and communities' empowerment. This
powerful book provides an analysis of how they can respond
to globalization – over key issues such as debt, gender rights,
education and poverty – and examples of how they have done
so.' – *Gary Craig, Professor of Social Justice, Hull University,
and President of the International Association for Community
Development*

'In clear and accessible language, Mayo brilliantly outlines
key theoretical debates about globalization, democracy and
social movements, linking them to concrete case studies of
citizen action. In so doing, she poses and explores critical
contemporary issues of how to build sustainable challenges
to global power through grassroots action. This book is a
must for all of those seeking to understand how to build
progressive movements for human rights and social justice in
the twenty-first century.' – *John Gaventa, Institute of Development Studies, University of Sussex and co-editor Global Citizen
Action*

About the author

Dr Marjorie Mayo is Head of Professional and Community
Education at Goldsmiths College, University of London.
Educated at St Hilda's, Oxford, the London School of
Economics, and South Bank University, she is the author
and editor of numerous scholarly books in the fields of
community action and adult education. Her single- authored
books include *Imagining Tomorrow: Adult Education for Trans-
formation* (NIACE, 1997), *Cultures, Communities, Identities:
Cultural Strategies for Participation and Empowerment* (Mac-
millan, 2000), and (co-edited with Gary Craig) *Community
Participation and Empowerment: A Reader in Participation and
Development* (Zed Books, 1995).

MARJORIE MAYO

Global Citizens

Social movements and the challenge of globalization

CSPI

Canadian Scholars' Press Inc.
TORONTO

Zed Books
LONDON · NEW YORK

Global Citizens: Social movements and the challenge of globalization was first published by Zed Books Ltd, 7 Cynthia Street, London N1 9JF, UK and Room 400, 175 Fifth Avenue, New York, NY 1010, USA in 2005.

www.zedbooks.co.uk

Cover designed by Andrew Corbett
Set in Monotype Dante and Gill Sans Heavy by Ewan Smith, London
Printed and bound in Malta by Gutenberg Press Ltd

Distributed in the USA exclusively by Palgrave Macmillan, a division of St Martin's Press, LLC, 175 Fifth Avenue, New York, NY 1010

A catalogue record for this book is available from the British Library.
US CIP data are available from the Library of Congress.

ISBN 1 84277 138 8 cased
ISBN 1 84277 139 6 limp

First published in Canada in 2005 by Canadian Scholars' Press Inc., 180 Bloor Street West, Suite 801, Toronto, Ontario M5S 2V6

www.cspi.org

Canadian Scholars' Press gratefully acknowledges financial support for its publishing activities from the Government of Canada through the Book Publishing Industry Development Program (BPIDP).

Library and Archives Canada Cataloguing in Publication
Mayo, Marjorie
 Global citizens : social movements and the challenge of globalization / Marjorie Mayo.
Includes bibliographical references and index.
ISBN 1-55130-294-2

 1. Social action. 2. Globalization. I. Title.
HM881.M39 2004   361.2   C2004-907288-9

Canadä

Contents

Acknowledgements

Many people have assisted with this project, giving generously of their time, despite being so busy themselves. I am particularly grateful to the following for providing materials and insights and/or for commenting on chapters in draft:

David Archer, Jean Besson, Frederique Boni, Tony Burdon, Nick Buxton, Roger Chisnall, Liana Cisneros, Richard Constant, Nick Dearden, Martin Drewry, Emanuel Fatoma, Martin Goodman, Ben Jackson, Ann Jellama, Joe Hanlon, Kate Hudson, Marion Kozak, Lucy Matthew, Ed Mayo, Andrew Murray, Nici Nelson, Ines Newman, Kate Newman, David Norman, Sheela Patel, Ann Pettifor, William Price, Michael Seifert, Jan Shaw, Trevor Sinclair, Claire Slatter, Michael Taylor, Viviene Taylor, Jane Wills and Jessica Woodroffe.

Many thanks to them all. Any remaining errors or misinterpretations are, of course, down to me.

Many thanks, too, to Goldsmiths for giving me a sabbatical term – and to colleagues in the Department of Professional and Community Education, especially Andy Gilroy, for adding my workload to theirs, over that period to enable me to finish the draft.

Finally, special thanks to Robert Molteno and Anna Hardman, at Zed, for providing invaluable advice and support.

Marjorie Mayo

Abbreviations and acronyms

ACHR	Asian Coalition for Housing Rights
AFL	American Federation of Labor
AMA	Association of Metropolitan Authorities
CBO	community-based organization
CIO	Congress of Industrial Organizations
CND	Campaign for Nuclear Disarmament
CUT	Central Unica dos Trabalhadores
DATA	Debt, AIDS and Trade in Africa
DAWN	Development Alternatives for Women for a New Era
GATS	General Agreement on Trade in Services
GCE	Global Campaign for Education
HERE	Hotel and Restaurant Employees
HIVOS	Humanist Institute for Co-operation with Developing Countries
IAF	Industrial Areas Federation
ICEM	International Federation of Chemical, Energy, Mine and General Workers' Unions
ICFTU	International Confederation of Trade Unions
IMF	International Monetary Fund
IPA	Institute of Public Affairs (Australia)
IUF	International Union of Food and Allied Workers and Agricultural Workers
MAI	Multilateral Agreement on Investment
MST	Movimento dos Trabalhadores Rurais Sem Terra
NGO	non-governmental organization
NSDF	National Slum Dwellers' Federation
OECD	Organization for Economic Co-operation and Development
PRSP	poverty reduction strategy paper
PT	Partido dos Trabalhadores
REFLECT	Regenerated Freirian Literacy through Empowering Community Techniques
REPEM	Red de Educacion Popular Entre Mujeres de America Latina y el Caribe
SCCD	Standing Conference for Community Development
SCF	Save the Children Fund

SDI	Shack/Slum Dwellers International
SEIU	Service Employees International Union
SEWA	Self Employed Women's Association (India)
SPARC	Society for the Promotion of Area Resource Centres
TJC	Trade Justice Campaign
TJM	Trade Justice Movement
TNC	transnational corporation
TRIPs	Trade Related Intellectual Property Rights
TUC	Trades Union Congress
UFCW	United Food and Commercial Workers
UNCHS	United Nations Committee on Human Settlements
UNDP	United Nations Development Programme
WFTU	World Federation of Trade Unions
WTO	World Trade Organization

to Scarlet and Clyde

Introduction

By the turn of the twenty-first century, the significance of global networks and social movements had gained widespread public recognition. Reflecting on its Millennium Campaign on Third World Debt, Jubilee 2000 argued: 'The world will never be the same again' as a result of this global people's mobilization, developing new North–South solidarity (Jubilee 2000), challenging the negative effects of globalization through citizen action, mobilizing people of all faiths and people of no faith, academics, pop stars, trade unionists and businessmen, boxers and artists, young and old, black and white, organizing in solidarity beyond the state, to transform global agendas.

The emergence of global citizen action has been widely recognized as having become key to the discourse and practice of democratic politics and social change. As Gaventa has argued, through 'community organizations, social movements, issue campaigns, and policy advocacy, citizens have found ways to have their voices heard and to influence the decisions and practices of larger institutions that affect their lives' (Gaventa 2001: 275). This global associational revolution has been seen as potentially 'as significant to the latter twentieth century as the rise of the nation-state was to the latter nineteenth century' (Salamon, quoted in ibid.).

As the United Nations Development Programme *Human Development Report* (1999) argued, 'Globalization is not new. Recall the early sixteenth century and the late nineteenth. But this era is different' with new markets, new tools (including the Internet), new rules and new actors, including the World Trade Organization (WTO), multinational corporations and 'global networks of non-governmental organizations (NGOs) and other groups that transcend national boundaries' (UNDP 1999: 1). The last decade of the twentieth century represented a turning point for capitalist globalization, it has been argued, and perhaps a turning point for humanity, as the World Trade Organization 'opened its doors for business (the ambiguity is intended)' in 1995 and the Organization for Economic Co-operation and Development (OECD) began to plan a Multilateral Agreement on Investment (Sklair 2002: 272). As Sklair went on to point out, 'the scope and level of organization and the ferocity of opposition on the streets in sites of resistance all over the world to various manifestations of capitalist globalization caught the pundits by surprise' (ibid.).

The emergence of organized resistance on the streets of Seattle in 1999 should not have been so surprising, however. Seattle was not the beginning of the anti-globalization upsurge, which had already been developing outside the United States, in Venezuela, South Korea, India and a dozen other countries (Katsiaficas 2001). While the movement had begun in other Western countries too (including Germany), protests against capitalist globalization had absolutely not been limited to relatively privileged 'masked anarchists' and students from rich countries, the 'usual suspects' according to various media representations. On the contrary, as the World Development Movement demonstrated, North American and European mobilizations were 'only one element of a much larger movement rooted in developing countries – showing that the fiercest critics of IMF (International Monetary Fund) and World Bank policies were the people most affected by them' (World Development Movement 2002: 4).

The demonstrators themselves were not necessarily the poorest of the poor, however. They included potentially broad coalitions of teachers, civil servants, priests, doctors, public-sector workers, trade-union activists and owners of small businesses, as well as poor farmers, indigenous peoples and the unemployed. Reporting on subsequent mobilizations in 2001, the World Development Movement pointed out that there had been protests in twenty-three countries, involving millions of people protesting about the global causes of their problems, causes rooted in the policies promoted by the IMF, the World Bank and the WTO. These policies were being blamed both for keeping the poor in poverty and for impoverishing wide sections of society, including those generally considered key to development. The *World Development Report* provided examples of these protests, ranging from strikes by students, teachers and the unemployed in Argentina, to public servants' strikes and riots in Zimbabwe (by way of Brazil, India, Mexico, Nigeria, Pakistan, South Africa, South Korea and Turkey).

The sheer breadth of these mobilizations against capitalist globalization has been key to their potential strength and effectiveness. Anti-globalization mobilizations had demonstrated 'the possibility of a deepening global alliance of workers, students, farmers, youth, indigenous people, immigrants and "marginals" whose potential', it was argued, was 'most alarming to the capitalist globalizers' (Yuen 2001: 7). Conversely, however, this breadth has presented its own challenges. It was not simply that there were differences of tactics, such as whether or how far to employ varying forms of direct action: the differences were more fundamental. The political Left was finding itself mobilizing alongside sections of the far Right. In the USA itself, there has been a history of politicians of the Right supporting small farmers, and business people arguing against international treaties that promote free trade. Discussions around the WTO, it has been argued, transcended 'the old borders between the left and the right' (Krebbers and Schoenmaker 2001: 212).

Anti-globalization has been described as a populist rather than a class-based movement – or perhaps more accurately as populist 'movements' rather than one single movement – including populisms of the Right as well as populisms of the Left (O'Connor 2001). In the USA and Europe, populisms of the Right have included extreme nationalist and overtly racist movements. These have included anti-Semitic mobilizations as well as mobilizations against refugees and asylum-seekers, especially refugees and asylum-seekers of colour, from the South.

There have been similarities with Right populisms in the South, which have included nationalist as well as fundamentalist movements. These movements have not necessarily been socially inclusive, let alone concerned with gender-equality agendas. Right populists in the South, however, have been characterized as anti-imperialist, while this has not been the case among Right populists in the North (ibid.).

There have been differences, too, in relation to the roles played by NGOs, organizations that have been seen as having gained unprecedented political influence following events in Seattle (Davis 2001). NGOs have been seen as doing vital work around the globe, promoting development, social justice and human rights. They have made valued contributions, including the provision of research to mobilizations against neoliberalism in policy programmes and in practice. For the media, it has been suggested, 'NGOs and protesters are virtually interchangeable and synonymous' (ibid.: 176).

To their critics from the Left, however, the roles played by NGOs may not be entirely benign. NGOs can be used as contractors to provide services, covering for gaps that emerge when public provision is being reduced – as a result of the cutbacks produced by the neoliberal economic policies in question. Most significantly, according to the critics, NGOs could be used to provide a 'responsible' leadership 'who could then negotiate on behalf of the hordes and diffuse the movement while recuperating it' (ibid.: 177). NGOs with profile and organizational ability, Davis argues, have been in a position to seize opportunities to gain places at negotiating tables, opportunities that could be used for varying ends, to promote the interests of the movement, or to promote the

NGOs' own brand and/or NGO careerists, whether these are careerist professionals or the careerist celebrities who provide brand endorsement. 'It could go either way' (ibid.: 182). Individuals and organizations make more – or less – well-informed choices, but they do not make their choices in a vacuum. As Marx argued in a much-quoted passage, men (and women) do make their own history, but they 'do not make it just as they please: they do not make it under circumstances chosen by themselves' (Marx 1968: 98).

The developing roles of NGOs need to be seen in the wider context of debates on the changing role of civil society more generally. While appreciating the radical changes that have placed civil society more centrally in international policy debates and global problem-solving over the past decade, Edwards, among others, has also cautioned that this is 'a highly contested debate in which questions abound and answers are in short supply. In reality civil society is an arena, not a thing, and although it is often seen as the key to future progressive politics, this arena contains different and conflicting interests and agendas' (Edwards 2001: 1). As Deakin has also pointed out, 'by definition, transactions and relationships which are located in the civil society arena take place on terms not wholly dominated by the state in its various forms or by the values or procedures of the market' with varying perspectives on 'the different type of engagement – close or distant – with the state on one side and the market on the other' (Deakin 2001: 7). From whichever perspective, Deakin continues, 'the boundaries of the space in which civil society activities take place are permeable' (ibid.). Like civil society more generally, NGOs are under pressure to become (literally) more 'businesslike', more formally/bureaucratically organized and more professionalized, if they are to be effective, working with international agencies and governments, in the context of capitalist globalization. But if NGOs become too 'businesslike' they risk losing legitimacy with those whose interests they set out to advance through the pursuit of transformatory agendas for social justice and human rights.

Similarly, as has already been suggested, global social movements may pursue regressive as well as progressive goals, just as they may lead to the incorporation of protest, rather than the challenging of social injustice (Castells 1997; Morris 1996; Mayo 2000). And global citizen action may be developed and led by professionals (often Northern professionals) with careers in the 'poverty' or the 'environmental' business, speaking on behalf of those directly affected in the South. Democratic accountability is potentially problematic at the global level, as well as, if not more than, at the local level, and global social movements are similarly faced with the challenge of how to represent diversity and difference effectively. Even the tools of direct democracy, such as referenda, are skewed, when big money, those with the greatest resources, dominate media debates (Cronin 1989). 'We may dream of a global community, but we don't yet live in one, and too often, global governance means a system in which only the strong are represented and only the weak are punished. Resolving these deficiencies is the essential task of the twenty-first century' (Edwards 2001: 1).

This book sets out to explore the context for anti-globalization movements and their potential implications for active global citizenship, for social justice, human rights and social transformation based upon new forms of solidarity between North and South. How can the history and contemporary development of this 'globalization from below' be explained in terms of critical theoretical debates on globalization, the changing relationships between the state, the market and civil society and theories of social movements more generally? What insights can be gained from community and progressive movement organizing, at local and national levels? And how can campaigning organizations and networks, NGOs and community-based organizations (CBOs) learn from such experiences of mobilizing for human rights and social justice in ways that are both democratically representative and accountable and effective, at the global level?

My personal interest in exploring these questions comes from my own experiences of community organization and development and adult, community-based learning at different levels, both in theory and in practice. These have been the dilemmas with which community organizers and development workers have been grappling at local level and beyond, dilemmas that have taken on increasing significance with the rediscovery of 'civil society' and renewed policy emphases on the 'third/not-for-profit sector', active citizenship, community participation and empowerment. Clearly, as Gary Craig and I suggest in a previous publication, community participation and empowerment are becoming 'more vital and yet more overtly problematic in the current global context' (Mayo and Craig 1995: 1). In this context, it is challenging enough for local community-based organizations to be effective in addressing immediate needs while building genuinely inclusive, democratically accountable campaigning organizations, resisting pressures for the incorporation of protest while working in partnership structures and developing wider alliances for social change.

To tackle these challenges globally seems even more problematic, but this is precisely what an increasing number of global social movements are doing. Building upon experiences of campaigning on the environment and on human rights issues, together with experiences of Southern-based campaigns, global social movements are developing their own critical analyses of capitalist globalization, taking on issues such as world debt and trade, directly linking the local with the global. This, it has already been suggested, is the background to the events that captured media interest in Seattle in 1999. It is these underlying challenges that are the subject of this book, which focuses on strategies to build effective, socially inclusive and democratically accountable alliances for social transformation globally.

The following chapters draw upon interviews with activists, advocates, campaigners, policy-makers, professionals and academics as well as policy researchers from a range of groups, organizations and movements, spanning the public, voluntary/NGO and trade union and community sectors. In addition, I attended a number of the events discussed in subsequent chapters, including NGO sessions at the World Summit on Social Development in Copenhagen in 1995 and the recall event in Geneva in 2000. I also participated in others, including one of the events linked to People to People exchanges and several of those supporting the Jubilee 2000 campaign. Many people provided information and added their own interpretations, sharing their enthusiasms and commitment, and their generosity is deeply appreciated.

Chapter 1 starts by exploring differing definitions and perspectives on 'globalization'. This is set in the context of debates on neoliberal economic policy agendas, as these have been developed in the 'post-Washington consensus'. Globalization has been presented by international organizations such as the World Bank as the only viable development strategy. In contrast, the critics whose work has informed so many global citizens' mobilizations have been exploring capitalist globalization's responsibilities for perpetuating inequality and indebtedness for the world's poorest people.

In addition, as has already been suggested, globalization has been linked to major shifts in governance and social policy, with changing roles for NGOs and CBOs, whether as active participants in the residualization of social policy or, conversely, as agents pressurizing supranational bodies on issues of social justice, social integration and equality (Deacon et al. 1997). Globalization has also been debated in terms of the globalization of culture, media and communications, similarly posing new challenges while opening new opportunities for communicating and indeed campaigning at the global level.

Chapter 2 takes up these themes of governance and the changing role of civil society. In the aftermath of the collapse of socialist states, at the end of the 1980s, state-led development strategies were widely seen as discredited; the market, it was argued, was the only possible alternative ('the end of history' thesis). Civil society needed to be strengthened, from this perspective, as a counterbalance and future guarantee against excessive state power.

In contrast, as has already been suggested, critics argued that the state, the market and civil society were far from being separate spheres. Neoliberal agendas were restructuring governance and impacting upon civil society, both locally and globally. How far, then, were strategies to promote 'capacity-building' and 'social capital' actually strengthening progressive democratic organizations and social movements? Or were these increasingly at risk of being colonized by capital itself, in the context of globalization? Chapter 2 concludes by exploring key implications for civil society (including NGOs, CBOs and social movements), together with key implications for strategies for 'capacity-building' and for the development of 'social capital' at the global as well as the local level.

Chapter 3 moves on to explore differing approaches to the study of social movements, locally as well as globally. Social movements have been analysed in terms of rational action/rational choice theories, together with resource mobilization and political process theories and in terms of the new social movement theories, the latter having been more prevalent in European than in North American debates (Della Porta and Diani 1999). In summary, the first approach has tended to equate people's participation in social movements with the pursuit of their own individual and/or group self-interest (an approach that would be consistent with neoliberal assumptions about human actors as rational consumers, although some theorists have developed resource mobilization and political process approaches from a more radical, political economy perspective). The latter approach, in contrast, has tended to focus upon new social movements as precursors of social transformation (often – although not necessarily – posed in libertarian socialist and/or postmodernist terms). More recently, social movements theorists have become increasingly concerned to cross-fertilize their ideas and to apply insights from both European and North American approaches to the analysis of global social movements, as these have been developing, historically and more recently over the last decades of the twentieth century and the beginning of the twenty-first (McAdam et al. 1996; Crossley 2002). Subsequent chapters draw upon insights from these more recent debates in particular.

Chapter 3 concludes by focusing on examples of international movements and campaigns on the environment and human rights. These range from campaigns with far-reaching agendas for social transformation, to those described as 'protest businesses' – organizations preoccupied with their own survival (Jordan and Maloney 1997). Unpacking these differences has increasing importance, given that there are wider opportunities (using information technologies) for movements to be effective at global level for better or for worse, depending upon the perspective, whether they are working for agendas of sustainable livelihoods, human rights and social justice or whether they are pursuing their own organizational self-interest – or even pursuing fundamentalist or socially abusive agendas (Castells 1997b).

Chapter 4 moves on to explore issues of structures and alliances for social change. Social networks and movements have been posited as representing alternatives, whether locally or nationally. In particular, new social movement theorists have contrasted their flexibility and direct democracy with the more bureaucratized structures of trade union organizations and political parties, characterized as pursuing traditional class politics in the old ways. In the new realities of the global context from the late twentieth century, it has been argued, new approaches are required (Laclau and Mouffe 1985).

Alternatively, it has been argued, the labour and trade union movement has a long, if problematic, history of international organization. In the current global context this is potentially more significant than ever. In particular, the fact that so many workers are not being organized in the workplace, because they are in marginalized, casualized employment, means that co-operation with community-based organizations and new social movements is more vital than ever (Waterman 1999). The trade union and labour movement has begun to recognize this, with increasing emphasis both on the need to develop global strategies in general and on the need to network and build alliances with new social movements, NGOs and CBOs more specifically.

Chapter 5 focuses upon a number of the issues already identified as the key dilemmas, opportunities and challenges for networks, campaigning organizations, NGOs and CBOs. This chapter also brings in insights and questions identified from community development and community education approaches. These include the following: how to be effective campaigning organizations without becoming over-bureaucratized/'protest businesses'; how to keep winning immediate gains to meet supporters' objectives and retain their support, without becoming – or at least being perceived as having become – incorporated, balancing the 'insider' and 'outsider' roles; how to build effective alliances while retaining independence from other organizations, including party political organizations as well as trade union organizations; how to learn from previous organizational experiences while developing ways of attracting newcomers, including those (especially many young people) who have found previous organizational approaches alienating; and how to work with diverse organizational cultures while ensuring effective democratic accountability and representation. Similar choices face networks, campaigning organizations, NGOs and CBOs operating at the local level; at the global level, as has already been argued, these pose even more problematic challenges. This chapter sets the specific framework for the discussion of the examples in subsequent chapters.

The first example, explored in Chapter 6, focuses upon networking based on concrete experiences of people-to-people exchanges, in different contexts. The chapter explores ways in which CBOs have been sharing experiences, and then reflecting upon these experiences, with a view to developing new and more effective ways of working. Through these international exchanges, CBOs have been enabled to share their learning and to support each other in campaigning at national level. This phenomenon is explored through homeless and landless people's exchanges, including the case of the Society for the Promotion of Area Resource Centres (SPARC), an Indian NGO working with homeless people, particularly women, the most vulnerable street dwellers. SPARC entered into a partnership with the National Slum Dwellers' Federation, and from that developed community exchanges in India, elsewhere in Asia and subsequently in South Africa and beyond, including Britain.

The focus of these exchanges has been upon empowerment and the development of earning within these organizations and federations, strengthening groups' capacity to work within their local environment, rather than on international policies and practices per se. Nevertheless, there have been wider implications and these have been fed back to donors and other agencies, internationally, both in the North and in the South.

Chapter 7 moves on from the exchange of experiences, to focus upon the development of alternative analyses and policies at global as well as local levels. In place of neoliberal agendas, these political economy-based alternatives emphasize holistic development, gender justice and freedom from discrimination and oppression. This chapter draws upon the case of Development Alternatives for Women for a New Era (DAWN).

DAWN is a feminist network of women activists, researchers and policy-makers from the South, committed to alternative approaches to economic development based on social justice, peace and freedom from all forms of oppression by gender and by class, race and nation (Taylor 2000). The network brings together shared theoretical analyses and experiences of policies in practice, country by country, and region by region and, on the basis of these, challenges global policies and campaigns for alternatives. DAWN's approach illustrates ways of building effective global lobbying on the basis of strong roots, supporting powerful theoretical analyses with empirical evidence collected locally, nationally and regionally, as part of campaigns to hold governments as well as international agencies accountable for their commitments (such as those on social development made at the World Summit on Social Development in Copenhagen in 1995). There are parallels with the approaches developed by other global campaigning organizations, and wider lessons, as subsequent chapters explore.

Chapter 8 draws on experiences of campaigning globally for rights to social welfare. In particular, the chapter explores the experiences of the Global Campaign for Education – a campaign based upon an alliance of international NGOs, working together with Southern NGOs, trade union organizations (including teachers' organizations) and campaigns around child labour. Like DAWN, the campaign has involved policy analysis and international lobbying, drawing upon evidence collected from monitoring at national level, and this has been rooted in local campaigning to hold governments accountable for commitments on education which they have entered into via international gatherings such as Jomtien in 1990 (when 155 governments promised education for all).

The Global Campaign for Education has been built on the experiences of NGOs such as ActionAID, developing participatory approaches to education, and addressing issues of equality and quality of provision as well as overall numbers enrolled. The campaign has raised key issues of global policy, including structural adjustment and Third World debt. It has also involved tackling issues of representation and accountability, while taking account of different organizational structures and cultures within this broad alliance, including trade union organizations as well as NGOs and CBOs.

Chapter 9 focuses on Jubilee 2000, which succeeded in building a major global campaign on an issue that might have appeared too abstract and too complex for any type of popular mobilization at all: global economic policy and Third World debt. In the space of four years, however, the campaign built a global coalition, based on a range of faith-based organizations as well as NGOs, CBOs and trade union organizations in both Northern and Southern contexts. While Jubilee 2000 represented a unique initiative, the campaign itself drew lessons from the experiences of previous international campaigns, including the movement to end slavery in the nineteenth century.

In 2001, representatives from Jubilee 2000 campaigns from both South and North met to evaluate their campaigns, to build on them, and to take the campaigning forward. The experiences of Jubilee 2000, as well as the experiences explored in previous chapters, have particular relevance for the questions explored in Chapters 4 and 5.

The final chapter, Chapter 10, reflects upon some of the issues raised in the previous chapters, taking account of the questions raised in Chapters 4 and 5. The chapter concludes by exploring the possible implications for building global solidarity, campaigning for human rights and social justice, combining democratic accountability and sustainability at global as well as local levels.

1 | Challenging globalization: developing alternative strategies

This chapter explores definitions and perspectives on 'globalization' and their varying implications for the development of alternative strategies. 'Globalization' itself is a contested term. As this chapter sets out to demonstrate, globalization bears different meanings and varying levels of significance, depending on the theoretical perspective underpinning the analysis in question. These are not simply semantic debates; different perspectives on globalization relate to differing and potentially competing political agendas, whether these agendas are pro- or anti-globalization in principle. As the Introduction suggested, mobilizations in Seattle, Prague and Genoa included protesters from the Right as well as the Left of the political spectrum, a blurring of the difference between left-wing approaches and right-wing approaches that led to considerable questioning and debate among anti-globalization activists and writers (Kessi 2001).

These debates have vitally important implications for the discussions of anti-globalization movements in subsequent chapters. The reader already familiar with these arguments about the nature of globalization and the impact of capitalist globalization, more specifically, may prefer to skip lightly over this chapter. In particular, the reader well acquainted with the criticisms of capitalist globalization, in terms of its effects on increasing poverty and social inequality worldwide, may choose to skip these sections.

Globalization has become a contemporary buzzword, but how new is it? In a much-quoted passage from the *Communist Manifesto*, in 1848, Marx and Engels described a number of key features that are typically considered characteristic of globalization in the twenty-first century. 'Modern industry has established the world market, for which the discovery of America paved the way,' they argued (Marx and Engels 1985: 81), going on to point to the constant processes of change inherent in capitalism, the 'everlasting uncertainty and agitation' that distinguish the 'bourgeois epoch from all earlier ones' (ibid.: 83). 'All fixed, fast-frozen relations, with their train of ancient and venerable prejudices and opinions are swept away, all new-formed ones become antiquated before they can ossify. All that is solid melts into air' (ibid.), a phrase that has been regularly quoted in the context of globalization and the increasing rate of economic, political, social and cultural change.

'The bourgeoisie', Marx and Engels argued, 'has through its exploitation of the world market given a cosmopolitan character to production and consumption in every country' (ibid.). So,

> in place of the old wants, satisfied by the productions of the country, we find new wants, requiring for their satisfaction the products of distant lands and climes. In place of the old local and national seclusion and self-sufficiency, we have intercourse in every direction, universal interdependence of nations. And as in material, so also in intellectual production. The intellectual creations of individual nations become common property. National one-sidedness and narrow-mindedness become more and more impossible, and from the numerous national and local literatures, there arises a world literature. (ibid.: 84)

In summary, according to Marx and Engels, the development of capitalist social relations was the key factor, leading to associated social, political and cultural changes on a global scale. The so-called McDonaldization of popular culture can be glimpsed in the future, along with the global popularity of Levi's jeans, Gap t-shirts, Hollywood movies and Starbucks coffee. Each of the features identified by Marx and Engels, the economic, political and social and cultural aspects, emerge in the discussion of more recent definitions of globalization.

Definitions and differing approaches

So what precisely is new about the notion of globalization? Not so much, some critics have argued. '"Globalisation" is an extension of the already existing power relationships in the world economy, in which the controllers of capital in the great powers seek to reinforce and intensify their exploitation of the rest of the world' (Murray 1997: 20). The novelty has been grossly overrated, it has been argued, by those who present globalization as an inevitable process, a juggernaut inexorably sweeping all before it (Hirst and Thompson 1996). 'Globalization', it has been argued, is a deeply ideological term. By implication, such critics have suggested, globalization is being defined as an irresistible contemporary process, a process portrayed as ultimately beneficial for humankind, or at least as inevitable.

Such a view of globalization has been characterized as 'globaloney' by critics who prefer to focus upon resistance, based upon alternative understandings, linked to fundamentally different political objectives and geared towards achieving very different policy outcomes. Before considering these critiques, however, the concept itself needs to be explored.

In established development discourse, definitions of globalization include a number of related features. The *World Development Report* produced by the World Bank for 1999/2000 (World Bank 2002) focuses on globalization in terms of technological advances in communication, which 'have made it possible to know in an instant what is happening in a household or factory or on a stock market half a world away' (ibid.: 4). Meanwhile, this report continues, in parallel with these advances in communication technology, multinational companies

> now rely on production chains that straddle many countries. Raw materials and components may come from two different countries and be assembled in another, while marketing and distribution take place in still other venues. Consumers' decisions in, say, London or Tokyo become information that has an almost immediate impact on the products that are being made – and the styles that influence them – all over the globe. (ibid.)

The products in question may be automobiles or items of clothing, but the globalization of the processes of design, manufacture and marketing may be comparable. There are parallels here with the factors identified by Marx and Engels, but with the emphasis upon technological advances in communications, rather than in the social relations of production per se.

With a similar emphasis upon capital and the social relations of production as well as an emphasis upon new technologies (including communication technologies) War on Want's website defines globalization as 'the way that world trade, culture and technologies have become rapidly integrated over the last 20 years, as geographic distance and cultural difference no longer pose an obstacle to trade. New technologies have increased the ease of global communication, allowing money to change hands in the blink of an eye.' Globalization, the website continues, involves

> the opening up of trade which allows goods and services to travel across the world more freely and increase in foreign investment – companies investing overseas by building plants, contracting subsidiaries or buying stock in foreign countries, the opening up of capital markets which increases the flow of money across the world, improved access to communication – from the development of new technology like the internet to cheaper plane tickets. (<http://www.globalworkplace.com>)

Summarizing the sociological literature on differing approaches, Cohen and Kennedy start from Albrow's definition of globalization as referring to 'all those processes by which the peoples of the world are incorporated into a single society, global society' (quoted in Cohen and Kennedy 2000: 24). Cohen and Kennedy then go on to identify six component strands of globalization:

- changing concepts of time and space
- an increasing volume of cultural interactions
- the commonality of problems facing all the world's inhabitants
- growing interconnections and interdependencies
- a network of increasingly powerful transnational actors and organizations
- the synchronization of all the dimensions involved in globalization

On the basis of the changes that have taken place in communications technologies this list starts from the impact of these changes on people's perceptions of time and space, the 'time–space compression', which has been speeded up so dramatically by the development of electronic media. The accompanying effects in terms of increasing cultural interactions have also been widely identified as key features of globalization: we live in a global village, it has been argued, albeit a global village which is effectively dominated by Western, and particularly US, cultural influences.

Globalization is not simply a matter of culture and communications, however. As the subsequent items in Cohen and Kennedy's list indicate, globalization is also defined in terms of increasingly interconnected problems, including problems of the environment – which cannot be confined within national borders – and problems of poverty and civil strife, which give rise to the mass movements of peoples, as refugees and asylum-seekers. These problems, in their turn, point to the economic and political dimensions of globalization, including the increasing power of transnational corporations, globally as well as locally. Their influence impacts on international organizations such as the World Bank, the International Monetary Fund and the World Trade Organization, as well as on national governments across the globe.

This links to debates about the changing role of the nation-state itself. As will be suggested below, one set of conclusions drawn from the increasing power of transnational corporations emphasizes the decreasing power of the nation-state – on its own, no national government can hope to influence, let alone control, the operations of transnational corporations. Total sales of major transnational corporations such as

General Motors, the Ford Motor Company, Mitsubishi and the Royal Dutch/Shell Group have exceeded the gross domestic product of nation-states (respectively Thailand, Saudi Arabia, Poland, South Africa and Greece) (UNDP statistics, quoted on War on Want website 2002). Half the largest economies in the world are transnational corporations, not nation-states (Cohen and Kennedy 2000). In an increasingly globalized context, it has been suggested, the nation-state has become, in many ways, redundant.

Alternatively, however, as will be suggested in more detail below, critics have also argued that the effective demise of the nation-state has been vastly overemphasized (Hirst and Thompson 1996). Nation-states, and particularly the most powerful nation-states and groupings of nation-states, can and do play key roles, too often facilitating the pursuit of the interests of transnational capital at the expense of the interests of labour and of the most oppressed and disadvantaged peoples, globally. So even in an increasingly globalized context, in which political mobilizations need to focus on international targets, the nation-state also needs to remain a key focus for strategies for social change.

Cohen and Kennedy conclude their discussion of definitions of globalization by exploring two related terms. 'Globalism', they suggest, quoting Albrow again, refers to 'values which take the real world of 5 billion people as the object of concern ... everybody living as world citizens ... with a common interest in collective action to solve global problems', consciousness of the world as a single entity, requiring common solutions to shared problems (Cohen and Kennedy 2000: 34). While this theme emerges powerfully in the subsequent discussion of global social movements, this has also been contentious from the perspective of those critics who emphasize the conflicting rather than the common interests between global capital and labour, between the most powerful and the most oppressed peoples worldwide.

The other term that Cohen and Kennedy explore in this context is that of 'glocalization'. Far from conceptualizing globalization as a one-way process, sweeping all before it, sociologists such as Robertson, for example, have pointed to its interactive features: the global is also affected by contact with the local. There are two-way processes at work here. Robertson has defined the dynamics of globalization in terms of the 'twofold process of the particularization of the universal and the universalization of the particular' (Robertson 1992: 177). One reaction to the apparent tendency towards cultural homogenization has been an increased emphasis upon ethnic cultures and indigenous peoples' artefacts (increasingly commodified as souvenirs, for the global tourist market). Alternatively, resistance may take the form of conservative cultural and/or religious movements, seeking to preserve an idealized past from the incursions of a globalized future. Subsequent discussions of global social movements include examples of this type, as well as examples of socially progressive global movements.

This makes it all the more relevant to distinguish between different approaches to globalization and their varying takes on what precisely needs to be challenged – if, indeed, anything does. This latter point needs to be emphasized because globalization has its admirers as well as its critics. From the neoliberal stance, after all, globalization is a positive phenomenon, representing the future, the way forward for humankind. Free-market economics, according to the neoliberals, offers the most effective strategies for economic development. Indeed, since the dissolution of the former Soviet Union and the demise of socialist states in Eastern and Central Europe, free-market economics represents the only viable strategy, from this perspective. In the Thatcher/Reagan-dominated 1980s, this approach was summarized by the slogan 'there is no alternative'. Or in the formula popularized by Fukuyama (1992), civilization had reached the 'end of history' by the end of the twentieth century, with the global triumph of free-market economics coupled with liberal democracy.

Neoliberal approaches

Neoliberalism started from what had been described as a 'tiny embryo at the University of Chicago with the philosopher-economist Friedrich von Hayek and his students – Milton Friedman amongst them – at its nucleus' (George 2001: 9). Neoliberalism took off from the 1970s and 1980s, as the long economic boom following the Second World War began to slow down and economic growth became more problematic. The neoliberal programme has been described as 'the way of handling this crisis' (Amin 2001: 19).

To summarize, the causes of this slow-down, according to the neoliberals of the Chicago School, were to be sought in the growth of state intervention, interfering with the operations of free-market mechanisms. As a result, resources were being drained away from productive investment to support ever-expanding state bureaucracies and inefficient public enterprises. Meanwhile, public services were increasingly being run for the benefit of self-interested professionals: the so-called producer culture that the neoliberals set out to replace with a consumer culture, based upon increasing competition to facilitate consumer choice. The solution, in summary, was to deregulate, to free market mechanisms and to roll back the state – the strategies broadly adopted by the Thatcher government in Britain and the Reagan government in the USA in the 1980s.

Neoliberal economic strategies were increasingly influential, too, at the international level, impacting upon a range of countries in the Third World in the South. Neoliberalism had become the new orthodoxy. Chicago School economists applied their solutions to particular economies (such as Chile after the military coup in 1973, which ended the Allende government's period of social reform). Neoliberal strategies were also applied via international organizations and agencies such as the World Bank, the IMF and, more recently, via the WTO, established in 1995.

The World Bank and the IMF had increasing influence, while the poorer countries of the South had less and less room for manoeuvre at this period, as prices for primary products fell in the 1980s, reducing their incomes from exports, just when they had taken on increasing liabilities, having borrowed heavily, when credit was relatively cheaper, in the 1970s (money they had been positively encouraged to borrow both by governments and international agencies). By the 1980s, when interest rates rose, many indebted countries in the South were forced to turn to the IMF and the World Bank for assistance. The IMF and the World Bank were therefore in particularly powerful positions to enforce neoliberal policy solutions. If they wanted to borrow, debtors had to put their houses in order, restructuring in neoliberal terms, via structural adjustment programmes.

In summary, these neoliberal strategies included measures to bring down the rate of inflation, to reduce public expenditure (to eliminate budget deficits) and to reduce the role of the state more generally (via privatization, as well as via increasing market mechanisms and charging for public services such as health and education). In addition, debtor countries had to open up their economies, liberalizing trade by reducing tariff barriers. The free market had to be allowed to flourish internationally, through free trade in goods and services, free circulation of capital and freedom of investment. This was supposed to be beneficial in terms of promoting economic growth, the benefits of which would then, it was argued, 'trickle down' to the rest of their populations.

These arguments emerge in more detail later in this chapter and in subsequent chapters, together with their critiques. The points to emphasize here are simply these: during the latter decades of the twentieth century, Third World countries in the South became increasingly directly affected by these neoliberal policy agendas and that these agendas were being promoted via international organizations and agencies, particularly the World Bank and the IMF (and more recently the WTO), described as the 'instruments of neoliberalism' (Houtart 2001: vi), pursuing these strategies on a global scale. The roots of global campaigning around issues such as tackling the debt crisis and promoting fairer trade can be identified from this period.

Shifts of emphasis

Meanwhile, there have been shifts of emphasis in the neoliberal discourse. From the 1980s and 1990s it was becoming increasingly apparent that neoliberal strategies were being accompanied by increasing problems, with increasing social polarization on a global scale, as the rich have become richer and the poor become poorer. The world's income distribution has been depicted as a champagne glass, with 82 per cent of the world's income being enjoyed by the richest 20 per cent, compared with the somewhat slenderer stem of 1.4 per cent of the world's income, which falls to the poorest 20 per cent of the world's population.

Faced with increasing concern, international agencies began to focus on the development of strategies to mitigate the negative effects of neoliberal globalization. Structural adjustment needed a human face, to protect the most vulnerable, including poor women and children. This trend developed in the 1990s. By 1999 the United Nations *Human Development Report* opened with a Foreword explaining that it 'comes down clearly in favour of globalization to bring economic and social benefits to societies: the free flow of money and trade is matched by the liberating power of the flow of ideas and information driven by new technologies' (UNDP 1999: v) (the emphasis upon technological change and information technology again as well as the emphasis on the free market). The report continued, however, by reiterating its commitment to championing 'the agenda of the world's weak, those marginalized by globalization, and calls for a much bolder agenda of global and national reforms to achieve globalization with a human face' (ibid.). The report also 'cautions that globalization is too important to be left unmanaged as it is at present, because it has the capacity to do extraordinary harm as well as good' (ibid.).

The United Nations' approach to economic and social development differs from that of the WTO, the World Bank and the IMF, it is argued.

> The latter promote the empowerment of the market, a minimal role for the State and rapid liberalization. Most UN agencies, on the other hand, operate under the belief that public intervention (internationally and nationally) is necessary to enable basic needs and human rights to be

fulfilled and that the market alone cannot do the job and in many cases in fact hinders the job being done. (Khor 2001: 15)

So the fact that a UN agency was arguing for some policy modifications was not so surprising, but it was not only UN agencies acknowledging the force of these criticisms; the World Bank itself was also recognizing the

World population
grouped by income level
(richest to poorest)

Richest group

The richest 20% share 82% of world income

Each division represents a fifth (20%) of the world population

Poorest group

The poorest 20% share 1.4% of world income

World income distribution (*source*: Houtart and Polet 2001)

need to modify neoliberal strategies. Trade liberalization, for example, continues to be presented as promoting economic development and thereby benefiting developing countries; however, 'the lack of attention given to the social consequences of reform has threatened a backlash' (World Bank 2000: 52), a potential backlash that needs to be averted.

The post-Washington consensus, in contrast, recognizes that market forces need to be balanced by strategies to reduce poverty, strategies that need to involve the active participation of the poor themselves, as part of wider strategies to strengthen civil society and decentralize governance. 'The concept of participation', it has been argued, 'has become central to the repertoire with which the Bank has sought to remake its public face' (Francis 2001: 72). Chapter 2 explores some of these strategies in more detail, examining different approaches to the notion of civil society and the contested concept of social capital. The point to emphasize here is simply this: despite these modifications, the post-Washington consensus remains rooted in the neoliberal paradigm. Globalization might need some managing, from this perspective, but globalization is still effectively being presented as the only realistic option for development, equated with the spread of the free market, worldwide.

This has been the dominant view, held from the World Bank in Washington to the proponents of New Labour in Britain. The increasing globalization of the world economy in terms of trade and finance, the White Paper on 'Eliminating World Poverty' argued, brings great new opportunities. Neoliberal economic policies encourage the private sector, which is seen as providing 'the main impetus for economic growth' (HMSO 1997: 15). Globalization does not necessarily benefit everybody equally, the White Paper points out. 'Globalisation, however, needs therefore to be accompanied by policies to help the poor' (ibid.: 10).

While the neoliberal paradigm continues to predominate, there have, then, been increasing criticisms. Broadly, these might be categorized in the following ways. First, critics, including those from within the World Bank itself, have continued to accept the basic premises of neoliberalism. Free-market economic strategies are still considered to be the only viable route to development, but these strategies need to be accompanied by compensatory mechanisms, to ensure that the costs are not borne disproportionately by the world's poorest and most disadvantaged groups, including poor women and children, indigenous peoples, ethnic minority communities or people with disabilities, for example. As the *Human Development Report* (1996) recognized, over the past three decades (as neoliberal agendas gained predominance) in seventy developing countries, income levels were less than in the 1960s and 1970s. 'Economic gains have benefited greatly a few countries, at the expense of the many' (*Human Development Report* 1996, quoted in Khor 2001: 17), with wider inequalities within countries as well as between countries. This recognition of increasing polarization, and the worsening plight of the world's poorest peoples, has justified the development of participatory poverty reduction strategies to redress these imbalances. Poverty reduction strategy papers (PRSPs) replaced structural adjustment as the framework for debt relief – outlining governments' strategies to reduce poverty, including plans for how money freed up by debt relief will be targeted.

Broadly, governments associated with 'third way' strategies, such as New Labour in Britain, have continued to support approaches to globalization based on neoliberal economic strategies, arguing that free trade benefits all – although they have also accepted that developing countries may need time to adjust to the effects of the reduction of trade barriers. As the White Paper on International Development argued in 1997, 'We will work within the EU and the WTO for increased multilateral liberalisation of trade in goods and services, and the continued dismantling of tariff and non-tariff barriers worldwide' (HMSO 1997: 58). 'For the future', the report continued, 'we are committed to negotiate further comprehensive trade liberalisation, in particular in the agriculture and services sectors.' (These sectors have particular significance, as the critics of capitalist globalization have argued, because of the potentially negative impact upon primary producers in developing countries as well as the potentially negative impacts upon education, health and other vital services.) The White Paper, however, was equally clear about the importance of supporting globally agreed strategies for poverty reduction with the target of halving the proportion of the world's population living in extreme poverty by 2015.

While the post-Washington consensus has been concerned with ameliorating the effects of neoliberal economic strategies associated with globalization (rather than fundamentally rethinking those strategies), this has also been associated with some shifts in attitudes to the state and civil society more generally. These aspects are explored in more detail in the following chapter. In summary, it has been argued, the post-Washington consensus has been associated with the view that rolling back the state can be carried to counter-productive extremes. A 'strong social and institutional infrastructure is crucial to growth and development', with a revised role for the state, working in more pluralistic ways with civil society (including NGOs) strengthening social capital and developing 'social consensus about structural changes in the economy and key reforms' (Edwards 2001: 2–3).

Such approaches to globalization have been associated with the 'third way' – aiming to square the circle – tackling the negative effects of neoliberal economics with doses of social democratic social policy remedies. 'Third way' policy papers do still contain elements of the social democratic perspectives that were more characteristic of previous decades, less dominated by the policy dictates of neoliberalism, globally. Whilst the White Paper firmly rejected past models of development, based on the view that the state was the key player, 'we have learned that the virtuous State has a key role to play in supporting economic arrangements which encourage human development, stimulate enterprise and saving and create the environment necessary to mobilise domestic resources and to attract foreign investment' (HMSO 1997: 12) as well as tackling poverty and social exclusion.

Social democratic approaches

In summary, social democratic approaches have tended to start from such an approach to the state, the market and civil society more generally. Rather than merely facilitating the operations of the market, the state has a more active role, promoting social as well as economic development, with particular responsibilities for ensuring that the interests of labour are represented effectively, as well as the interests of capital, the interests of the disadvantaged as well as the interests of the most powerful. This type of thinking can be identified, for example, as underpinning the arguments for promoting adjustment with a human face, to protect the most vulnerable groups from the ill-effects of structural adjustment policies (Cornia et al. 1987).

Similarly, an Oxfam publication, *A Case for Reform: Fifty Years of the IMF and World Bank*, argued that 'the policies of the Bretton Woods institutions (i.e. the IMF and World Bank) do not sufficiently reflect the needs of the majority of the world's citizens' (Oxfam 1995: 2). Too often, it claims, blueprints for structural adjustment are 'drawn up in Washington in accordance with the dictates of free-market ideology, and applied with insufficient regard to the circumstances of individual countries' (ibid.: 3). 'Half a century on from the establishment of the Bretton Woods institutions, now is the time for a fundamental reappraisal of the roles and policies of the World Bank and IMF and their impact on the world's poor' (ibid.: 48). The paper concludes with a call for reform – reform of particular policies such as structural adjustment and debt, as well as reform of the system itself, to make it more transparent and democratically accountable in the South as well as in the North.

Social democratic perspectives have featured within international agencies, as well as within NGOs and within particular national states. As will be suggested below, many of the critiques of capitalist globalization, developed through a range of social movements and campaigns, have been compatible with social democratic perspectives. As has also been suggested, however, these perspectives have been contested.

For the far Left, including the libertarian socialist/anarchist Left, social democratic reformism can become part of the problem, rather than part of the solution. From these perspectives, campaigners such as some of those involved with major NGOs become identified by elite decision-makers as 'potential allies in the delicate work of diffusing this new opposition' (to globalization), 'the respectable face of dissent, with whom firms and governments are suddenly eager to do business' (Davis 2002: 176). According to these critics, 'NGOs such as Oxfam, for example, were all but co-opted into designing debt relief strategies' (*Economist*, quoted in ibid.: 177). The following chapter explores the contradictory pressures on NGOs and civil society more generally, in more detail. The point here is simply to identify the differences of perspective between those campaigning to reform the international agencies that promote capitalist globalization and those who have been campaigning on the basis of a more fundamental rejection of capitalist globalization per se.

As Epstein has argued in relation to Seattle mobilizations,

> the coalition that opposed the WTO in Seattle was held together by a common perception of the global corporations as the main threat to environmental standards, labor and human rights, and to democracy generally. There were differences among the various constituencies in Seattle over how far the critique of the corporations should go, and what solution should be proposed to growing corporate power. Radicals in the direct action movement and left-leaning environmental and human rights groups argued that the WTO should be abolished; more mainstream environmental and human rights organizations, and trade unionists, argued for reforming the WTO, demanding that its powers be restricted. (Epstein 2002: 54)

In the debate between abolition and reform, she continued, 'the WTO also stood as a metaphor for the global corporations that it serves, and for a global capitalist system that the radicals want to dismantle and which others hope can be brought in line with democracy' (ibid.).

These debates can be illustrated, for example, in relation to campaigning for fairer trade. As has already been argued, the liberalization of trade and investment has been key to globalization, linked to the growing power of transnational corporations and international financial institutions. While neoliberals have argued that for developing countries free trade frequently represents 'the primary means of realizing the benefits of globalization' (World Bank 2000: 51), enabling them to access new markets, increase production, transfer new technologies and improve productivity, the critics have argued that the reality is far more problematic. Globalization is a very uneven process, and while some groups in some countries have benefited, a majority of those in developing countries 'are excluded from the process, or are participating in it in marginal ways that are often detrimental to their interests: for example import liberalization may harm their domestic producers and financial liberalization may cause instability' (Khor 2001: 16).

Among campaigners, there are those arguing that the system, as it stands, is currently unfair, and very far from representing a level playing field. On the contrary, while the WTO argues for free trade in theory, in practice the most powerful interests in the industrialized North, particularly in the USA and the European Union, continue to protect particular industries and sectors (such as steel and agriculture). Meanwhile, the critics point out, trade liberalization has, in many cases, resulted in 'a vicious cycle of trade and balance-of-payments deficits, financial instability, debt and recession' (ibid.: 34).

The liberalization of trade in services would be particularly problematic, with potentially far-reaching damage to the education, health and welfare of the world's poorest peoples (Woodroffe 2002), not to mention the damage to the education, health and welfare of all those who need public services in the industrialized North, services provided for social needs rather than private profits. The countries of the developing South, it has been argued, 'enter into supposedly equal negotiations with very different levels of capacity' over issues such as GATS (General Agreement on Trade in Services) and these inequalities are compounded by 'the close relationship between corporations and some governments and the influence that this has had over GATS' (ibid.: 7).

While the critics of capitalist globalization might agree on this diagnosis of the problem, however, differences emerge when it comes to proposing ultimate solutions. One view focuses upon the importance of getting a more level playing field, challenging the ways in which the most powerful interests in the North preach free trade while practising protectionism, whenever this suits them better, and gaining more realistic timescales to enable developing countries in the South to adjust. Alternatively, others argue that it is neoliberal globalization itself that needs to be challenged, and replaced with alternative strategies for development and social transformation.

Alternative approaches

There have been differences here over strategies as well as over tactics. Among those advocating more radical transformative strategies, there has been a libertarian socialist/anarchist view. Broadly, these types of approaches question the development roles of the state as well as the market (or more specifically, of big business and transnational corporations). Like the neoliberals, they reject bureaucratic, statist solutions, but unlike the neoliberals, they are also suspicious of big business, preferring small-scale co-operative developments that enable people to have more direct control over their lives.

While libertarian socialist/anarchist approaches cover a wide range of views, broadly these tend to be characterized by their commitments to mutuality and co-operation, based upon relatively small-scale, local developments, respecting people's autonomy and their rights to self-organization and self-determination. These approaches have been linked with strategies for decentralization, for delinking from the global corporate economy and for emphasizing the importance of working for sustainable development and sustainable livelihoods. As Starr's study of anti-corporate movements confronting globalization has demonstrated, anarchism is 'alive, youthful and international' (Starr 2000: 112), having been actively engaged in campaigning against globalization, as well as actively engaged in related campaigning on environmental issues, feminism, anti-racism and the rights of indigenous peoples.

While anarchists have been popularly associated with violent protest, this is a misleading stereotype. Anarchists have been just as, if not more, frequently associated with peaceful, non-violent tactics. As one of the commentators on events in Seattle in 1999 reflected, while the 'century-old stereotype of anarchy as mayhem defined the media coverage' (Kauffman 2002: 125), for many of those organizing against corporate globalization in the United States the key lesson was 'not to allow our movements to be divided and conquered over the question of property destruction'. There were groups of anarchists dressed in black, masks over their faces, using militant tactics, but these groups had their roots in environmental protest and self-management principles, which used a *range* of tactics. There were heated debates, both before and after Seattle, about the non-violence code, which had been adopted by the Direct Action Network.

While there were indeed lively debates about tactics, other commentators have regretted that there was not more vigorous debate over *ideas*. Reflecting upon the significance of the fact that the Seattle mobilizations were clearly not just anti-globalization but more specifically anti-capitalist globalization, Aronowitz went on to put the question: if 'anti-capitalism is the leading edge, what are the alternatives?' (Aronowitz 2002: 200). 'Is resistance enough to persuade more than an elite of semiprofessional organizers to stay the course of opposition? Or does the movement need a rich address to the cultural, educational and social dimensions of life?' Socialism, he concluded, carried a great deal of baggage, in the wake of the demise of the Soviet Union, as did perhaps its libertarian socialist/anarchist variety. Many of those at Seattle were clearly still aiming at reform rather than more fundamental socialist transformation. 'They believe that the nation-state still has enough juice to yield concessions.' So, in Aronowitz's view, 'the problem is to think and debate the alternatives, to experiment with reform even if it yields very little or nothing, and to craft a new politics of internationalism that takes into account the still potent force of national states and their identities. The hardest work is thinking' (ibid.: 22).

This type of approach is actually compatible with a more orthodox Left position, arguing for the importance of working for immediate reforms while building a movement with longer-term goals for social transformation, a movement in which critical theory is seen as key as well as militant practice and solidarity, internationally. Clearly, as Aronowitz points out, there most evidently *has been* a crisis of confidence on the Left, particularly since the demise of the former Soviet Union and the widely proclaimed view that capitalism has triumphed as the only viable alternative globally. This makes the case for developing coherent challenges all the more urgent and compelling for the Left.

This book starts from the position that movements against capitalist globalization could – and should – be supported by the development of critical theory as well as by building solidarity in practice, within national borders and across them, internationally. Alliances for long-term strategies for social transformation could be strengthened through reflecting upon struggles for immediate gains, for improved conditions for labour and greater opportunities for sustainable livelihoods, for working towards poverty reduction and for improving access to education, health and welfare.

Without suggesting that the *Communist Manifesto* provides the deepest insights of Marxist analysis, let alone that any text from the mid-nineteenth century necessarily provides relevant contemporary guidance, the following quotation may still have some resonance. 'The Communists fight for the attainment of the immediate aims, for the momentary interests of the working class; but in the movement of the present, they also represent and take care of the future of that movement' (Marx and

Engels 1985: 119), allying themselves with the most progressive forces while reserving the right to take up a critical position, when critical thinking needs to be developed. The *Communist Manifesto* concludes with a rallying call to internationalism.

Alternatively, however, the *Communist Manifesto* also includes some critical reflections on those who oppose capitalism from what Marx and Engels define as 'petty-bourgeois' positions (ibid.: 108). Small business people and peasants were also adversely affected by the development of modern industry, and individual members of the 'petty-bourgeoisie' were 'being hurled down into the proletariat by the action of competition, and, as modern industry develops, they even see the moment when they will completely disappear as an independent section of modern society' (ibid.). In response to these perceived threats from the development of capitalism, worldwide, small business people and farmers were attracted, Marx and Engels argued, to backward-looking forms of opposition, seeking to return to an idealized past, a romanticized approach that can be identified in more recent forms of protest. Petty-bourgeois critics pointed to

> the disastrous effects of machinery and division of labour; the concentration of capital and land in a few hands; over-production and crises; it pointed out the inevitable ruin of the petty-bourgeois and peasant, the misery of the proletariat, the anarchy in production, the crying inequalities in the distribution of wealth, the industrial war of extermination between nations, the dissolution of old moral bonds, of old family ties, of the old nationalities. (ibid.: 109)

They were looking back to the old property relations and former social ties. There are connections here with particular populist traditions.

Populism from the Right as well as from the Left

Populism has a powerful tradition in the United States, in particular, a tradition with varieties of the Right as well as varieties of the Left. The right-wing populism of Pat Buchanan, for example, has been associated with opposition to globalization, having attacked international trade treaties; from his perspective the decent hard-working productive middle class and working class – and small farmers – are being 'squeezed from above and below' – by 'lazy social parasites' from below, and from transnational corporations from above (Kessi 2001: 203). Right-wing opposition to globalization campaigns against free trade because this is seen to benefit transnationals and global elites, globally, rather than small businesses and farmers, locally. Opposition to globalization can also take on extreme nationalist and explicitly racist connotations, as exemplified by the positions of far-Right groups in France and Holland for instance, as well as by extreme-Right Republicans in the USA or conservative environmental groups. As Kessi has argued, traditionally 'leftist ideas about self-management and autonomy get mixed with discourses on regionalism which tend towards racism, and leftist criticism of technology receives support from essentialist and fascist discourses about living in harmony with "nature"' – opposing 'the destruction of "Mother Earth" by a "modern world" gone astray' (ibid.: 205).

Some campaigners on the Left have argued that they need to work together with the Right in one big movement against globalization. Such an alliance, it has been suggested, gives the anti-globalization movement strength and legitimacy. Others, conversely, have argued that this is potentially dangerous as a strategy (Krebbers and Schoenmaker 2001), pointing to the dangers of allying with racists and homophobes. While Pat Buchanan was passionately defending 'the legitimate expectations of working families in the global economy' in the presidential campaign in the USA in 2000 he was supporting American workers, it was argued, 'as long as they are conservative and obedient and not unemployed, black, gay, female, lesbian or Jewish. He's not particularly fond of left-wing workers' either (Dolan, quoted in ibid.: 211). As this commentator points out, Buchanan's views on Argentina might also give cause for alarm on the Left, he having argued that with military and police and freelance operators (i.e. death squads) at work 'between six thousand and one hundred and fifty thousand leftists disappeared. Brutal yes; also successful. Today peace reigns in Argentina; security has been restored' (a view that, with the wisdom of hindsight, might be considered to be as inaccurate as it was vicious).

So far the discussion of populism has been related to populism in the North. In the USA, for example, O'Connor has argued that anti-globalization is 'a populist movement, not a class-based movement' (O'Connor 2001: 360). This label, however, has also been applied to the movement in the South as well as to the North. While right-wing populism in the USA and Europe, for example, has been characterized as nationalist and often anti-immigrant and racist, rather than internationalist, in the South the situation is somewhat different. 'In the South', according to O'Connor, Right populists 'are anti-imperialist while their opposite numbers in the North are pro-imperialist' (ibid.: 361).

'Of equal importance,' O'Connor continues, 'right populists in the South are people of color and antiracist while their counterparts in the North are (often proudly) racist. In most countries I would guess that right populists regard themselves as patriotic. This all means that the likelihood of a right-wing global populist movement is zero while the odds are much better for an international populism of the left', a point he regards as important because 'the political terrain of both capital and antiglobalist movements is itself global' (ibid.). Whether or not Right populists in the South are less likely to be racist than Right populists in the North may be more questionable than this might suggest, as may their potential for international mobilization. Either version may be problematic enough in terms of the potential for building alliances for social justice and social transformation, on a global scale – anti-capitalist global social movements that are the focus of subsequent chapters.

Building alliances

How then to evaluate the potential for building alliances among the varying interests that may be engaged in opposition to globalization? Very broadly, this potential may be summarized as follows. Globalization, when defined in terms of 'those processes by which the peoples of the world are incorporated into a single society, global society' (Cohen and Kennedy 2000: 24), may be opposed by a very broad coalition of organizations and individuals, in both North and South. Globalization, thus broadly defined, may be resisted by those with a wide range of concerns, whether these are primarily economic, political, social, cultural and/or environmental concerns.

As has already been suggested, Right as well as Left populists may come together to protest against what they perceive to be the increasing power of the transnational capitalist class – transnational corporations, together with 'globalizing state and inter-state bureaucrats and politicians (state fraction), globalizing professionals (technical fraction)', and 'merchants and media (consumerist fraction)' (Sklair 2002: 99). The ways in which transnational capital shifts investment and jobs from region to region in the search for profit maximization concerns labour too, as jobs are lost in one area, all too often to be replaced by lower-paid jobs, with worse conditions, in another – just as labour is also potentially concerned by nation-states' failures to intervene to regulate these processes. The social polarization that has accompanied globalization has mobilized responses from human rights groups and women's organizations, from trade unions and faith-based organisations, from NGOs as well as from government and intergovernmental organizations. Opposition to the 'McDonaldization' of local cultures – the perceived loss of local cultural identities and the destruction of indigenous heritages – may be rooted in similarly broad bases. Likewise with opposition to the degradation of the environment, on a global scale.

So far, so good, in terms of the case for bringing Left and Right together to campaign around globalization, the case for building 'the greatest possible unity' (George, quoted in Krebbers and Schoenmaker 2001: 212), giving campaigns strength through the diversity of views and constituencies involved. As has already been suggested in this chapter, however, alternative definitions and perspectives point towards more ambiguous conclusions. The commonality of problems may point towards the need for common solutions globally, but not necessarily towards the existence of common interests in working for these.

In summary, as has also been suggested, there are important differences, in terms of economic, social, political and cultural interests. From a Left perspective, labour and capital have different underlying interests, whatever their common concerns on particular presenting issues. So while trade unionists may join together with small business interests to oppose the negative effects of trade liberalization, they cannot realistically expect so much support, when it comes to issues of trade union rights or the rights of unemployed people, whether globally or locally.

Similarly, anti-globalization campaigners may build a broad coalition to combat poverty and social exclusion, and to work for human rights for all, including women, ethnic minorities and indigenous peoples, people with disabilities, refugees and political prisoners, globally. When it comes to taking on the vested interests, including the vested interests concerned with the arms trade, this becomes more problematic, however. Increasing the supply of arms may fuel the very conflicts that are creating cripples and forcing refugees to seek asylum elsewhere. But this is not how the increasing flows of refugees and asylum-seekers are being perceived by anti-globalists of the far Right.

The erosion of the power of the nation-state has been an issue of widespread concern, globally, the debates about the extent to which this has actually been the case notwithstanding. Here, too, there are significant underlying differences of view. From the far Right's perspective, the goal of global campaigning must be to restore the power and influence of the nation-state, rolling back the incursions of international governmental agencies as well as containing the operations of transnational corporations.

From the Left's perspective, internationalism per se is to be welcomed rather than resisted – so long as this is based on solidarity between peoples rather than the pursuit of capitalist profitability. While libertarian socialists/anarchists might share this commitment to internationalism, however, this, in their view, would need to be rooted in decentralized communities, rather than the state, whether nationally or internationally. For others on the Left, as has already been suggested, the nation-state remains a vital focus for campaigning. Both national governments and international governmental agencies need to be pressurized – although the ultimate extent to which they will be prepared to work towards social transformation tends to be viewed more optimistically by some and considerably more sceptically by others, including those most directly influenced by Marxist analyses of the state in capitalist society.

Finally, there are differences as well as points in common, when it comes to issues of culture, communications, new technologies and the media. While the so-called 'McDonaldization' of culture has been widely criticized, the alternatives are more open to question. The far Right has been associated with backward-looking forms of nostalgia, seeking to preserve national heritages whether or not, in practice, these visions of the past are more mythical than real. Such approaches have been associated with exclusionary and often xenophobic forms of cultural politics. On the Left, in contrast, alternative approaches to cultural politics start from the value of diversity and difference, celebrating hybridity and creolization rather than attempting to freeze traditional cultures and identities into essentialized versions of the past (Gilroy 1987; Hall 1990).

Meanwhile the protagonists of technological explanations of social change tend to emphasize the role of new technologies, particularly new electronic communications technologies, as causal factors in the development of globalization over the last decades of the twentieth century and beyond. In contrast, anti-globalization campaigners may differ among themselves as to the relative importance of technological change and the mass media, compared and contrasted with the relative importance of underlying changes in the processes and relations of production (the Marxist approach). Whatever differences they may have on these analytical issues, however, anti-global campaigners would seem to have shared a common understanding of the immense creative potential of new communications technologies. E-mail and access to the worldwide web open up amazing possibilities, transforming the nature of campaigning against capitalist globalization, as will be discussed in subsequent chapters.

2 | Democratization and marketization: the state, the market and civil society

As Zygmunt Bauman has argued, 'We live in a globalising world' characterized by increasing mutual interdependence but increasing polarization between rich and poor both within and between nations and regions. According to the UN Development Agency, 'less than 4% of the personal wealth of the 225 richest people would suffice to offer all the poor of the world access to elementary medical and educational amenities as well as adequate nutrition'. But even 'such a relatively minor redistribution of basic necessities is unlikely to occur; not in the foreseeable future at any rate'. When a survey of 10,000 of the world's poor asked what aspect of their plights were most demeaning and painful, Bauman reflects, two themes 'crop up with amazing regularity – insecurity and powerlessness' (Bauman 2001: 2).

The previous chapter focused on debates on globalization in economic terms, and more specifically on neoliberal economic agendas and their implications for developing alternatives via global social movements. This chapter moves on to focus on debates on globalization and political power – and powerlessness. Globalization has been associated with increasing democratization, both locally and internationally. And conversely, globalization has been associated with growing concerns about the health of democratic forms of governance. There has been increasing emphasis upon the role of 'civil society' (however defined, from differing perspectives, whether considered locally or transnationally). And there has been increasing emphasis on the importance of capacity-building to strengthen 'civil society' and to promote the development of 'social capital' (another contested term).

This chapter starts by exploring the differing ways in which globalization has been associated with increasing – or decreasing – democratization. Is the trend towards the development of more democratic forms of governance, globally? Or is democracy being eroded, as power has been increasingly concentrated, transnationally; devalued, in addition, as electorates become more sceptical both nationally and locally? This leads into the discussion of what types of democratic processes have been proposed as alternatives, whether more transnational and/or more decentralized processes and structures, more representative and/or more direct approaches to democracy. The latter approaches contain their own inherent dilemmas, too – how to ensure that these alternative approaches are also genuinely representative and democratically accountable? These dilemmas apply to social movements as well as to the structures of governance. As will be suggested in subsequent chapters, democratic accountability is potentially just as, if not even more, problematic in the NGO and community sectors and, more specifically, within global social movements.

This leads into the discussion of competing approaches to the concept of 'civil society' and civil society's relations with the market as well as with the state, at different levels. The chapter concludes by exploring some of the key implications for global social movements, faced with the prospect of potentially increasing political space for their mobilizations, internationally, yet increasingly pressured by the constraints of neoliberal economic agendas, as these impact upon the institutions of governance, whether locally/nationally or transnationally.

The 'end of history' and the triumph of Western liberal democracy following the collapse of the former Soviet Union?

Francis Fukuyama's book, *The End of History: The Last Man*, published in 1992, typified a widely held, if highly contentious, interpretation of the significance of the collapse of the Soviet Union and of the previously existing socialist states in Eastern and Central Europe from 1989 (Fukuyama 1992). According to Fukuyama, history as we knew it came to an end with the ultimate triumph of Western liberal democracy. Free-market economics and Western parliamentary democracy won out over state planning and state controls. The freedom of the individual consumer was to be mirrored by the newly acquired freedoms of the individual as citizen. Democratization has been presented as one of, if not the single most important theme of the twentieth century (Potter et al. 1997) – the story of the ultimate victory of Western democracy, despite decades of fascism and military dictatorships in Europe as well as in the South, in a century which has been characterized as an 'age of extremes' (Hobsbawn 1994).

Fukuyama's view of this triumph of liberal democracy in the 'new world order' was soon challenged, as critics pointed to a range of countervailing arguments in the context of the 'new world disorder'. Without in any way accepting his conclusions, however, this chapter starts from the common ground of the global significance of the collapse of the Soviet Union. In summary (and without attempting to go into the underlying causes or the wider impact here) it needs to be acknowledged that the demise of the Soviet Union left the United States significantly less challenged in the global arena, politically and ideologically as well as economically.

Meanwhile, on the Left, there was seen to be an ideological vacuum (Fraser 1997). Socialism was represented as discredited, as neoliberals proclaimed that there neither was, not could be, any viable alternative to liberal (free-market) Western-style democracy. There were powerful pressures to promote the development of market mechanisms in the former socialist countries, together with the development of Western democratic forms, and the strengthening of 'civil society' to guarantee their future stability. In face of all this, then, there were processes of rethinking on the Left, including rethinking about the role of the market and rethinking the significance of democracy in general and, more specifically, the role of civil society.

One view, the 'new realist' view, was that the new Right had triumphed globally. All that was possible, in these circumstances, was to accommodate to this situation and to settle for pressing for the humane management of global capitalism – neoliberal agendas plus a dose of human rights. As will be suggested subsequently in this chapter, there are affinities, here, with 'third way' perspectives.

Alternatively, however, others argued that it was vital to address the underlying causes of past failures with a view to reinvigorating socialist theory and practice (Blackburn 1991). One of the key themes here was the issue of democracy – and, more specifically, how to build on previous democratic gains, in capitalist states, such as the right to vote, and equal rights to due legal process, and to work towards a more democratic future socialist society. This would be characterized by economic and social rights as well as civil and legal rights (Miliband 1991).

A series of debates ensued, on the Left (and former Left), about different approaches to democratization. These included debates about the limits of traditional Western representative forms of democracy and the need to explore alternative approaches, including those drawing on traditions of direct democracy and deliberative democracy. These were approaches that also had histories on the libertarian socialist Left as well as within populist traditions (Hirst 1990; Mouffe 1992; Mouffe 2000; Elster 1998).

There were, then, widespread concerns with processes of democratization, coming, as these did, from different sections of the Left as well as from the political Right and from those more sympathetic to the perspectives of the 'third way'. Democratization was being promoted within the context of strategies to make the world safe for neoliberal capitalism, globally. And democratization was being promoted within the context of alternative agendas for social transformation.

Meanwhile, there was increasing recognition that however desirable in theory, liberal democracy was manifesting major shortcomings in practice, in its Western heartlands. Perhaps the events of 1989 had not represented such a straightforward triumph, after all? For whatever reasons, whether from satisfaction, from complacency or even from profound alienation and disenchantment, the fact was that a significant proportion of electors – and particularly the next generation of young electors – were failing to cast their votes in the old established democracies such as Britain and the USA. There were, in addition, associated anxieties about the potential decline of citizen engagement and civic trust, the possible reduction in 'social capital' that has concerned Putnam and other much-quoted authors on this subject (Putnam 1995). Here too, then, there seemed to be a need for strategies to promote active citizenship, and to strengthen 'civil society' more generally. As has already been suggested, however, like 'democratization', 'civil society' and 'social capital' are terms that have been used with varying meanings and differing policy implications, depending on the underlying perspectives of those concerned to promote them.

Globalization and democratization: some paradoxes?

Capitalist globalization has been described as paradoxical (Cohen and Kennedy 2000), generating similar experiences on the one hand – including common aspirations for greater personal freedom and democracy – while generating increasing complexity and polarization on the other. As has already been suggested, capitalist globalization has been associated with the spread of Western democratic forms in the former socialist states and in former dictatorships, whether in Europe or the South. Globalization has also been associated with the spread of civil and political rights, as these have been enshrined in the 1948 Universal Declaration of Human Rights. Since then a series of UN Conventions and treaties have established more detailed provisions for individuals, with positive duties for states to protect these rights (Sklair 2002). And NGOs, along with a range of human rights organizations and movements, have developed advocacy and campaigning work to try to ensure that these rights are effectively enforced. The following chapter explores an example of international advocacy and campaigning on human rights in more detail.

However vitally important they are, civil and political rights do not constitute the sum total of human rights. As critics of capitalist globalization have argued, human rights need to be expanded from the civil and political spheres to the economic and social spheres, extending from the rights to due legal process, freedom of speech and the right to vote – spheres in which, it has been argued, capitalist globalization 'has often had a relatively positive influence' – to the more challenging freedoms of sustainable livelihoods and access to health, education and welfare provision (ibid.: 299). Far from automatically guaranteeing these latter rights, it has been argued, capitalist globalization, dominated by neoliberal economic agendas, has been upholding the freedoms of transnational corporations to pursue the interests of profitability, at the expense of the economic and social interests of the poor and the poorest, and at the expense of environmental considerations, globally. From this perspective, democratization has been and continues to be a paradoxical process.

In addition, the role of the nation-state, itself, has become increasingly contentious. Citizenship rights and responsibilities have typically been defined in national terms (although increasingly taking account of the provisions of regional groupings of nation-states, such as the European Union). From the late 1960s onwards, however, the nation-state has had to face challenges as a result of the rapidly increasing power of transnational bodies, transnational corporations in particular.

The extent to which globalization has actually involved the decline of the nation-state has been a matter of contention. On the one hand, as the previous chapter explored, the nation-state has been considered as an increasing irrelevance in the face of globalization, having progressively lost some of its autonomy, in face of the pivotal role of transnational corporations, the requirements of international governmental organizations such as the IMF and the World Bank, the requirements of international law (including that impacting on human rights) and the power of international arrangements governing security, weaponry and foreign policies more generally (Held 1989). As McGrew has summarized the position, constrained by 'global market forces and confronting problems which, like ecological degradation, deny purely national resolution, the liberal democratic state ... has only limited control over the forces which shape its destiny' (McGrew 1997: 236).

Alternatively, it has been argued, the demise of the nation-state has been much exaggerated (Hirst and Thompson 1996). Most transnational corporations do still have some national base and nation-states can and do differ significantly in the extent to which they facilitate neoliberal global agendas – or attempt to offset the negative effects on their most vulnerable citizens and their environments. By implication, politics at the level of the nation-state do still matter – considerably.

Meanwhile, nation-states differ most significantly in the degree of autonomy that they do – or do not – continue to enjoy, just as they vary in terms of their overall wealth or poverty, economically. At one end of the spectrum, the United States of America wields very extensive political power and influence internationally, imposing its will on other nation-states and international organizations, if not without provoking resistance, globally. The USA stands in sharp contrast with the recipients of its power and influence, towards the other end of this spectrum.

There are key implications here for global social movements. As it will be suggested, through case study examples in subsequent chapters, national governments, and particularly the government of the USA and those of other G8 states, continue to control key levers of power. So these national governments need to be pressured into wielding their power in progressive ways, both nationally and globally – to abide by international agreements on environmental protection, for example, or to vote for less regressive policies on world trade. Chapter 9, on the experiences of the Jubilee 2000 campaign, illustrates the importance of lobbying at national level, trying to win over the governments of the most powerful states, to support more progressive policies on debt relief, at international levels.

This still leaves the question of how to promote democratization at the transnational level per se. Arguing the case for a cosmopolitan approach, Held has pointed to the need to secure democracy 'in a series of interconnected power and authority centres' (Held 1995: 106). Democracy, in the context of globalization, could be fully sustained, he argued, only 'in and through agencies and organizations which form an element of and yet cut across the territorial boundaries of the nation-state' (ibid.). This would be a democracy beyond borders. Such an approach to cosmopolitan democracy would start by strengthening the United Nations, building regional parliaments, and extending democratic representation on such bodies, supported by the development of grass-roots movements, regionally and globally. As Held himself has recognized, however, there are serious obstacles to the realization of such a potentially Utopian approach to cosmopolitan democracy, in practice. Not least of these may be the extent to which, in the current context, such proposals might be seen as simply one more instance of attempts to consolidate Western dominance, worldwide.

Critics from the Right as well as from the Left of the political spectrum have pointed to the inherent difficulties of persuading the powerful and their political representatives to cede power voluntarily in the pursuit of human rights and social justice agendas, globally. While the former emphasize the imperatives of a 'realist' approach, the latter focus on the importance of setting this in the context of the underlying interests at stake. How might the World Bank, the IMF or the WTO be effectively democratized from above, without taking on the neoliberal economic assumptions that underpin their strategies? Could political power be challenged globally without challenging the economic interests of global capital? Or could human rights be guaranteed, internationally, without pressures from below, as well as from above, pressures from women's organizations and trade unions, for instance, as well as from global social movements more generally (Dickenson 1997; McGrew 1997)?

On the other hand, radical communitarians have argued for alternative approaches to global democratization, rooted in direct and participatory forms. These would be based upon self-governing communities, locally, encouraging and developing in citizens 'a sense of simultaneous belonging to overlapping (local and global) communities of interest and affection', an approach that has been linked to the politics of the new social movements (McGrew 1997: 247) (more fully explored in the following chapter). How effective such an entirely bottom-up approach might be in taking on the interests of global capital has also been subjected to questioning. Nor can it be taken for granted that alternative forms will necessarily be more fully representative of minority as well as majority interests, or more effectively accountable. This brings the discussion to debates on alternative approaches to democracy, including direct and participatory approaches, more generally.

Alternative approaches to democracy

Just as Western-style parliamentary democracy was being spread globally, critics from within were arguing the case for developing alternative approaches. Critics such as Hirst started from the position that representative democracy was much better than none. But representative democracy was still too limited (Hirst 1990). Theoretical debates have drawn extensively upon concepts developed in ancient Greece, concepts rooted in the experiences of democracy in city-states. In ancient Athens, for example, citizens (although not women or slaves) enjoyed the right to engage in political debate; decisions could be reached on this basis. Active participation was perceived as a right and a duty. It was, indeed, key to achieving the good life. Only in such association with others, as Dahl has summarized this view, 'can we hope to become fully human or certainly to realize our qualities of excellence as human beings' (Dahl 1989: 14). And conversely, a good city was characterized as one 'that produces good citizens, promotes their happiness, and encourages them to act rightly', taking account of the general interests, rather than simply pursuing their own self-interest (ibid.: 15).

As theorists of different approaches to democracy have also pointed out, however, this type of direct democracy represented an ideal – even in its own time, in city-states where citizens shared sufficient common interests to achieve relative consensus, on the basis of face-to-face interactions. In larger, more complex and more significantly differentiated states, this approach has been far more problematic – hence the development of representative democracy, characterized by parliamentary systems and competing political parties. Representatives, once elected, are not mandated by their electorates. They deliberate, and then take decisions accordingly, using their judgement as they think fit, on behalf of their constituents. Elections do, of course, provide the voters with regular opportunities to change their governments, and competing political parties can represent some at least of the divergent interests within modern nation-states. But representative democracy bears 'only a weak resemblance', it has been argued, 'to the political institutions of classical Greece' with its ideals of active citizenship (ibid.: 14). However limited representative democracy at the national level, how much more problematic is it on the global scale? As Dahl pointed out, one 'consequence of the change in the scale of democracy is to magnify the already significant utopianism of the democratic ideal' (ibid:. 5).

Although alternative approaches have been attracting widespread interest in the contemporary context, these actually have a longer history too. The previous chapter referred to long-standing debates within libertarian socialist and anarchist traditions. In addition, populist approaches also have long histories, in the United States and elsewhere. And as suggested in the previous chapter, too, these approaches have been developed from different ends of the political spectrum. While direct democracy and participatory approaches have been explored on the Left, the Republican Right has also embraced traditional concerns with democracy on a small scale, the suspicion of big government and the preference for local democracy expressing 'America's desire to return to the good and decent values of small-town society' (Berry et al. 1993: 4). This was, for example, the tradition of the New England town meeting.

A number of states in the USA, along with a number of other democracies such as Swiss cantons, continue to practise elements of direct democracy (Budge 1996). For example, there are provisions for Californian voters who collect sufficient signatures on a petition to propose a particular law (a provision that has been used to press for cuts in property taxes, for instance). Other provisions include the right to file a petition to remove a particular public official. Clearly, new electronic technologies enable such devices to be practised far more widely too, beyond the local level. Direct democracy does not have to be confined to the small-scale. Citizens everywhere could play more proactive parts.

So why have these alternative approaches to democracy not been practised far more widely? One explanation offered refers to the inherent elitism lurking within societies that claim to be more democratic than their reality warrants. 'Fears of the great unwashed', it has been suggested, 'are an enduring part of American politics' (Berry et al. 1993: 8). Mass participation would dilute the expertise of those who 'know best' and could be potentially divisive and destabilizing.

Against such fears, it has been countered that where more participatory approaches to democracy have actually been tried out, the results have generally been relatively positive. 'Instead of chaos' in fact 'there is a degree of empowerment' (ibid.: 14), because participation can nourish democracy, providing people with opportunities to learn active citizenship in practice – far fuller lessons than those offered simply by voting for elected representatives, every five years or so. This potential for experiential learning and empowerment through active engagement in more participatory forms of democracy emerges as a theme in subsequent chapters (Holst 2002).

Anxieties about the limitations of more direct forms of democracy, however, have not been confined to the proponents of elitism. There have also been concerns about the potentially negative effects of introducing political changes without taking account of their economic and social contexts. These concerns may be summarized as follows. In societies characterized by deep underlying conflicts of interest, divided in terms of class, race, gender, ethnicity, age and abilities/disabilities, the political arena cannot be assumed to be a level playing field. So opportunities for proactive participation are unlikely to be taken up and used equally effectively, regardless of these underlying socio-economic differences. On the contrary, in fact, there is a wealth of empirical evidence to demonstrate the opposite.

Those who participate most effectively tend to be those from higher-income groups, with most advantages of education and access to decision-making processes in any case (Hirst 1990). Berry and colleagues' study of attempts to strengthen participatory democracy in five US cities came to precisely this conclusion about the relative lack of involvement of blacks and Hispanics too (although social class emerged as the single most significant factor) (Berry et al. 1993). Despite this, the authors concluded that strategies to promote citizen participation (through decentralization in these cases) were worthwhile overall. These processes of democratization were potentially empowering and participation itself was a learning process, even if this tended to be somewhat uneven in practice. There is a long tradition of writings about the potentially educative effects of participatory democracy, from classical Greek theorists onwards to more contemporary debates on social learning and capacity-building (Sirianni and Friedland 2001). But strong participation was no panacea and distortions caused 'by wealth and social status are not eliminated' even if they were not being exacerbated (Berry et al. 1993: 189) in decentralized neighbourhood structures.

Approaches emphasizing the importance of deliberation and public debate have potentially contributed to such notions about social learning. Elster's approach to 'deliberative democracy', for example, focuses upon the importance of argument and bargaining to improve decision-making (whether via representative or more direct democratic structures). This also, in his view, 'improves the moral or intellectual qualities of participants' (Elster 1998: 11). Hannah Arendt developed similar arguments when she emphasized the value of civic engagement and collective deliberation that would develop citizens' judgement as well as increasing their political effectiveness (quoted in Passerin d'Entrèves 1992). Such approaches might be empowering for participants, offsetting initial inequalities of access to knowledge and critical understanding, even if they could not, on their own, be expected to reverse underlying inequalities of power and material resources.

More populist approaches to direct democracy – approaches emphasizing the importance of involving 'the people' as an undifferentiated entity, without taking account of differing interests or social divisions among the 'people' – may achieve even less in these respects. On the contrary, in fact, some processes might actually reinforce such underlying inequalities. For example, devices associated with direct democracy, devices such as the right to call for referenda or for the recall of officials, have been associated with a number of pitfalls (Cronin 1989). As Hirst pointed out, simplistically formulated referenda on lowering taxes in California have been criticized for effectively promoting the interests of the relatively well-off – at the expense of those who most need the public services which such taxes might have provided (Hirst 1990). Well-heeled interest groups are much better placed to finance such campaigns, including paying for advertising in the mass media. Who else could afford to subsidize teledemocracy? The rights of disadvantaged minorities are inherently less likely to be safeguarded in such a context.

Comparable arguments have been applied to provisions for the recall of particular public officials. While this could be a useful device to root out corruption, it could also be misused, in the pursuit of particular interests (Cronin 1989). Such provisions have inherent dangers, and especially so in the context of societies where power and resources are very unequally divided. The recall of the Governor of California in 2003 illustrates a number of these potential contradictions.

Similar findings about the inherent limitations as well as the potential benefits of such approaches to democratization have emerged from a range of other studies. In the context of development projects in the South, participatory approaches have been questioned as potentially representing a 'new tyranny' (Cooke and Kothari 2001) reinforcing the interests of the most powerful, internationally as well as locally, despite the rhetoric of empowerment. Similar arguments about the potentially negative aspects of apparently positive strategies for participation and empowerment have emerged both in general (Craig and Mayo 1995) and in relation to gender issues (Gujit and Shah 1998).

Studies of urban regeneration and community development programmes in the North have raised comparable questions about their inherent biases. The voices of the poorest and the least powerful are not necessarily more likely to be effectively represented and heard in decentralized structures or in other processes to promote direct democracy or community participation more generally (Anastacio et al. 2000). Without going into detail here, the point to emphasize is simply this: whatever the limitations of representative democracy, as this has developed in Western parliamentary systems, there are no simple solutions which promote more genuinely inclusive and more fully accountable forms – without taking on the underlying biases in the socio-economic context. Unless there are powerful pressures – backed with resources, including access to technical resources such as professional advice and expertise and information technology – to support them, working-class voices tend to be under-represented in mixed-class contexts, just as black and ethnic minority voices tend to be under-represented in areas in multi-ethnic communities. And there are genuinely complex questions to be resolved about who can legitimately speak for whose interests.

Democratic representation and accountability are inherently problematic, then. As has already been suggested, there are vitally important implications here for global social movements, setting out, as so many do, to be more democratically representative and accountable than the governments and the international organizations and agencies that are to be challenged. Some of these implications, and their associated dilemmas, emerge in more detail in subsequent chapters.

Meanwhile, this chapter concludes by focusing on strategies to strengthen democracy by supporting the development of 'civil society', 'social capital', capacity-building, active citizenship and community empowerment.

'Civil society', 'social capital' and capacity-building for active citizenship and community empowerment

Despite their widespread usage, the above are contested terms, with varying meanings relating to differing theoretical perspectives. A widely quoted definition considers 'civil society' as 'the space of uncoerced human association and also the set of relational networks – formed for the sake of the family, faith, interests and ideology – that fill this space' (Waltzer 1992: 89). This definition encompasses the widest range of voluntary and community organizations and networks, both formal and informal, local and global, including those based around churches, mosques, synagogues and temples, ethnic organizations, those concerned with advocacy and campaigning on particular issues or human rights more generally, those concerned with cultural issues, the arts, sports, leisure and the environment.

The case for building and maintaining a strong civil society has been put forward because this has been seen as providing a bulwark for democracy, limiting the potentially excessive powers of the state. This argument was used to justify programmes to strengthen civil society in Eastern and Central Europe, post-1989, just as similar arguments have been used to support the development of more decentralized and more participatory approaches to development in the South, with correspondingly enhanced roles for NGOs and community-based organizations.

Debates among Marxists have highlighted more problematic aspects of the concept of civil society, however. Turner, for example, referred to Marx's view of civil society as the 'real theatre of all history'. By implication, this implied that, far from representing any neutral counter-weight, civil society was actually imbued with the social relations and the associated conflicts of interest that characterized capitalist societies, more generally. Drawing upon the writings of Gramsci, Turner emphasized the importance of exploring the interconnections rather than the separations between civil society and the market as well as between civil society and the state (Turner 1992).

Gramsci's writings, which developed Marxist debates on civil society, have been immensely influential in subsequent discussions, being quoted in support of varying positions on the Left, including positions that have been criticized for their retreat from class politics (Holst 2002). Although Gramsci did indeed emphasize the importance of civil society and its potential role in struggles for social transformation, he was not suggesting that this could be achieved in isolation either from the state or from the economy. On the contrary, in fact, he emphasized the importance of understanding the inter-relationships between civil society, the state and the market. According to Gramsci, the concept of the state included more than the formal institutions of government.

The state, more broadly conceived, included elements of civil society, elements such as educational institutions (voluntary as well as statutory, informal as well as formal), through which the interests of the dominant class may be reinforced and indeed legitimized – or challenged from below. Capitalist social relations are not simply – or even predominantly – reproduced and maintained through the use of force, although the police and the courts do have roles to play in containing strikes and demonstrations, for example. The reality is far more complex, as people come to accept the 'common-sense' assumption – reinforced by the mainstream mass media – that the existing (capitalist) social framework is broadly reasonable and indeed acceptable as the basis for social relations. Civil society, according to this more complex view, is potentially a key site of struggle, particularly key when it comes to the battle of ideas about capitalism and the extent to which it may even be feasible to consider alternatives for social transformation (Sassoon Showstack 1991). Far from seeing capitalist globalization as necessarily linked to the strengthening of civil society, whether as cause or effect – or both – such approaches see civil society, then, as an increasingly important arena for these struggles, globally as well as locally.

So how might these debates relate to those concerned with social capital and capacity-building? As Fine's critical study has argued, social capital is a notion that has risen with 'a specific burst to prominence within and through the World Bank' as well as through debates in the social sciences (Fine 2001: 131). 'The traditional composition of natural capital, physical or produced capital, and human capital needs to be broadened to include social capital' according to the World Bank.

> Social capital refers to the internal social and cultural coherence of society, the norms and values that govern interactions among people and the institutions in which they are embedded. Social capital is the glue that holds societies together and without which there can be no economic growth or human well-being. Without social capital, society

at large will collapse, and today's world presents some very sad examples of this. (quoted in ibid.: 158)

Social capital was being defined, then, as the missing link to development, with the capacity for making those well endowed with it healthier as well as wealthier. Such extensive claims would seem to warrant further investigation.

In Fine's view, there are connections to be traced, here, with the shift in the World Bank's stance in recent years, from out and out neoliberalism to the post-Washington consensus, a shift outlined in the previous chapter. Social capital has shot to prominence as a research topic for the World Bank, Fine argues, as part of wider efforts to find ways of managing criticisms of the negative effects of neoliberalism, as this had been promoted in the past. Neoliberalism, in its more rampant forms, had stood accused of promoting increasing marketization at the expense of humanitarian considerations, neglecting 'the poor, women, popular participation, the environment, etc.' (ibid.: 153).

In addition to demonstrating concern about these social and environmental aspects, the World Bank's increasing focus upon social capital was part of wider agendas to legitimize 'more extensive intervention in "Civil Society"' (ibid.). The aim, in Fine's view, was to strengthen the voluntary and community/NGO/CBO sectors, thereby contributing to the construction of bulwarks against the state, bulwarks that would also be acceptable to the interests of transnational capital. This would be a more sophisticated – and more politically acceptable – version of neoliberalism. In place of privatization, per se, the voluntary and community sectors would be actively involved as partners in the processes of marketization.

There are parallels between Fine's view of the post-Washington consensus and the concerns of communitarian theorists such as Etzioni (Etzioni 1993) and those of particular politicians espousing the so-called 'third way' (Blair 1998). They, too, have shared anxieties about the negative social effects of rampant neoliberalism, fearing that unfettered individualism could become too socially divisive for anyone's ultimate comfort, breaking down traditional ties of trust, leading to a Hobbesian state of the war of all against all. Social trust and citizen responsibility needed to be rebuilt if liberal – free-market – democracies were to be safeguarded, whether locally or globally. The 'third way' has been promoted as representing a middle course between rampant neoliberalism on the one hand and discredited forms of state socialism on the other. Alternatively, critics such as Stuart Hall have argued that, far from being 'neither Left nor Right', the third way, as pursued by New Labour in Britain, has been characterized by an unequal struggle between the two. Increasingly the goals of social democracy, Hall argues, are becoming absorbed into the more dominant strand of neoliberalism (Hall 2003).

The concept of social capital is open to criticism, then, for its theoretical and political ambiguity, for carrying so many meanings as to be effectively meaningless. It has been criticized extensively, too, on empirical grounds. Putnam's assumptions about the potential benefits of social capital have been challenged (and the potentially negative effects of close social networks have also been highlighted, including the negative effects of such close ties among the Mafia and other such groupings). In addition, cross-cultural studies of social and political trust have provided empirical evidence to suggest that Putnam's assumptions about declining trust need to be disaggregated. While there would seem to be evidence of considerabe widespread scepticism about politicians and political parties, this does not necessarily imply a corresponding lack of social trust. On the contrary, in fact, 'social and political trust are not necessarily related' and voluntary organizations and associations do not necessarily affect this very significantly, having an influence which is 'generally weak, although not trivial' (Newton 1999: 185).

Broadly, in summary, supporters and critics of the notion of social capital could be categorized in the following ways, as the term has emerged from competing perspectives in the social sciences. The most frequently quoted sources have been rooted in the liberal pluralist political science studies in the USA already referred to, particularly the work of Putnam (Putnam 1995; 1996), Coleman (Coleman 1988) and Fukuyama (Fukuyama 1995). These sources have also been quoted and developed in the context of debates on communitarianism and the 'third way'. As has already been pointed out, both of these approaches have been the subject of considerable controversy.

Alternative approaches have emerged from the Left: European socio-logical perspectives, rooted in critical political economy, particularly the work of Bourdieu and others (Bourdieu 1977; Bourdieu and Passeron 1977). While these latter approaches have also been contentious, they have particular relevance in the context of this chapter, because they have begun to address issues of power and conflicting interests, with a critical focus upon the ways in which individuals and groups are more – or less – able to be effective through mobilizing their social networks, including mobilizing via global social movements.

The first set of approaches focus upon social capital in terms of the importance of relationships of trust in civil society and support networks as a means to generate economic development/renewal and to focus upon addressing problems such as health and well-being, as well as education and childcare (Giddens 1998). Social capital can also be sub-divided into 'bonding capital' – meaning the networks and relationships of trust *within* communities – and 'bridging capital' , the networks and inter-relationships *between* communities and external organizations, and agencies providing resources and services to communities. The overall emphasis, in either case, focuses upon economic development and the provision of cost-effective services within the framework of existing social relations. From this perspective, there are concerns with social capital as a means for the promotion of self-help – to reduce demands on overstretched services – concerns with social capital as a mechanism for strengthening social control, and concerns with social capital in the context of capacity-building for participation and the ability to gain access to external resources more effectively. Social capital is seen as providing mechanisms for reinforcing and stabilizing social relationships within liberal democracies, rather than for challenging them. The im-plications of such approaches to the concept of social capital may be summarized as follows.

- social capital may be positively (or negatively) related to commu-nication networks: so, for example, those who have strong social networks may be better informed and therefore better able to make informed choices and to access relevant services, and to participate more generally
- social capital may be positively (or negatively) related to particular subcultures: so, for example, young people may belong to social net-works that discourage or which reinforce deviant and/or unhealthy behaviour such as smoking and substance misuse, which need to be controlled
- social capital, more generally, may be related to the strength or weak-ness of social ties that promote self-reliance, self-help and caring within communities and
- social capital may be related to local cultures that may be more or less socially cohesive and inclusive: so, for example, in areas with strong ties, fewer people may suffer from social isolation and depression and this, in turn, may be expected to have positive effects on their physical as well as their mental health and well-being.

Alternative approaches, in contrast, focus on social capital in terms of its relations with other forms of capital, economic capital in particular, as well as cultural capital and symbolic capital. Just as the previous section argued that political power needs to be understood in the context of the underlying relations of production, so does social capital need to be understood in its wider context. For Fine, in fact, capital is social – capitalism being rooted in capitalist social relations (Fine 2001). By definition, from this viewpoint, 'social capital' cannot logically be separated out from these underlying structures.

While still coming from a perspective which has been broadly rooted in political economy, other critics have conceptualized social capital somewhat differently rather than rejecting the notion altogether. According to this type of approach, social capital can be considered as one particular aspect of capital more generally. As with any other form of capital, it has been argued by Bourdieu and others, the effectiveness of social capital is unevenly distributed, and those with the most social capital tend to be those able to put their social networks to most effective use. Even if fewer city bankers, for example, have social networks based upon public school education these days, they may still enjoy access to massively more effective social networks than do unemployed residents in inner-city areas. Social networks of trust do matter, from this perspective, and those with the most powerful networks can – and do – use these networks to reinforce their wealth and power.

Conversely, those with access to less powerful networks may still use these as best they can, to pursue their common interests. For example, working people can and do belong to trade unions to safeguard and to improve their wages and working conditions. Being an active trade unionist can offer opportunities for gaining access to other relevant networks, including access to political parties of the Left, and to organizations campaigning for a variety of related causes, including the environment, peace and human rights, more generally. As will be suggested in more detail below, such networks are key to the development of effective alliances for social transformation.

Programmes to strengthen social capital need to be evaluated, then, in terms of the extent to which they support such potentially progressive networks – or, conversely, the extent to which they bypass them, thereby contributing to their effective marginalization. Are inequalities being reinforced or are they being effectively challenged by initiatives to strengthen social capital, and to provide for capacity-building to promote community participation and empowerment?

The implications of this alternative approach to the concept of social capital may be characterized as follows:

• those with the least effective social capital and/or the weakest networks may be least likely to benefit from policy interventions to promote user and community participation (unless corrective measures are built into programmes and monitored continuously to ensure that programmes are socially inclusive and that community participation structures are both representative and effectively democratically accountable)

- those with the most social capital, initially, may be best placed to increase their social capital through such policy interventions – becoming the acceptable faces of the NGO/community sectors, the 'stars' of community participation (unless corrective measures are built into programmes and monitored continuously)
- even those with strong social capital locally, *within* their own communities, may fail to develop effective networks *beyond* their communities – i.e. networks to organizations and individuals responsible for decision-making in general and resource allocation more specifically. Strong local ties in deprived areas and regions may also be associated with limited knowledge of wider opportunities for development and change. Here too, whether consciously or not, programmes may reinforce rather than redress these forms of inequality in relation to effective social capital.

While these differing perspectives on the concept of social capital have been set out as polar opposites, however, it has also been suggested that it may be more useful to approach the study of social capital in terms of a continuum (Gamarnikow and Green 1999). At the progressive end, Gamarnikow and Green suggest, is a concern with citizenship, empowerment, democratization and social justice. At the other end, in contrast, social capital may be associated with strategies to strengthen traditional family and community structures and the remoralization of the social order, stressing the contribution of families and communities to self-help and social control in their neighbourhoods.

Possible implications for global social movements?

Global social movements face competing pressures. Paradoxically, capitalist globalization can be perceived to have opened up political spaces while simultaneously increasing the countervailing pressures on movements for democratization and empowerment. The spread of Western forms of liberal democracy has been associated with increases in particular aspects of human rights, such as the right to vote, but decreases in other aspects, such as the right to a sustainable livelihood, for all too many of the world's poorest peoples.

The post-Washington consensus has been associated with increasing opportunities for the organizations and agencies of civil society – within the context of the continuation of neoliberal agendas more generally. NGOs have been invited into international policy fora in addition to being invited to tender to provide policy research as well as services for development. As the World Bank's paper on partnerships with NGOs argued,

> The increased recognition of the limitations of the public sector and a greater reliance on the private sector to effectively address the problems facing developing countries have led to a greater awareness of what different actors in civil society can contribute to national development [...] In this context, the World Bank recognises the important role that nongovernmental organisations (NGOs both local and international) play in meeting the challenges of development. (World Bank 1996: 1)

In parallel, major international gatherings have come to include spaces (albeit, often, peripheral rather than central spaces) for alternative assemblies. Democratization is being promoted both locally and globally, whether this takes the form of policies to promote decentralization, or policies to encourage more direct approaches to democracy, including the promotion of citizen participation and empowerment. But democratization emerges as a complex process, with no easy answers to the dilemmas inherent in representation and accountability. Here, too, political power and powerlessness cannot be addressed without taking account of the underlying socio-economic context.

Widespread concerns with strengthening civil society, enhancing social capital through capacity-building, have resulted in increased opportunities for the NGO and community sectors. These opportunities can be used in different ways, however, depending – at least in part – on the perspectives and the interests of those involved. Those with the most effective access could use this to reinforce their own positions as the organizations that can most effectively represent the interests of others. As they gain increasingly valuable contacts and expertise at the international level, the social capital of larger NGOs in the North, for example, could be further enhanced, along with that of their partners in the South. While these pressures may be more acute, the more professional an international organization or agency becomes, active grass-roots campaigning groups face not dissimilar dilemmas about who represents whom, and in whose ultimate interests. These are dilemmas that reappear in subsequent chapters.

3 | Social movements: competing approaches

Social movements have been analysed by sociologists, as well as political theorists, from differing intellectual traditions and perspectives. This chapter focuses upon those aspects of the debates around these approaches, which have particular relevance for the analysis of global social movements, 'globalization from below' as they have been categorized (Falk 1995). Social movements in general, like global social movements more specifically, span the range of the political spectrum (Castells 1996; 1997; Falk 1995; Harvey 1998). Definitions have varied and so have the theoretical perspectives that underpin them.

Rather than attempt a comprehensive account of social movement theory, this chapter focuses on summarizing two broad schools of thought that have been particularly influential: 'rational actor' theories, as these have been developed and built upon, in varying ways, in North American debates, and 'new social movement' theories, more prevalent in European debates (Della Porta and Diani 1999). The first approach, in summary, started from explaining people's participation in social movements in terms of the pursuit of their own self-interest (an approach that would be consistent with neoliberal assumptions about individuals as rational actors and consumers in the marketplace), although subsequent theorists have developed more radical structuralist interpretations. The second approach, in contrast, has tended to focus upon social movements as precursors of social transformation (often – although not necessarily – posed in libertarian terms), emphasizing the development of new identities, and new, less bureaucratized and more fully participatory forms of organization.

More recently, there has been growing interest in cross-fertilization, drawing upon insights from both approaches. North American approaches have contributed to our understanding of how social movements develop, it has been suggested, while new social movement approaches have contributed to our understanding of why (Klandermans 1991). Recent studies have, more specifically, also been concerned to explore the inter-relationships between structure and agency, the ways in which individuals and groups/organizations shape events and/or are shaped by the structures of their social contexts, the material opportunities and constraints and the cultural influences and values that affect their choices (Crossley 2002). As this chapter will suggest in more detail subsequently, there are potentially key implications, here, for the analysis of social movements in general and global social movements more specifically – even if there are still gaps to be filled, in theorizing the latter.

The chapter concludes by focusing on examples of international movements and campaigning social movement organizations concerned with the environment (including organizations such as Friends of the Earth and Greenpeace) and human rights (such as Amnesty International). None of these examples would seem to be explained fully by either of the approaches that have been summarized – although elements of each would certainly seem to have relevance. There would also seem to be implications from the previous chapter's discussion of civil society and the conflicting pressures from the market as well as from the state. As Deakin has pointed out, 'by definition, transactions and relationships which are located in the civil society arena take place on terms not wholly dominated by the state in its various forms or by the values or procedures of the market', but they are affected by both, with varying perspectives among participants about how to respond to these pressures from *both* sides, 'the different type of engagement – close or distant – with the state on one side and the market on the other' (Deakin 2001: 7).

Differing approaches to studying social movements and social movement organizations

The definition of what constitutes a social movement has been contested, just as their roots and wider potential significance have been, depending upon the perspective in question. It has even been suggested that 'the whole idea of a "social movement" as a description of collective action should be abandoned because it traps our language in conceptual traditions that have to be discarded' (Escobar and Alvarez 1992: 7). But varying attempts at definition have been offered.

In summary, these tend to include collective mobilizations with socio-economic, political and/or cultural dimensions, mobilizing around issues of identity as well as around more specific rights (and social movements – such as feminism, for example – may include each of these). Blumer defines social movements as 'collective enterprises seeking to establish a new order of life' (Blumer 1969: 99), implying long-term goals for social change. Eyerman and Jamison, in contrast, focus upon the transitory nature of such mobilizations, which they define as 'temporary public spaces, as moments of collective creation that provide societies with ideas, identities, and even ideals' (Eyerman and Jamison 1991: 4), although others have seen social movements as more durable phenomena.

In addition, the four social movement themes that have been identified by Della Porta and Diani have relevance, to add to these varying definitions. These themes include *informal interaction networks* (as well as more formal ones, because formal organizations such as churches, trade unions and political parties can and do participate in social movements too) *based upon shared beliefs and solidarity, engaging in collective action with a focus upon conflicts,* and *including the use of protest* (Della Porta and Diani 1999). As Della Porta and Diani also recognize, however, shared beliefs and solidarity are not simply to be taken as givens in social movements. There are two-way processes at work here, as individuals and groups join on the basis of shared beliefs, which may then become strengthened through processes of participation in collective action and collective reflection on these shared experiences. As the previous chapter suggested, adult and community education perspectives may be of relevance here, focusing on the potential for experiential learning, backed by critical analysis, enabling social movement participants to strengthen their shared understandings of the causes as well as their shared commitments to the resolution of the issues around which they mobilize (Holst 2002).

Such approaches to the definition of social movements could encompass a very wide range of mobilizations. The women's movement and environmental and green movements would be included, for instance, together with movements for peace, civil liberties and human rights (including rights to self-determination and respect for a range of minorities – and indeed majorities in the case of the women's movement). The trade union and labour movement would also be included, comprising, as it does, a range of networks and adherents, over and above the paid-up members of any particular constituent organization. So would fascist movements, as well as anti-fascist and anti-racist movements (there being nothing inherently progressive about social movements per se), pro- and anti-abortion movements and animal rights movements. All of these could be described as comprising networks sharing beliefs and solidarity, with commitments to collective action, including the use of varying forms of protest (whether violent and/or non-violent).

Della Porta and Diani's definition of social movements would not include single formal organizations, however. So particular trade union organizations, religious organizations or political parties would not be defined as social movements per se, although they might well participate in social movement mobilizations, along with other organizations and individuals. Movements, according to Della Porta and Diani, are 'by definition fluid phenomena' with broad collectives with 'blurred boundaries' (Della Porta and Diani 1999: 17). 'Strictly speaking, social movements do not have members but participants' (ibid.). In practice, however, the term 'social movement' has often been used less tightly, to include specific social movement organizations, as well as applying to looser groupings. Summarizing the problems of definition, Crossley has suggested that none of the definitions is watertight; social movements 'share a family resemblance rather than a fixed essence and their definition inevitably rests upon the *fuzzy* logic of ordinary language use' (Crossley 2002: 7).

Starting from collective mobilization as rational action

Della Porta and Diani and others have explained the origins of rational actor approaches to the study of social movements (Klandermans 1991; Canal 1997; Della Porta and Diani 1999; Crossley 2002). The background to the development of these approaches to the study of social movements in the USA from the 1970s was the previous predominance of functionalism in sociological explanations of collective behaviour, emphasizing, as functionalist sociologists did, the ways in which society functioned as a coherent whole. Functionalism placed less emphasis upon the motivations and actions of individuals and groups – and could be taken to imply that collective action and social conflict more generally were aberrations, evidence of deviancy in an otherwise well-functioning social system.

Counteracting such approaches, rational actor theory started from the desires of individual social actors, and the rational ways in which they evaluated and acted upon the opportunities and constraints that faced them in attempting to realize these desires. As has already been suggested, rational actor theory has been described as methodological individualism (Crossley 2002), consistent with neoliberal economic approaches to society, based upon rational individuals realizing their own self-interest. But this could be and was applied to the study of collective action. Approaching social movements as rational responses, rather than as examples of deviancy, was a step forward, although rational actor theory has also been widely criticized for its inherent limitations, offering at best a very partial account, focusing on actors' choices, without taking sufficient account of the complexity of human motivations, political beliefs and emotions, altruistic as well as self-interested, and without sufficient emphasis upon the wider structural context.

In addition to being critiqued, these approaches were drawn upon and developed by resource mobilization theorists. They were concerned to take more account of the availability or non-availability of the resources, such as the political freedom to organize, together with a minimum of time, energy and access to material resources, which made it more – or less – likely that social actors would participate in collective action. So, for example, organizational resources were identified as a potentially relevant factor, including access to external resources such as the resources provided via support from powerful allies.

As has been pointed out, however, relying upon powerful allies can be a mixed blessing (McAdam 1982). There may – or may not – be members of a 'liberal left elite who, when they have excess resources, in the form of time or money, etc. are both willing and able to inject them into good causes' (Crossley 2002: 82). And those struggles that are effectively patronized by middle-class elites may then become subjected to pressures and 'preferences from above'. 'Struggles against the establishment may succeed because some members of that establishment wish them to' (ibid.). Elite sponsorship may also divide social movements, defining their acceptable and their non-acceptable faces, the former to be supported, the latter to be marginalized and if possible discredited (Piven and Cloward 1992).

Similar issues have been raised in previous chapters, including criticisms of the ways in which 'elite decision-makers evaluate the NGO world with a quick and pragmatic eye and see potential allies in the delicate work of diffusing this new opposition', seeking out the respectable face of dissent (Davis 2001: 176) in the context of mobilizations around Seattle. Such a view could, incidentally, be seen as consistent with rational actor theory, although that is not necessarily how such arguments have been developed. Liberal elites may support some, but by no means all, social movements as part of coherent strategies for taming them, thereby preserving the status quo for the longer term.

On the other hand, to dismiss any external support would seem unnecessarily limiting. As the case studies demonstrate, subsequently, social movements and social movement organizations have, in many cases, relied extensively on such support, engaging with the ensuing dilemmas rather than rejecting them as a matter of principle. There are, in any case, definitional problems about notions of elites and concepts of social class, relating to differing theoretical perspectives. Marxist approaches define classes in terms of the relations of production ('captains of industry' versus 'workers by hand or brain') and differentiate between 'class in itself' and 'class for itself' (or degrees of class consciousness) – which would certainly not exclude Left intellectuals and organizers from active participation in movements for social transformation. More generally, it could also be pointed out that if labour and progressive movements and liberation struggles had rejected any support or involvement from middle-class intellectuals and organizers they would have dispensed with the contributions of Marx and Engels, Lenin, Gramsci, Rosa Luxemburg, Fidel Castro and Nelson Mandela, to name but a few examples.

Meanwhile theorists of social movement organizations, such as McCarthy and Zeld, have also compared them with 'businesses or entrepreneurial units which are found in economic life and which respond to economic demand. They emerge in response to demand, or perhaps in some ways pump prime to create demand, which they then seek to satisfy' (Crossley 2002: 85–6; McCarthy and Zald 1977). Once they have been formed, McCarthy and Zald suggested, social movement organizations have to look to their own organizational survival, so they have to become concerned, even preoccupied, with securing resources. The better-established may be more likely to succeed in this, in the long term, having a stronger market position, an achievement that involves developing a public profile in competition with others. If this also sounds somewhat reminiscent of neoliberal economics, that does not necessarily make it inherently less relevant. As will be suggested below, the impact of market forces can indeed be traced, as social movement organizations cope with pressures to become what have been questioned as effectively 'protest businesses' (Jordan and Maloney 1997).

Resource mobilization approaches have been criticized from the Left, for over-emphasizing the 'how' questions rather than the more fundamental 'why' questions in general. More specifically, they have also been criticized for over-emphasizing the role of formal organization and support from liberal elites that can lead to deference and the incorporation of protest rather than more challenging mobilizations for social change. Rather than exploring wider challenges, Melucci and Lyyra argue, through such approaches 'we are, instead, confronted with strategically oriented reform actors, analytically indistinct from political pressure groups, even when they do not act within the formal frame of a political system' (Melucci and Lyyra 1998: 216). This latter question about formal organizational structures, and their strengths as well as their limitations, emerges in subsequent discussions. Meanwhile, resource mobilization theories have also been developed in explicitly radical ways.

Resources and networks have been explored from within as well as from without. So, for example, McAdam's study of the civil rights movement in the USA valued the contributions of existing organizations and networks, particularly those of the black churches. Participation in social movement activities can also develop networks and organizational resources, both for the individuals and for the organizations and groupings involved. McAdam completed a follow-up study of white college students who had taken part in civil rights campaigning in the southern states of the USA in the 'Freedom Summer' of 1964 (McAdam 1988). Through this he traced the long-term impact, as so many of those who had been radicalized by their experiences went on to play active parts in the peace movement against the Vietnam War, in the student movement, the women's movement and in local community mobilizations.

There are important implications here for social movements more generally, including global social movements. McAdam's work underlined the importance of pre-existing networks and organizational experiences, together with the ways in which these resources can be strengthened and developed through active participation. Even when social movements are at a relatively low ebb, these resources can survive, to be revivified, if and when the climate for social action becomes more favourable again, subsequently. As Crossley confirmed on the basis of his own studies of anti-psychiatric and mental health survivor movements, 'the history of any movement is often punctuated by the rise and fall of specific organizations and organizational cells within it, each new group breathing life into the movement and its struggle, directing it in a specific way, before finally dying off or burning out and leaving room for the next contender' (Crossley 2002: 97). Networks can and do survive and develop through these processes, and there are typically linkages and friendship networks between social movement organizations that can sustain them, both within their field (as with Greenpeace, Friends of the Earth and Earth First, for example) and more generally. The importance of such networks emerges from the subsequent case studies, ties of cooperation as well as the relationships of competition already identified. And as individuals move jobs from one social movement organization to another, such networks can be further reinforced.

McAdam and others have seen such networks as only one of a number of aspects to be explored. 'Political process' approaches include the structures of political opportunity, as these impact upon social movements, creating more – or less – space for effective mobilizations. This type of approach focuses on interactions with mainstream politics as well as upon the social movements per se. As McAdam, Tarrow and Tilly and others have developed their analyses, in fact, there is potentially far more emphasis upon the underlying structural factors (McAdam et al. 2001). Mobilizations are set within the framework of the wider political environment, taking account of the potential links between structural issues, industrial conflicts, the student movement and violent police responses to social mobilizations in Italy at the end of the 1960s, for example. This includes (if not emphasizes) underlying grievances, the socio-economic cleavages as well as more individual and group motivations, the structures of opportunity (including the political space or lack of space for protest) and the resources (including the networks and organizational resources) available for pursuing these as well as the actions of social actors. These action strategies include putting forward demands ('framing' them, according to this terminology), in ways that maximize support, and developing effective tactics ('repertoires of contention') such as teach-ins, sit-ins and other innovative forms of direct action that challenge previous ways of expressing and managing social conflicts.

Taken together, these are conceived as dynamic processes, processes that inter-relate and develop accordingly, over time, in 'cycles of contention'. People's consciousness and commitment can and do develop over time, as issues are 'framed' and participants avail themselves of the opportunities and resources to mobilize. And through such involvement, collective consciousness can develop, along with networks of solidarity.

Political process approaches would seem to offer a number of valuable insights that could be applied to the study of global social movements. These include the emphasis upon the importance of movement networks as well as access to external resources, the focus upon the wider political context and the links with other mobilizations, the notions of 'framing', 'repertoires of contention', and the links between these and the development of collective consciousness and commitment, in 'cycles of contention', over time. Each of these aspects emerges in the discussions of case study experiences in subsequent chapters.

Summarizing such approaches, Crossley concluded that this 'has a great deal to offer to the analysis of social movements', but that there were also 'significant weaknesses which must be addressed' (Crossley 2002: 126). In summary, one of his concerns was that the emphasis upon political opportunities was not sufficiently precise, nor did it take sufficient account of other structural factors. Some of these aspects were more fully explored by new social movement theorists. In addition, Crossley argued, the inter-relationships between socio-economic structure and human agency were still insufficiently developed.

Before moving on to summarize the new social movement theorists approaches, it is important to recognize, however, that over the past two decades US scholars such as McAdam, McCarthy and Zald have been getting together with new social movement theorists from Europe.

'The intellectual impact of this cross-fertilization', they argued, 'has been dramatic and salutary' (McAdam et al. 1996: xii) as they move towards a synthetic, comparative approach to the study of social movements. Authors such as Tarrow have also been explicitly concerned to build towards enhanced understanding of transnational social movements. So what was it about new social movement approaches that they were interested in exploring?

New social movement approaches

Much has been written about new social movement theories (such as those developed by Gorz 1982; Melucci 1988; Touraine 1974) and their critics (Scott 1990; Shukra 1998; Mayo 2000; Holst 2002). In summary, these approaches were developed in Europe, in response to the rise of new movements in the 1960s and 1970s. This phase of protest in Europe began with the student movement, which erupted in 1968 (coming close to toppling the government in France, according to some interpretations). The peace movement developed in solidarity with those protesting against the US war in Vietnam and the women's liberation movement/second-wave feminism developed in Europe as well as North America in the 1970s, along with gay and lesbian liberation, the green and environmental movements, black and ethnic minority movements. More recently, disability movements have developed, together with a range of others, including various brands of fundamentalist movements.

The movements were not so different in practice in Europe, but theoretical responses varied, being more overtly focused upon debates within Marxism and its critics, including former Marxists. They were concerned to analyse not only how, but also why, some movements were emerging, as the result of what underlying forces of socio-economic and political change. In particular, those coming from a Marxist tradition were concerned to explore the reasons why these apparently new forms of social conflict did not seem to fit neatly into previous categories of class conflict, rooted in the working class and the trade union and labour movement (although, as a matter of fact, there were also major industrial struggles in the late 1960s and early 1970s in a number of European countries, including Britain, France and Italy).

One of the strengths of the new social movement theorists, a strength already identified, was that they focused on these broad underlying socio-economic and political questions (Della Porta and Diani 1999; Crossley 2002). Typically, however, they started from the 'new' movements' emphasis upon issues of identity, ideology and culture, issues of social integration and social and cultural reproduction, rather than upon the material issues around production and distribution that had been seen as the bread and butter of class conflict in capitalist societies. In the post-Second World War boom, with a larger 'cake' of resources to be distributed, there were greater opportunities for some of the material benefits to be spread more widely. The class structures of advanced industrial countries were, in any case, undergoing processes of change. Overall, service sectors increased and occupational structures shifted accordingly, as white-collar jobs expanded. These changes did not, of course, mean that social conflicts were outmoded. On the contrary, expectations rose, and so did demands. But as the boom began to slow down, there was increasing frustration as a result of attempts to improve private profitability through industrial restructuring and through measures to control public spending on welfare.

The new conflicts, according to Habermas, one of the thinkers who particularly influenced new social movement theories, were 'not ignited by distribution problems (such as wages struggles) but by questions having to do with the grammar of forms of life' (Habermas 1987: 392, quoted in Crossley 2002: 160). This gave the second-wave feminist slogan, 'the personal is political', a particular meaning – politics was now being widened to include issues of identity, culture and lifestyle.

The reasons for this fundamental shift in the nature of social conflict could be explained, new social movement theorists such as Touraine suggested, by the development of post-industrial society, a context in which new classes developed critiques of the very nature of capitalist society. Traditional forms of class politics were being challenged by these new ways of doing politics, raising more basic questions and raising them in new ways, more decentralized and more participatory than conventional working-class politics. One of the key texts here was Gorz's *Farewell to the Working Class* (Gorz 1982). While traditional class politics had been concerned to achieve immediate material gains, these new forms of politics were far less readily satisfied, it was argued, because they were challenging the very basis of politics and society.

There are parallels here with aspects of libertarian socialist traditions. The emphasis upon decentralization and active participation was a characteristic of both. And both expressed very considerable scepticism about strategies that relied upon the state, or even the formal organizations of the trade union and labour movement to achieving meaningful steps towards social transformation.

Some of these assumptions have already been subjected to questioning, including questions about the supposedly inherent shortcomings of the 'old' movements and organizational structures, issues which will be explored further in the following chapter. With 2.5 billion in the global workforce – almost twice as many as in the mid-1960s (Munck 2002) reports of the supposed death of the working class might seem to have been somewhat exaggerated (to borrow a phrase from Mark Twain). Indeed, Gorz himself has subsequently revised his views on this. Meanwhile, as has also been pointed out, some of the new social movements of the 1960s and 1970s have subsequently been on the wane (Holst 2002). Aspects of the new social movement's approaches may seem irrevocably dated, then, in the contemporary global context.

As the following chapter will argue, they are also problematic politically, in so far as they marginalize the organizations and struggles of the workers and their allies in the trade union and labour movement, worldwide. Setting up the 'new' against the 'old' is also inherently problematic, as will be suggested below. As a number of critics have pointed out, many of the features, including many of the issues addressed and the organizational appoaches and tactics employed, have actually already been tried and tested. First-wave feminists used imaginative forms of direct action, for example, including chaining themselves to railings, just as protesters took direct action for the right to access to the countryside in the inter-war period in Britain. Nor have the new social movements necessarily pursued more progressive goals. On the contrary, in fact, they have covered the range of the political spectrum (Castells 1997a; Mayo 2000). And they have developed and changed over time, both in terms of their politics and in terms of their organizational structures (Scott 1990) as some of their more far-reaching, more transformatory goals have been adjusted over time, to become more realistically achievable within the current socio-economic framework (ibid.).

So why have these approaches been of continuing interest? A cynic might suggest that they have been more acceptable to the Right than have the alternatives, more rooted in Marxist analyses of the continuing relevance of class conflict, with the working class as the key force for social transformation. Meanwhile, as has been pointed out, the Right has been actively waging class war on 'the unemployed, the unemployable and the working poor' (Piven and Cloward 1982) both locally and globally.

But critics on the Left have also pointed to the value of the questions that the new social movement theorists were posing. Whatever their inherent limitations, they were raising key issues for the development of a more transformatory politics of the Left (Harvey 1990). As Paterson summarized this, despite doing away with the universalistic concept of rights themselves, through their emphases on particularistic identity politics, they 'have radicalised left-wing politics in an irrevocable way. They have also indelibly marked our understanding of society and of the political sources of social change' (Paterson 1999: 51). Left approaches pay more attention to issues of culture and identity and how to relate these to other struggles. And whatever the remaining battles that need to be fought, the rights of women, black and ethnic minority communities, gays and lesbians and people with disabilities, along with green and environmental issues, are now firmly on labour and trade union movements' agendas.

The new social movement's search for the underlying structural causes, the whys as well as the hows of social movements' emergence, successes and shortcomings has been recognized and valued (McAdam et al. 1996) and this has led to a multiplication of 'attempts to meld different theoretic perspectives into a new synthesis' (Della Porta and Diani 1999: 14). One of the most promising of these attempts to achieve a new synthesis has been explored by Crossley, seeking to build upon the theoretical work of Bourdieu – who, as Crossley points out, did not focus upon the study of social movements per se, although his theoretical work can usefully be applied to this – to develop a framework that would encompass both the 'why' and the 'how' questions, focusing upon the inter-relationships between human agency on the one hand and socio-economic structures on the other. In summary, Bourdieu built upon Marxist approaches to the analysis of structural relations in capitalist society, developing the concept of the 'habitus' to understand the two-way relationships between people's structural situations and their own agency as humans acting upon this. As the previous chapter summarized, Bourdieu also developed the concept of 'fields', the different aspects of the structures in which and with which people act and interact, the economic field, the political field, the social field and the educational, ideological and cultural fields, each of which relates to particular aspects and forms of capital. Although this has been criticized for stretching the concept of capital (Fine 2001), Bourdieu's approach offers promising lines of development in constructing a coherent analysis of global social movements from a Left perspective.

Meanwhile, before exploring debates around the extent to which social movements might offer potentially radical alternatives to – or might be building alliances with – the organizations and groupings of the political Left and the trade union and labour movement internationally, in more detail, this chapter concludes by focusing on some examples. These draw upon experiences of social movement organizations of the green and environmental and human rights movements. How might these illustrate the relevance of the insights from either or both of these types of approaches to the study of social movements?

Social movements and social movement organizations concerned with green and environmental issues and with human rights

The green and environmental movement has already emerged as an example of a new social movement, challenging existing social relations, an embryo of future societies based upon alternative relations and organizational forms. Deep ecologists clearly have challenged productionism and proposed alternative ways of living sustainably, with different relations between humans and nature. At the other end of this spectrum, however, environmental campaigners have been concerned with far more immediate issues and gains, including the defence of people's own space from toxic waste, for example, or from unwanted developments more generally ('Not in My Back Yard'), as a more urgent priority than the defence of nature – 'Not in Anyone's Back Yard' – as this position has been summarized by Harvey and others (Harvey 1998; Castells 1997a).

Environmental campaigns have actually spanned the range of the political spectrums then, from 'back to nature' fascists to libertarian socialists and anarchists (Morris 1996). It has been suggested that rather than one green movement, in fact it might be more relevant to refer to varying shades of green (Jordan and Maloney 1997). Alternatively, as one of the founders of Greenpeace, Robert Hunter, has been quoted as arguing, environmentalists have seen themselves as neither needing to move further to the Left nor further to the Right – rather, we must seriously begin to inquire into the rights of rabbits and turnips, the rights of soil and swamp, the rights of the atmosphere, and ultimately, the rights of the planet (quoted in Dalton 1994: 49).

Nor are environmental campaigns actually so new, the National Trust, for example, having been founded in 1850. The term 'ecology' itself was coined in the latter half of the nineteenth century, subsequently emerging as an identifiable academic study in the 1930s (Morris 1996). More recently, however, the green and environmental movement has had renewed support – although this may have reached a plateau, it has been suggested (Jordan and Maloney 1997). And with the slogan 'Think global, act local' they have been in the forefront of developing environmentalism as a global social movement. In a study of the characteristics of the transnational social movement sector Smith quoted evidence to demonstrate that the environment was the focus for 14 per cent of these organizations in 1993 (compared with 6 per cent in 1973) – the second largest single category, after human rights (the focus of 27 per cent of transnational organizations in 1993, compared with 23 per cent in 1973) (Smith 1997: 47). Rather than attempting to cover this range and diversity, this chapter merely summarizes some of the issues that relate to debates on social movements more generally, as these issues emerge from writings on two well-known social movement organizations within the green and environmental movement: Friends of the Earth and Greenpeace.

Friends of the Earth dates back to the early 1970s. The British organization is linked to Friends of the Earth International (founded in 1971) and there are local campaigning networks that come together via an annual conference. The local groups are separate legal entities operating under licence. By the 1990s, there were approaching a quarter of a million supporters in Britain, with nearly a hundred paid staff, over a hundred thousand supporters and an annual income of over £5 million. Friends of the Earth International had over twenty organizations in industrialized countries, fourteen in the developing South and three in Eastern and Central Europe.

Friends of the Earth covers a wide range of activities, including work with local community projects, on issues such as recycling, anti-road campaigns and campaigns for cycling and healthier cities. They provide educational materials on environmental issues, and they act as a think tank and watchdog, monitoring, for example, pollution, toxic waste, acid rain and vehicle emissions and the ozone layer and global warming. Friends of the Earth also engages in parliamentary lobbying and in campaigning at different levels. For example, these have included environmental campaigns to save the rainforest and wider campaigns with other organizations and movements on issues such as fair trade and world debt. Briefings for global events such as the 1992 Earth Summit explained both the issues and the processes leading up to the Rio summit, educating supporters in how to lobby and campaign effectively at this global level.

Greenpeace developed over a similar period, from 1971, focusing upon the environment and peace (Kozak 1997). The organization set out to campaign 'to prevent people from damaging or destroying our world' (Hurley 1991: 2). The initial impetus came from Canada, although this spread rapidly and the German organization has been a key source of support, from the 1970s onwards. The Quakers were also a significant source of support in the early days. The first international office was in London, and this then moved to Amsterdam. National organizations provide resources for this, and support the development of organizations in developing countries in the South and in ex-communist countries. By the mid-1990s Greenpeace had a staff of a thousand or so, with over forty offices worldwide. In the UK there were over a quarter of a million local supporters with some 150 local groups (Kozak 1997) with some two and a half million supporters worldwide by the beginning of the 1990s (Hurley 1991). Like Friends of the Earth, Greenpeace supporters come from a range of perspectives, and the leadership has been described as not being especially concerned with traditional Left policies, although they do typically support movements for women's equality and participation more generally (Dalton 1994).

Each of the national offices elects a representative who goes to the annual meeting of councillors. This is where campaigns and policy are developed. The international board, which is the overall governing body, then decides whether or not to confirm these decisions. The major spectacular international events have been under the control of Greenpeace International. Greenpeace is totally independent of any political party and all its funding comes from supporters and the general public, plus any funds raised (from the sale of t-shirts and badges, for example).

Greenpeace's focus on the environment and peace, initially, came together in campaigns against nuclear testing and nuclear dumping, with considerable emphasis upon direct non-violent action. There have been some spectacular events, including campaigns against French nuclear testing in the Pacific in the 1970s and the loss of the ship the *Rainbow Warrior*, which was blown up by French secret agents, killing one of the crew, in 1985 (not sharing Greenpeace's commitment to non-violence, evidently). Since then there has been more emphasis upon more complex aspects such as environmental monitoring, focusing on issues such as the ozone layer. Campaigning tactics focus on non-violent direct action. There is less emphasis upon lobbying politicians, the organization being more focused upon applying pressure on corporations to change their ways. Successes here include the fridge companies' recognition that they needed to negotiate, when Greenpeace exposed the impact they were having on the ozone layer. In summary, then, there are differences of focus and of organizational culture and style between Friends of the Earth and Greenpeace, although there are also considerable parallels between these two social movement organizations, both of which have a very considerable degree of support and networks with the wider green and environmental movement and beyond.

Amnesty developed somewhat earlier, founded in 1961, the brainchild of Peter Benenson, a Catholic lawyer of Jewish descent, who had grown up in the wider context of a period dramatically affected by the Spanish Civil War and by Nazism. As the *Amnesty International Handbook* explains, 'More than four decades ago, two Portuguese students lifted their glasses and raised a toast to freedom. For that simple act, they were sentenced to seven years' imprisonment. The story horrified the British lawyer Peter Benenson, who decided to take action' (Amnesty International 2002: 9). He wrote to the *Observer* newspaper calling for an international campaign to protect 'forgotten prisoners'.

Historically, Amnesty International has campaigned to: 'free all prisoners of conscience; ensure a prompt and fair trial for all political prisoners; abolish the death penalty, torture and other cruel, inhuman or degrading treatment or punishment; end extrajudicial executions and "disappearances"; fight impunity by working to ensure that perpetrators of such human rights abuses are brought to justice in accordance with international standards' (ibid.: 12).

Benenson involved a number of prominent figures from the law and the mass media who shared his concern with prisoners of conscience. These were defined as those detained because of their beliefs, colour, sex, ethnic origin, language or religious creed – provided that they had not used or advocated the use of violence (Power 1981). The focus was 'to work impartially for the release of those imprisoned for their opinions, to seek for them a fair (and public) trial, to enlarge the right of asylum, to help political refugees find work, and to urge the creation of effective international machinery to guarantee freedom of opinion' (Power 1981: 10).

Amnesty set out to take up their cases, through tactics such as sending postcards to prisoners of conscience to express support, writing letters to take up their cases and lobbying on their behalf with the authorities in question. Local Amnesty groups were set up, and these groups adopted particular prisoners. From the start, though, Amnesty was an international as well as a national and locally based organization.

The early 1960s were still affected by the Cold War (although this was not its peak) and Amnesty set out to be politically neutral. For each political prisoner from the Eastern bloc, one would also be adopted from the West, starting with political prisoners such as Augustino Neto, a political prisoner held by the Portuguese, and a Hungarian cardinal, held in the East, for instance. There was major controversy over the case of Nelson Mandela (because, by 1964, he had supported going beyond non-violence in the struggle against apartheid in South Africa – a controversy eventually resolved by a compromise agreement to press his case without formally adopting him).

There were some difficult times, when Amnesty was involved in splits over allegations about key figures' involvement with the Foreign Office and even the CIA. The organization really took off in the 1970s, around the same time that Friends of the Earth and Greenpeace were growing. The bloody coup in 1973 which ended the socialist developments under the Allende government in Chile was seen as a factor in this growth, in response to the civil liberties abuses of the Pinochet regime (ibid.). By 2002 there were nationally organized sections in some fifty countries, with other co-ordinating structures in more than twenty others, with over a million members and subscribers worldwide (Amnesty International 2002).

In addition to campaigning for the rights of individual prisoners of conscience, Amnesty also undertakes research, sends special missions to particular countries to collect evidence and promotes special campaigns. These have included campaigns against capital punishment, against torture and against the torture trade (trade in the instruments and techniques of torture, such as the use of electric shocks, which were supplied to Chile, for example). Amnesty has also campaigned around children's rights.

Amnesty, like Greenpeace and Friends of the Earth (at least initially), is financed mainly from its membership and from donations from wider networks of supporters. The *Amnesty International Handbook* explains that the organization is democratic and self-governing (ibid.). Groups of members discuss issues and propose resolutions to the general meetings of their national section and governing bodies. These sections hold general meetings that debate policy proposals and vote on resolutions, and these resolutions then go forward to the international council. This international council is the main governing body, made up of representatives from every section, who meet every two years at the international council meeting (ibid.). The international council meetings elect the international executive committee, which implements the decisions of the international council through the international secretariat. While these are democratic structures, however, it has been suggested that, in practice, much decision-making is actually taken within the secretariat.

Jordan and Maloney's study concludes that these new social movement organizations cannot accurately be described as decentralized, non-hierarchical or particularly participatory in organizational style. In practice, Jordan and Maloney argue, Greenpeace, Friends of the Earth and Amnesty 'are similar in that like many other large-scale public interest groups, they operate along corporate lines. Amnesty and Friends of the Earth adopt a business strategy to ensure efficient use of resources, to maximise effectiveness and, probably above all, to ensure organizational survival in a highly competitive market' (Jordan and Maloney 1997: 19).

They have to service their membership to keep the organization going and to raise funds from their supporters. In fact, according to Jordan and Maloney, they have to walk a tightrope here, as supporters want to see effective actions, real successes, but they also want the organization to resist becoming incorporated, being seen to remain independent. Movements need high-profile events, including stunts, which was how they described Greenpeace's Brent Spar campaign, to keep supporters interested. But they also need to be working within the policy-making process, coming under pressure to maintain dialogue with business interests as well as with government and international governmental organizations.

While social movement organizations such as Amnesty and Greenpeace respect democratic decision-making processes, including participatory processes, they themselves would not necessarily claim to exemplify direct democracy in action. Dalton, for example, suggested that mass membership organizations do, in practice, tend to be relatively centralized, and although they have annual general meetings, it would be unrealistic to expect an attendance of more than 10 per cent of the membership. 'Simply put,' Dalton concludes, 'most voluntary environmental associations are not vehicles for extensive citizen participation, and most group representatives openly acknowledge the fact' (Dalton 1994: 105). Although he suggested that environmental organizations tend to emphasize the importance of democratic participation, some achieve this more fully than others. He quoted one Greenpeace official's comment that the role of individuals was to provide money and leave the organizers to get on with it, while another representative suggested that effectively members could 'only vote with their feet' (ibid.: 107).

But this does not at all imply that such views were – or are – generally held. Nor does it actually demonstrate that these organizations were, or are, out of touch with the views of their members and wider supporters. On the contrary, in fact, there was evidence that they do know what their supporters will wear – or what they could become convinced about – and they do tend to do market research to check this out systematically (Jordan and Maloney 1997). Most members seemed contented, and studies of why people were leaving such social movement organizations have revealed that very few people were leaving because of policy differences (ibid.). They were far more likely to be leaving for more practical reasons, such as that their subscriptions had become overdue and they had neglected to renew them.

Friends of the Earth is somewhat different, placing far more emphasis upon democratic representation and local participation. The local groups are autonomous, operating under licence to use the name and logo (licences which have very rarely been withdrawn, and then only in exceptional circumstances). In England and Wales, the local groups have their own department at head office and their conferences pass resolutions, offering advice to the executive, which directly impacts upon the policy-making process. Two-thirds of the board is elected via the local groups, while the remaining third are appointed for their specific expertise.

Membership in these social movement organizations has also varied to some extent (with Friends of the Earth members tending to be younger). More generally, though, according to Jordan and Maloney's study, the membership was relatively middle-class, professional and well-educated (35 per cent of Friends of the Earth and 26 per cent of Amnesty's members had a degree, according to Jordan and Maloney's survey, compared with 8 per cent of the population overall). Women were more likely to be members than men (unlike the membership of political parties in Britain, which is more likely to be male). And members of Amnesty and Friends of the Earth in Britain were more likely to be members of a political party (and not necessarily a green party) than the population at large.

So the composition of the membership did seem to relate to the new social movement theorists' views about the mobilization of the 'new middle classes'. But the evidence was contrary to their assumptions about these social groups being fundamentally alienated from formal/ traditional politics. The members of Amnesty and Friends of the Earth were more not less likely than the population at large to be joiners, and they were also more likely to be networked with other social movement organizations and with other organizations more generally.

Jordan and Maloney concluded, overall, that the new social movement literature did not contribute very much to understanding these social movement organizations. Nor did rational actor-type approaches, which seemed unable to account for the values and the commitments of so many people, worldwide, as a result of their general concerns for the environment and for human rights, values and commitments. These altruistic commitments tended to be strengthened as people became more involved (although a minority did refer to other less entirely self-less reasons too, including personal reasons such as wanting to meet other like-minded people). Dalton concluded, similarly, that rational actor and resource mobilization approaches failed to take sufficient account of the politics and of the ideologies involved more gener-ally (Dalton 1994). While valuing the new social movement theorists' emphasis upon these, however, Dalton also concluded that while these mattered, environmental organizations were not necessarily providing case studies of decentralized, participatory, alternative-style politics in practice (ibid.).

Neither approach seems entirely satisfactory, then. Having summarized some of their shortcomings, how might their more positive relevance be summarized? Rational actor approaches could provide potential insights into the wider contextual pressures on social movement organizations to become 'protest businesses', concerned with their own organizational survival in a competitive market. Resource mobilization approaches add a potentially relevant focus upon the ways in which social movement organizations take opportunities and draw upon elite sponsorship in doing so, as well as drawing upon their own networks and organizational experiences. Political process approaches provide useful ways of exploring the ways in which they mobilize in particular political, social, cultural and ideological contexts, 'framing' issues and developing 'repertoires of contention' including novel tactics and media-grabbing stunts to appeal to supporters as well as to put forward their arguments to decision-makers and the wider public.

New social movement theorists add key questions about the underlying socio-economic, political and cultural/ideological contexts and the structural cleavages that give rise to these forms of social conflict. These insights could contribute to an understanding of the potential connections between social movements and social movement organizations and their phases, or 'cycles of contention'. But the particular ways in which these connections have been traced have been fundamentally contested. The reality of these social movements and social movement organizations' experiences and organizational styles, as they take account of the competing pressures of the state and the market, whether locally and/or globally, sits awkwardly with many of assumptions of the new social movement theorists. The following chapter takes up some of these debates in more detail, focusing upon the potential for building on the common interests as well as understanding the differences between the so-called 'old' and the so-called 'new' social movements.

4 | Social movements old and new: alternatives or allies?

'Globalization in all its facets presents new problems that the old (social) movements failed to address' (Brecher et al. 2000: 17) it has been argued, while the new social movements have been seen to represent 'a qualitatively different form of transformative politics' (Munck 2002: 20). The old social movements have been characterized in terms of class politics, 'anchored in traditional actors who struggled for the control of the state, particularly the working class and revolutionary vanguards'; whereas, in the new situation, 'a multiplicity of social actors establish their presence and spheres of autonomy in a fragmented social and political space' (Escobar and Alvarez 1992: 3). The old social movements were seen to privilege the transformatory role of the working class, with a particular emphasis upon industrial struggles – struggles that could be bought off, with relatively minor concessions on wages and conditions. In addition, the old social movements were criticized for their bureaucratic organizational forms, which routinized conflict and facilitated the emergence of professional leaderships rather than galvanizing grass-roots mobilizations. In the new realities of the global context, from the late twentieth century, new approaches have been required, it has been argued (Laclau and Mouffe 1985).

In contrast, new social movement theorists have been more concerned with the transformatory potential of movements rooted in a wider range of social actors, focusing on 'life world' issues that are not so easily accommodated within the existing social order. New social movements, it has been argued, have developed new forms of politics, autonomous from party politics and free from 'the problems of routinisation and bureaucratisation which have bedevilled the labour movements at certain points' (Munck 2002: 20). Or so it has been suggested.

This chapter takes up aspects of these arguments, taking account of the debates that have already been summarized in previous chapters. Do the new social movements genuinely represent alternative, more fully democratic and more transformatory approaches to politics in the context of globalization, replacing the politics of the 'old' social movements? Or conversely, should the Left be celebrating labour 'rising from the ashes', with renewed energy in the trade union movement, as a marker of a return to orthodoxy? Alternatively, as this chapter suggests, the 'new' may not be so 'new' in practice, or the 'old' so 'old', whether nationally or internationally. Rather than simply contrasting them as alternatives, global social movements have also been developing on the basis of learning from each other and building alliances.

While there have been and continue to be significant theoretical differences between the new social movements theorists and others on the Left, labour movement organizations have actually been developing new ways of working, in practice, in the context of globalization, and these have included the development of 'social movement' unionism. There are particularly relevant issues here for women, who face new challenges in organizing as workers, whether in the formal or the informal economy, as well as users, or would-be users, of services, as carers and as community mobilizers, the 'triple burden' of women globally (Moser 1989). The chapter concludes with a study of union revitalization in the American labour movement, breaking out of bureaucratic conservatism and pursuing an organizing agenda that owed much to leaders' experiences of activism outside the labour movement, as well as to the influence of international trade union pressures (Voss and Sherman 2000).

How new?

The previous chapter explored some of the criticisms of new social movement theorists' contentions about the demise of the working class and the decline of class politics more generally. On the contrary, it was argued, class politics was certainly still being waged – by the Right against the unemployed and the working poor (Piven and Cloward 1982), if not always as effectively by the working class and its allies. And far from 'fading away', as Castells had suggested (Castells 1997a), the labour movement's potential base had grown, as the workforce in manufacturing, distribution and services had expanded (Munck 2002) – not to mention the potential for developing support among those in the informal sector, globally. The new social movement theorists' assumptions about the end of the industrial era and the rise of post-industrial society (Touraine 1974) were also questioned, together with related assumptions about the supposedly more revolutionary/transformatory potential of the emerging politics of Habermas's lifeworld.

How might these arguments relate to the actual experiences of the new social movements? How new were they in reality, and how much more transformatory in principle or in their approaches to organization and participatory democracy, in practice? How far were these distinctions based upon particular circumstances in a specific period of Western European history, in any case, a particularly eurocentric view with far less relevance elsewhere, globally. As Foweraker has suggested, for instance, in relation to Latin America, 'there is some doubt whether new social movement theory may be properly applied to the continent' (Foweraker 1995: 24). These have all been contested questions.

As Holst pointed out, critics have argued that whether 'these new movements actually exhibit "new" characteristics is debated' (Holst 2002: 36). Rather than seeing them as replacing working-class struggles, new social movements could be seen as 'part of the working class' (ibid.: 43). The fact that many of the participants could be described as middle-class was not necessarily a barrier to this view, because a Marxist approach to social class would include 'white-collar' and 'white-blouse' workers as well as the more traditional 'blue-collar' members of the working class. According to Marxists, including contemporary theorists such as Olin Wright (Olin Wright 1985), it is the relations of production that are key here – whether and how people sell their labour power to their employers – rather than the extent to which they work by hand or by brain (or both, of course).

Other writers have developed similar arguments about the potential connections between new social movements and the labour movement. Shukra, for example, questioned the way in which a number of key black radicals effectively wrote off the organized labour movement, in the 1980s, accepting the notion of 'the decline of the workers' movement' (Touraine 1981: 11) and defining the trade union movement and the white working class more generally as part of the problem, rather than as being potentially part of the solution too (Shukra 1998). Clearly the trade union movement had much to answer for, in terms of past failures to challenge racism (and indeed, past collusions with racism) (Ramdin 1987). But this did not mean that the organized labour movement was irrelevant – on the contrary, she argued, it needed to be challenged and won over. Shukra concluded that the new social movements 'can evolve in different directions; they can forge different alliances and have different outcomes' with the most promising outcomes for fundamental change being closely connected with 'advanced sections of the working class, with a view to politicising all groups to develop a liberatory working-class consciousness independently of the state' (Shukra 1998: 109). As will be suggested below, the labour movement has more recently been making significant moves to address racism and to build a more inclusive, more effective progressive movement.

Comparable arguments have been developed in relation to the

women's movement and the organized labour movement. As Davis, for example, has argued, in her study of the history of the British labour movement, one of the movement's key weaknesses has been its failure to tackle the divisive forces of either sexism or racism effectively, thereby obstructing the vital contributions of women and black workers (Davis 1993). Reviewing the prospects, in the 1990s, in a difficult period of declining trade union membership, she drew very different conclusions from those of Touraine, however, pointing to the movement's 'uncanny ability to renew itself' (ibid.: 213). Munck made a comparable point when he argued that, 'As with capitalism, labour would seem to have a great ability to regenerate and transform itself, adapting to new situations, mutating organizational forms and strategies, and living to fight another day' (Munck 2000: 90). Democratic collective involvement, Davis concluded, must be key to reviving the labour movement as a vehicle for socialist politics, and this means

> consciously extending its appeal, as some of the early socialists attempted, to *all* workers and in particular those most vulnerable to superexploitation because of their race or gender.
>
> This in turn entails an understanding that working-class unity is not just a desirable but an essential goal, and that its achievement is only possible if differences born of life experiences of centuries of disunity founded on oppression are recognised and respected. (Davis 1993: 215)

The politics of identity and culture needed to be related to, rather than opposed to, the politics of class. As Aronowitz has pointed out, comparable arguments apply elsewhere. Although social movements in the USA have, in the past, 'as often as not, perceived class politics as inimical to their aims' (Aronowitz 1992: 67), class remains key in its impact upon life chances, including its impact on the life chances of women and black and ethnic minorities.

Nor has it been the case that the new social movements have been confined to issues of identity, culture and the 'lifeworld' while the labour movement and the political parties of the Left have confined themselves to issues of political economy. Although the previous chapter illustrated some of the boundaries around particular environmental campaigning, for example, there have been overlaps too. Tarrow, for example, has explored the links between ideological conflicts and the emergence of the student movement in 1968–69 in Italy and the explosion of class politics, including the upsurge of industrial unrest at the same period (Tarrow 1990). Meanwhile, Shore's anthropological study of Italian communism has provided evidence of the importance of issues of culture and identity in a mass Left party that included intellectuals and white-collar workers as well as the more traditionally defined industrial working class (Shore 1990). The Italian Communist Party had women's groups and youth groups, with its own bars, clubs and community festivals, the 'Festa dell' Unita', as well as the organizational forms and mobilizations more usually associated with the political Left. Although these features were, perhaps, particularly marked in the Italian Communist Party, this was by no means the only example of Left political parties with their own emphases on working-class culture and identity, from the Fête de l'Humanité in France to miners' galas in Britain.

Previous chapters have already raised doubts about the extent to which new social movements could be described as inherently more committed to new ways of working in terms of organizational structures and procedures, whether in principle or in practice. The old social movements had been critiqued by the new social movement theorists for their bureaucratic organizational structures and their formal approaches to representative democracy – structures and approaches that led, it was argued, to Michels's 'Iron Law of Oligarchy' (Michels 1949). Power became increasingly concentrated in small professional cliques of trade union bureaucrats or party hacks, principally preoccupied with preserving their own positions. Organizations, according to Michels, had inbuilt tendencies towards the development of such ruling elites, cut off from their rank and file. Formal organizational structures have been criticized more specifically too, for their inherent tendencies towards conservatism and deference, with excessive formal organization potentially leading to political co-optation, 'such that movements lose their critical edge' (Crossley 2002: 92).

In contrast, it was argued, effective challenges to the status quo would be mounted by the new social movements with their greater flexibility and enhanced ability to develop innovative tactics. As the previous chapter argued, however, there was no necessary connection between these claims and the realities in practice. Nor could new social movement organizations necessarily be assumed to be more democratically accountable to their members. And whatever the inherent limitations of formal organizations and representative structures, labour movement organizations' accountability structures were at least relatively transparent – which was not automatically the case with new social movement organizations.

Summarizing these debates about the distinctions between the old and the new, Crossley has concluded that, in pointing to the similarities, he was not meaning to deny that there is a genuine difference between old and new movements, or indeed that they are not periodically prone to come into conflict with one another. It is important to appreciate that they overlap, however, and the extent to which the new movements grew out of the old – albeit sometimes also out of disgruntlement with the old movements and their own particular brand of conservatism. (ibid.: 165)

Escobar and Alvarez have added reflections about the changing social realities within which social movements operate. Many of the supposed differences vanish, when account is taken of changes in consciousness and collective action more generally. To deny that there is anything new in today's collective action would be to 'negate the changing character of the world and its history' (Escobar and Alvarez 1992: 8).

So what about the old?

Meanwhile, the old social movements, the labour and progressive movement and the peace movement, have long histories of organizing across national boundaries, just as the women's movement and anti-slavery movements in the nineteenth century did. Chatfield, for example, has traced the history of international mobilizations for peace from the nineteenth century, along with campaigns for women's suffrage and mobilizations of the labour movement, internationally. To a greater or lesser extent, these involved campaigning transnationally as well as nationally (Chatfield 1997). In their study, *Activists Beyond Borders*, Keck and Sikkink explore the histories of transnational advocacy networks, including those addressing human rights, international issues, peace and development, women's rights, ethnic minority and indigenous peoples' rights and the environment (Keck and Sikkink 1998). This is not, of course, to suggest that there has been nothing new about global mobilizations in more recent decades, 'negating the changing character of the world and its history', simply to set this in historical context.

Marx and Engels's analysis of the development of capitalism saw this in relation to the growth of the world market. As the *Communist Manifesto* concluded in 1848, to challenge this required that 'working men of all countries unite' (Marx and Engels 1985: 121). The First International Working Men's Association, set up in 1864, was clearly influenced by Marx's ideas, although Marx himself did not claim to have initiated this. This was the first of a number of attempts to develop an international approach to the movement, bringing together socialists and progressive trade unionists across national boundaries.

Without attempting to go into any detail here, the points to note are simply these. First, the importance of organizing internationally was established from the second half of the nineteenth century and pursued through three attempts at building the International, up to and during the Second World War, and then again subsequently with the Fourth International. The second point of relevance here is that right from the start there were differences of view over organisational structures and styles. Broadly these differences have been summarized in terms of flexible decentralization versus centralism, debates over which Marx himself, incidentally, was reported to be ambivalent (Drachkovitch 1966), and there were differences about the relative merits of direct action strategies and the General Strike (favoured by the anarchists) versus strategies to capture political power (favoured by Marx and Engels). The Second International (1889–1914), which broke up with differences over peace and internationalism in the context of the outbreak of the First World War, like the First (which fragmented and dissolved in 1876), was characterized by a similar diversity of views. These included debates about strategies for reform or for revolution, more generally, the third point to note in this context. (The Fourth International was founded in opposition, on the initiative of Trotsky, in 1938.) Without suggesting that there are direct parallels, there would seem to be some room for comparisons as well as contrasts with more recent debates such as those reflected in the 'fix it or nix it' slogan from Seattle.

The Third International, set up in 1919, following the 1917 Bolshevik Revolution, lasted until the Second World War, effectively dominated by the Soviet Communist Party. Its dissolution, in 1943, has been seen as a move by Stalin to placate his Western allies. This wartime alliance was, of course, short-lived, and the post-war context was dominated by the Cold War – with major implications for the development of international solidarity. As Munck argued, 'Following the Second World War, the development of the international trade-union movement was dominated by the Cold War between the West and the "communist" East' (Munck 2002: 140). This, he pointed out, was the period when 'trade-union imperialism' took shape, with the British Trades Union Congress (TUC), for example, effectively acting as 'the labour arm of the Foreign and Colonial Offices' (ibid.: 141).

In summary, two rival international organizations emerged after the Second World War. The World Federation of Trade Unions (WFTU) was founded in 1945, at a congress that represented some 67 million workers, from fifty-six national organizations from fifty-five countries and twenty international organizations – including the US Congress of Industrial Organizations (CIO). But it did not include its then rival, the

American Federation of Labor (AFL), which held aloof. The WFTU was to be the 'child of unity' committed to the need for 'trade union unity on a world scale' (Ganguli 2000: 2). This unity was not to survive for long, however. By 1949, the US CIO and the British TUC, had withdrawn from the WFTU to form the anti-communist international, the International Confederation of Free Trade Unions (ICFTU). This set the scene for the divisions that persisted through the Cold War period. International mobilizations were correspondingly limited. Despite these divisions, however, Munck points to the ways in which there were, nevertheless, instances of genuine international solidarity (including considerable solidarity against apartheid in South Africa).

More recently, though, the ICFTU has come to develop its understanding of globalization as representing one of the most significant challenges for the labour movement, if not the most significant. With the fading of Cold War rivalries, Thorpe, for example, has argued that the ICFTU was in a better position 'to provide a progressive, identifiable trade union voice within the intergovernmental agencies, old and new, that preside over the New World Disorder' (Thorpe 1999: 227). Ashwin made a similar case when she argued that, with the collapse of the former Soviet Union, debate within the international trade union community came to be refocused 'on the common problems faced by all trade unions in responding to the challenges of the global market. In effect,' she continued, 'the ICFTU was forced to find a new role now that the enemies against which it had defined itself were either collapsing or clamouring for ICFTU affiliation' (Ashwin 2000: 102). 'With its major affiliates all suffering from declining membership and revenue,' she concluded, 'the ICFTU has come under increasing pressure to define a new role for the international trade union movement, and in particular to develop a trade union strategy in the face of the global market' (ibid.: 109). By 1992, she argued, the ICFTU was already beginning to shift.

At its sixteenth world congress, in 1996, the ICFTU's main position paper argued: 'The position of workers has changed as a result of globalisation of the economy and changes in the organisation of production' (ICFTU 1997: 4, quoted in Munck 2002: 13). This, in Munck's view, signalled a significant move. 'Now the ICFTU – still bureaucratic, but with a new post-Cold War identity – could state quite categorically that "one of the main purposes of the international trade union movement is the international solidarity of workers" ' (ICFTU 1997: 51, quoted in ibid.).

The irony of this scarcely needs underlining. As Chapter 1 argued, the end of the Cold War was marked by a new triumphalism as US-dominated capitalism was thought to have won out, signalling the end of history, in terms of any possibilities of alternatives. Seven years on, the ICFTU was posing precisely such alternative possibilities in terms of the need for 'globalization from below'. Without overestimating the significance of such attempts to develop an 'anti-systemic alliance' globally – or even to overestimate the durability of the more local alliance between labour and the environmentalists, encapsulated in the US slogan 'Teamsters and Turtles' – Munck concluded that globalization was opening new possibilities for transformative social movements – old as well as new (ibid.).

Globalization and the need for international solidarity – at the centre of labour movement concerns

As Chapter 1 pointed out, neoliberal capitalist globalization has been challenged not only for its impact on the world's poorest peoples, but also for its impact upon organized labour. While the liberalization of finance has been the most pronounced of the three aspects, trade and investment have also been liberalized, and this has been accompanied by increasing concentrations of power and economic resources by transnational corporations and by global financial firms and funds (Khor 2001). Transnational corporations can and do shift their operations, depending on where these can be carried out most profitably, moving manufacturing jobs away from relatively high-wage contexts in the North, when they can find cheaper labour in the South.

Meanwhile, as the better-paid and more organized jobs were disappearing in the North, workers were becoming more vulnerable to the spread of employment patterns more typical of the South. Beck has described this process as follows. 'The social structure in the heartlands of the West', he argued, 'is thus coming to resemble the patchwork quilt of the South, characterised by diversity, unclarity and insecurity in people's work and life' (Beck 2001: 1). While Munck cautions against over-emphasizing the novelty of this situation – work having always been unstable rather than secure, for the majority of the world's workers – the problems for the labour movement are real enough, in the North as well as the South. Pay and conditions are under pressure in the North (a situation variously described as the Third World coming to the First, or 'Brazilianization').

This has been described as a global 'race to the bottom'. As companies are free to move without restraints, the real competition, it has been argued, is among people and communities for a declining pool of jobs, competing by offering the lowest wages, the poorest working conditions and the least environmental restraint. Korten has summarized this as follows.

What the corporate libertarians call 'becoming more globally competitive' is more accurately described as a race to the bottom. With each passing day it becomes more difficult to obtain contracts from one of the mega-retailers without hiring child labor, cheating workers on overtime pay, imposing merciless quotas, and operating unsafe facilities. If one contractor does not do it, his or her prices will be higher than those of another who does. With hundreds of millions of people desperate for any kind of jobs the global economy may offer, there will always be willing competitors. (Korten 1995: 229)

'The global system,' Korten continued, 'is harmonizing standards across country after country – downwards towards the lowest common demoninator' (ibid.: 237). Brecher, Castells and Smith put this in similar terms when they argued:

Globalization promotes a destructive competition in which workers, communities and entire countries are forced to cut labor, social and environmental costs to attract mobile capital. When many countries each do so, the result is a disastrous 'race to the bottom' [...] This race to the bottom brings with it the dubious blessings of impoverishment, growing inequality, economic volatility, the degradation of democracy, and the destruction of the environment. (Brecher et al. 2000: 5–6)

While workers, and those struggling to get into waged work, in the South, may be desperate for these jobs, racing to the bottom, as a strategy, has severe limitations for organized labour in the South, then, just as it does in the North – although that is not necessarily how the problem may be perceived by those concerned.

Globalization, then, brings increasing competition between workers. Paradoxically, however, it is also potentially bringing them closer together. As Munck has pointed out, globalization for workers 'means many things; not all of it is positive, but it has created an objective community of fate, in so far as workers' futures in different parts of the world are becoming more integrated' (Munck 2002: 65). This opens up new opportunities as well as posing new challenges. Workers are generally less mobile than capital is – with the exception, perhaps, of a small but rapidly growing segment of professionals and scientists, as Castells has pointed out (Castells 1998) – with fewer resources for organizing across national boundaries and across cultural and language barriers. There are genuine differences of interests to be addressed, within and between regions as well as internationally – as differences between North and South over the 'social clause' debate have illustrated. In summary, the inclusion of social clauses – such as a clause to proscribe child labour – in multilateral trade agreements has been an approach that has been supported by trade union organizations, including the ICFTU. This approach has, however, been criticized by those in the South who have feared that such clauses would simply be used/abused to protect jobs in the North, while potentially leading to even worse conditions in the South. Child labourers, for example, might be forced into alternative and even more damaging forms of income generation such as prostitution. (This issue will be dealt with in Chapter 8, with special reference to education.) But despite all these differences and genuine difficulties, labour is not simply to be seen as the victim, it has been argued, passively suffering the negative effects of globalization. On the contrary, the labour movement has been developing its own international agendas. 'The reality', Munck concludes, 'is that labour has been back centre stage since the mid-1990s at least' (Munck 2002: 68).

Losing members as the more organized jobs came under increasing threat, particularly in the anti-union climate of the Thatcher/Reagan years in the 1980s, or the neoliberal context of New Zealand, for example, the trade union movement urgently needed to find new ways to organize, both locally and internationally. And that is precisely what they began to do. By the mid-1990s, in the USA, the AFL-CIO was beginning to embrace a new 'organizing' agenda, an agenda also being developed in a number of other countries.

This 'organizing' agenda has been characterized by an emphasis upon active recruitment strategies, with a particular focus on recruiting groups that had been harder to organize, women and black and Hispanic workers in casualized employment who were becoming proportionately more important as the more readily organized jobs disappeared. In Britain, for example, there have been a number of campaigns to recruit casualized workers, such as the three-year campaign to organize hotel staff at one of London's most exclusive hotels, the Dorchester, owned by the Dorchester Group, which is owned by the Sultan of Brunei, one of the richest men in the world. The workforce included migrant workers from other countries, including Ghana, Italy, the Philippines, Somalia, Sri Lanka and the former Yugoslavia (Wills 2002). With a 40 per cent turnover of staff to add to the problems of organizing such a potentially vulnerable workforce, this determined campaign illustrates many of the challenges involved.

To meet these types of challenges, the TUC in Britain has been pursuing an organizing agenda, setting up the Trade Union Academy in 1997. This has trained organizers, particularly young organizers, including women and young people from black and ethnic minority communities, to go out and recruit (based upon the principle that 'like' can be most effective in recruiting 'like'). The issue of racism was seen as particularly important to address, and the new unionism has also consciously built on initiatives such as anti-racist summer 'Respect' festivals to challenge racism within the movement as well as outside it in the wider society (Mayo 2000).

A novel feature, which has been particularly significant, it has been argued, has been 'a major emphasis upon unions as organizers of a social movement' (Munck 2002: 100), promoting a new community unionism built on links with social movement networks. And this emphasis, in turn, has related to a new focus upon internationalism – at a time when trade union organizations, elsewhere, were coming to similar conclusions and were similarly motivated to share experiences of developing these new organizing agendas. As Waterman has pointed out, 'From the "social movement unionism" of Brazil, South Africa and the Philippines to the "new Realism" of Western Europe and elsewhere, labour has been seeking ways out of the apparent impasse of the old tactics, organizational modes and even objectives' (Waterman 1999: 13). A new social union model was needed for a new world order.

Without suggesting that these new approaches were likely to be unproblematic, Hyman, for example, has argued that these were particularly relevant in the context of strategies to reach the least readily organizable sections of the labour force. Where trade union membership was unstable and traditional resources unreliable, there was considerable pressure to 'embrace at least some elements of the social movement model' (Hyman 1999: 130). This applied in the North as well as in the South, with the growth of 'flexible' ways of working, part-time, casualized and often geographically dispersed forms of employment, including homeworking. New York's garment district, for example, has been quoted as an example of the 'Third World in the First', with sweated, overwhelmingly female labour at the machines, representing a range of ethnic minorities. As many of them spoke little or no English, they were correspondingly even less likely to be in a position to claim whatever limited rights they may have had, in the workplace, in principle (Wichterich 2000).

There have been particular issues here for women, as has already been suggested, and women have been organizing in response. Chapter 7 explores these mobilizations in more detail. Women have been described as representing a 'comparative advantage' for employers, enabling them to increase their profits because they can get away with paying them comparatively less, and offering even less favourable working conditions (ibid.: 1). Globalization has been associated, then, with the feminization of employment and with the growth of flexible labour more generally.

The reality would seem more complex, however. Women have indeed been affected in particular ways, but the gender division of labour takes varied forms in different cultures. Men have also been affected by flexibilization, and women have been losing jobs faster than men in some contexts.

Whatever the context, however, whether they are gaining some types of jobs or losing others faster than men, women are disproportionately likely to be particularly vulnerable to exploitation in the workplace. This is the result of the burdens that women are so typically expected to bear. Their experiences in the world of work are often inextricably bound up with their experiences in their families and their communities. In developing challenges to the impact of globalization, as a result, women have been in the forefront of strategies to build links between the workplace on the one hand and community networks and social movement organizations on the other.

The Indian Self Employed Women's Association (SEWA) provides a well-known example of these interconnections. SEWA's history goes back to women's mobilizations around their problems as workers in the informal sector, in the wider context of their struggles in challenging the dominant power structures of caste and patriarchy (Abbott 1997). SEWA was set up in 1972, combining the functions of a trade union for self-employed women and women in the informal sector with those of a bank and co-operatives. The co-operatives complement the trade union functions, strengthening the bargaining position of the workers by offering alternatives sources of livelihood – vitally important given the vulnerability of women in the informal sector, liable as they are to victimization if they demand that employers pay the minimum wage (Hensman 2000). SEWA has been described as 'a very diverse and broad-based organization, and this has been its strength' (ibid.: 254). 'In particular', it has been argued, 'the combination of union and co-operatives has given it a great deal of flexibility, enabling it to offer credit, union organization or income generation to its members as the need arises' (ibid.: 254) and strengthening their bargaining power accordingly. In addition, by developing service co-operatives, providing functions such as childcare, usually performed by women as housewives and mothers,

SEWA has offered 'a low-cost service which helps to reduce their double burden' (ibid.). This demonstrates ways of addressing the links between the workplace, the home and the community. SEWA has also taken on issues that affect the members' abilities to earn a living more generally, issues such as obtaining licences for women street traders (which were being denied because of their illiteracy and difficulties in taking on the highly bureaucratic structures that controlled the issue of these licences) (Abbott 1997). And SEWA has also played leading roles in campaigning on wider gender issues 'such as those of dowries, domestic violence, male alcoholism and sex-discrimination tests which encourage female foeticide' (ibid.: 204). Following a memorable study visit, Abbott concluded: 'This process of collective defiance and organisation thus leads to individual empowerment and the poor feel that they can achieve almost anything' (ibid.). There was, she concluded, 'a new type of women's movement emerging in India. These organisations have allowed the poor and the invisible to gain international recognition and power to defy and change existing structures. Their success is so unexpected that it is little wonder that development agencies are desperate to replicate these models elsewhere' (ibid.: 208). The women's earnings, however, sadly remain very low, competing as they do with sweated labour in the informal economy more generally. However valuable in themselves, such initiatives do also illustrate the importance of wider campaigning.

This brings us back to the significance of the links between social movement unionism and internationalism, more generally. However modest its achievements so far, in the international arena, the ICFTU has at least some potential, it has been argued, 'to attain a new prominence in world politics' (Ashwin 2000: 111). While recognizing its limitations, the difficulties of enforcing international agreements on labour standards and the potential for divisions between trade unions in the developed and developing worlds, Ashwin nevertheless pointed to the prospect that the 'participation of the trade unions in a process of global rule making' could 'make a real difference' (ibid.: 112). Most importantly, she argued, the organizing agenda and the developing alliances with NGO campaigns on issues such as child labour could open up new possibilities. So, eventually, might the development of international trade union groupings, such as the International Federation of Chemical, Energy, Mine and General Workers' Unions (ICEM) and the International Union of Food and Allied Workers and Agricultural Workers (IUF) (Thorpe 1999). As Wills has concluded, drawing upon experiences of social movement organizing, taking on international as well as local interests, trade unions 'need to extend beyond the workplace to develop multi-scalar networks, reaching from the local to the global arena' (Wills 2002: 6). The potential importance of widening networks emerges in the following case study, in the context of unionism's potential for change more generally.

Union revitalization in the American labour movement: a case study from California

Until recently, the authors of this case study of revitalization among trade unions argued, 'the American labor movement seemed moribund, as unions represented ever-smaller proportions of the workforce and their political influence dwindled' (Voss and Sherman 2000: 303). Some unions have started to change, however, organizing new members using a variety of tactics, including massive street demonstrations and other forms of direct action. 'These organizing and contract struggles look very different from the routinized contests that have typified labor's approach since the 1950s,' the authors argued (ibid.: 304).

Voss and Sherman set out to investigate these apparently unlikely changes in the trade union movement, characterized, as it was, by formal bureaucratic organizational structures and entrenched leadership that seemed to typify Michels's Iron Law of Oligarchy. As Michels had asserted, such organizations tended to be characterized by increasing numbers of professional staff, over time, and a growing distance between staff and members, allowing leaders to 'mold the organization in their interests rather than in those of the members'. In such a context, goals and tactics became 'transformed in a conservative direction as leaders become concerned above all with organizational survival' (ibid.: 305).

How then, they asked, had some trade union organizations been able 'to break out of this bureaucratic conservatism' (ibid.: 304)? Through in-depth interviews with union organizers and staff, as well as via secondary data on particular campaigns and tactics, the researchers set out to explore the factors that enabled some unions to make these organizational breaks – and to analyse the reasons why some achieved these changes more successfully than others. The literature on organizational structures in social movements had tended to focus upon the dangers of bureaucratization – with very little evidence on the issues that preoccupied the researchers, the question of how these processes might be reversed.

The context, the underlying structural features, were key, in their view. More aggressive tactics from employers – in the face of increasing global competition – were resulting in job losses, and most particularly to the loss of unionized jobs. Trade unions' share of the workforce in the USA dropped from 37 per cent just after the Second World War to less than 14 per cent at the time of writing, with only 9.5 per cent in the private sector. Unions needed to fight back. The revitalized 'repertoire' of tactics included targeting particular industries and workplaces, staging direct actions, pressurizing public officials to influence local employers and allying with community and faith-based groups, taking up issues of fairness in addition to more specific material issues in the workplace.

The researchers quoted studies to document the success of such tactics, particularly when used together. Unions that innovate in general, they argued, 'and in terms of organizing in particular are more successful in recruiting members – including formerly excluded minority and gender groups – than unions that do not' (ibid.: 312–13). Conversely, studies have demonstrated that only one-third of the loss of trade union membership in the USA could be attributed to structural changes in employment, the remaining two-thirds being 'a result of the labor movement's inability to deal effectively with an anti-union climate' (Savage 1998: 227). The above-mentioned recruiting tactics, in turn, have required significant organizational changes. The new organizing campaigns have required resources and to find resources for organizers has involved shifting resources away from more traditional preoccupations, servicing existing members. Innovating unions have therefore looked to find new ways of supporting members, including training members to solve more of their own problems on the shopfloor. These types of shifts, the researchers argued, 'fly in the face of conventional theorizing about social movements, which indicates that once institutionalized, movements remain conservative' (Voss and Sherman 2000: 313).

Focusing upon union revitalization, Voss and Sherman were concerned to analyse the reasons why some unions were achieving this far more effectively than others – and not only in principle, but also in practice. They focused upon fourteen Californian 'locals', union organizations mostly affiliated with three 'internationals', Service Employees International Union (SEIU), Hotel and Restaurant Employees (HERE) and United Food and Commercial Workers (UFCW). They compared unions' performances, both in terms of their formal commitment and in terms of their overall programmes, their organizational changes and uses of resources, and their tactical repertoires. Taking account of these factors, they identified five of the fourteen union organizations as fully revitalized and nine as partially revitalized. How could these differences be explained?

Structural factors such as the degree of membership loss that the organizations had suffered, however important, did not, by themselves, explain the differences. Nor did the degree of employer opposition. The researchers concluded that explanations that 'economic crisis (which arises from membership decline) or countermobilization lead to innovation fail to explain the differences among these locals' (ibid.: 320). The other key factors they identified as also needing to be taken into account were as follows.

First, revitalized unions had succeeded in changing the culture of the union, where strong leadership had been prepared to challenge resistance to change from members, and from staff. This involved convincing staff of the value of working in different ways, and addressing their concerns about losing control. As one informant recognized, if sharp young organizers were brought in, existing officers might well start to feel 'nervous that they're going to lose their jobs' (ibid.: 322). Support and training were required here to persuade existing officers that change was both necessary and, ultimately at least, in everyone's interests, including their own.

The role of leadership was key in promoting these changes in union culture. In some cases, there were changes of leadership, following particular crises (such as strike defeats), which enabled a new slate of elected leaders to come forward. The key factor, though, was not simply that there were leadership changes. The type of leadership also mattered significantly, whether these were 'people who have a vision and who are willing to take political risks', as one commentator expressed this (ibid.: 328). These 'leaders with vision' were, it emerged, thought to be particularly likely to be people 'steeped in the struggles of the sixties, you know, in terms of civil rights, the women's movement, probably the war in Vietnam, the fight against racism, all that stuff' (ibid.: 329).

Others referred to the importance of having a wider vision more generally. One commentator referred, for example, to the importance of having a 'world view of poverty and power' (ibid.). These organizers, the researchers concluded, were 'less caught up in traditional models of unionism and were familiar with alternative models of mobilization' (ibid.). They quoted comments about the lessons to be learned from community organizing, both in terms of tactics and in terms of political analysis. They include, for example, the following comments – although referring to earlier corporate campaigns in the 1970s and 1980s.

'I can't minimize the influence of the Vietnam War' not only in terms of tactics but also in terms of political understanding. 'The teach-ins (about the war) weren't just to tell about the atrocities being committed, but to explain the economics behind the war' and the ways in which corporations were making 'a huge amount of money off the war' (ibid.).

In sum, the researchers concluded, 'activists with experience outside the labor movement brought broad visions, knowledge of alternative organizational models, and practice in disruptive practice' (ibid.: 333).

The significance of having such a vision has emerged from other studies, too. Fletcher and Hurd, for example, concluded that transforming unions required a vision 'that offers a clear alternative to business unionism, a vision that can touch a large segment of members and be relevant to everyday life. Consistent with the experience of the organizing locals, this vision should encompass principles such as empowerment, social justice, and equitable distribution of wealth' (Fletcher and Hurd 1998: 33).

When such a vision was combined with support from the relevant international union, revitalization was even more likely. International union leadership was crucial, the researchers argued, in leading to full revitalization. Pressure for change was coming from the top as well as from the bottom. These factors all interacted with each other, in a climate in which the organizing agenda was beginning to become the norm. And these cultural shifts in the labour movements were, in turn, encouraging a new generation of young activists to get involved. As one informant reflected, 'I think the labor movement is becoming a little more dynamic, so young, progressive activists think that's a cooler thing to do than maybe was true at another time' (Voss and Sherman 2000: 340).

The researchers concluded with some reflections about entrenched organizational cultures and how these could be shifted. It was commonly believed, they suggested, 'that only democratic movements from below can vanquish bureaucratic rigidity. Our research challenges this view, for in the locals we studied, this was not the means by which change happened' (ibid.: 343). Pressures from below were not automatically democratic. And in the labour movement, 'rather than democracy paving the way for the end of bureaucratic conservatism, the breakdown of bureaucratic conservatism paves the way for greater democracy and participation, largely through the participatory education being advocated by the new leaders' (ibid.: 344).

Old and/or new? Alternatives or allies?

The Californian study has relevance for a number of the debates identified at the beginning of this chapter. The revitalized unions demonstrated ways in which social movement unionism might be developed, overcoming bureaucratic conservatism. Old social movements were rediscovering their radical roots, drawing on the knowledge and skills that key leaders had acquired, in other contexts, contexts that had included the civil rights movement and campaigning against the Vietnam War. To pose the 'new' versus the 'old' would be to set up false dichotomies, missing key points about the ways in which these interactions had been taking place. Concluding on the lessons of joint community and union campaigning to organize low-wage workers, Needleman suggested that community-based organizations need to be patient about these processes. But Needleman did recognize that although building alliances takes time, there was real potential for developing joint action because: 'The AFL-CIO and many union affiliates have begun a process that is altering the faces and methods of unionism, enabling them to work more effectively and democratically at the grass roots' (Needleman 1998: 86).

Nor could the view that bureaucratic rigidity could be shifted only by democratic movements from below be sustained. On the contrary, in fact, the Californian study demonstrated that the reality was more complex. Movements 'from the bottom up' were not necessarily more democratic, and pressures for change could also be effective when coming from the top, opening up opportunities for strengthening democracy and participation. Support from the top could, indeed, prove vital, enabling resources to be redistributed to support the organizing agenda. As Walldanger et al. commented in relation to the Justice for Janitors campaign in Los Angeles: 'JfJ (Justice for Janitors) is widely seen as a bottom-up campaign. That it is, but it also has a crucial top-down component' including resources, which were being redistributed top-down from organized to unorganized labour (Walldanger et al. 1998: 112). Justice for Janitors operated at the level of a national campaign, as well as working flexibly, taking account of very local conditions, building upon previous trade union members' experiences as well as working with local community organizations, combining workplace issues with broader concerns for 'social justice in our community, for these workers' (Savage 1998: 242). Far from seeing trade unionists as being outside communities, it was argued, 'They are us and we are them' (ibid.). Rather than simply contrasting the 'old' with the 'new', organizational change needed to be understood in terms of interactive processes, involving cultural transformations as well as structural re-organizations, or leadership shifts.

The role of different types of leadership emerged as crucially important, more generally. However significant the structural factors, these alone could not explain the differences between the extent to which particular trade unions had revitalized themselves. The role of human agency also needed to be taken into account, including the extent to which these leaders' knowledge and tactical skills *and* wider understanding were rooted in an internationalist vision. This final point relates back to the previous chapter's discussion of Bourdieu's approach to the analysis of human agency and socio-economic structures, and the ways in which these inter-relate. There are links with the following chapter, too, in relation to debates about teaching as well as experiential learning through participation in social movements.

5 | Empowerment, accountability and participation: challenges for local and global movements

This chapter sets out to provide a bridge between the previous chapters and the case studies that follow. The aim is to summarize the key issues that have emerged so far, setting out the implications for the opportunities and the challenges that global networks and social movements face. In addition to the debates that have already been explored in previous chapters, this chapter includes differing perspectives from the fields of community development and community education. Together, these differing approaches highlight strategies for addressing the dilemmas that face global social movements aiming to build broad and democratically accountable alliances that are also effective in working towards social transformation.

The first part of this chapter summarizes the varying ways in which the opportunities and challenges for global social movements have been conceptualized, depending upon the differing theoretical perspective adopted. Globalization, it has been argued, can be seen as opening up new opportunities for achieving more equitable and more sustainable development, based on alliances of professionals and policy-makers, working with international NGOs, trade union and community-based organizations, using new information technologies to promote more effective democratic participation and empowerment. Alternatively, it has been argued, participatory approaches to development can be manipulated by the powerful, to bypass or 'override existing legitimate decision-making processes' and/or to 'reinforce the interests of the already powerful' (Cooke and Kothari 2001: 5–6). And even where these approaches do open up new spaces, it has been argued, these new spaces may be incorporated, if social movement organizations become increasingly bureaucratized, decreasingly disruptive and ultimately decreasingly threatening – 'protest businesses', with power increasingly centralized among professional organizers.

How, then, can global social movements take up these opportunities for reform, in the current policy context, meeting their supporters' demands for immediate gains without losing sight of their longer-term aspirations for wider social transformation? How can they be effective campaigning organizations – maintaining a mutually acceptable balance between ends and means, outcomes and processes? And how can they benefit from much-needed professional expertise – without becoming dominated by professional organizers, ambitious to pursue their own careers in the international NGO sector? How can they succeed in balancing the 'insider' and 'outsider' roles, without being incorporated? And how can they build broad and sustainable alliances around common interests without losing focus, and without ending up with the lowest common denominator for their programmes? Most importantly, how can they combine organizational effectiveness with genuinely democratic forms of representation and accountability? And how can they avoid becoming an ossifying clique, by implementing strategies to recruit and actively involve newcomers, including young people, in live organizations, which are continually developing and renewing themselves?

These are dilemmas that have faced community and trade union organizations and social movements more generally, over the years. At the global level, given the scale of operations and the diversity of interests and organizations involved, it will be argued, these pose even more problematic challenges. Without in any way suggesting simple answers, the second part of this chapter explores debates about ways of addressing some of these challenges, based on experiences in community development and community education.

Opportunities and challenges for global social movements

The *Communist Manifesto* pointed to the world that was to be won. As Chapter 1 argued, however, there have been widely differing perspectives on what precisely needed to be won, by whom and for whom, in the context of globalization. As Epstein summarized these differences in relation to Seattle, the coalition that opposed the WTO was held together by 'a common perception of the global corporations as the main threat to environmental standards, labor and human rights, and to democracy generally' (Epstein 2002: 54). Beyond this, however, there were differences of view about whether the WTO should be abolished or whether it could be reformed. This debate stood as a metaphor, she argued, for wider arguments about the global capitalist system, more generally, a system 'that the radicals want to dismantle and which others hope can be brought in line with democracy' (ibid.).

This debate about short-term reforms versus longer-term social transformation emerges as a continuing theme, both in global social movements and in social movements more generally. As Chapter 1 also pointed out, however, the *Communist Manifesto* argued against posing one against the other in this way, suggesting that communists needed to do both. Communists, Marx and Engels argued, fight for the 'attainment of the immediate aims, for the momentary interests of the working class; but in the movement of the present, they also represent and take care of the future of that movement' (Marx and Engels 1985: 119). Given the degrees of diversity among anti-globalization movements, this might be easier said than done, taking account of the different perspectives and objectives, let alone the tactical preferences of social democrats, leftists, populists and environmentalists of every shade of red and green. This diversity has been hailed as a sign of strength and vitality rather than a sign of weakness or lack of focus (Klein 2002). But that does not make it any less inherently challenging, in terms of building alliances to campaign for short-term reforms as well as for longer-term social transformation.

One of Chapter 1's conclusions was to emphasize the need for *more* rather than *less* vigorous debates over these differing ideas. As Aronowitz suggested, resistance may not be enough to persuade more than 'an elite of semiprofessional organizers to stay the course of opposition' (Aronowitz 2002: 20). The problem, in his view, was 'to think and debate the alternatives, to experiment with reform even if it yields very little or nothing, and to craft a new politics of internationalism that takes into account the still potent force of national states and their identities' with the hardest work being the thinking (ibid.: 200). But without such theoretical work, rooted in clear understandings of the differing theoretical perspectives and the underlying interests of the various organizations and groupings involved, he suggested, anti-globalization movements lack the basis for building effective alliances.

There has to be clarity about shared aims and objectives and the boundaries to these common interests, the issues that divide the individuals, groups and organizations involved within anti-globalization movements. As Chapter 1 also pointed out, for example, trade unionists may join together with small businesses to oppose the negative effects of trade liberalization, but they are less likely to be able to work together on trade union rights, for example. Similarly, politicians of the far Right may join anti-global campaigners in resistance to the increasing powers of multinational corporations. But 'whoever starts working with the right automatically drops migrants, women and gays as potential allies', it has been argued, 'for they are always under attack from the right' (Krebbers and Schoenmaker 2002: 212). The importance of engaging in theoretical work, including self-educational work, to develop these debates within anti-globalization movements emerges, subsequently, in the context of the discussions on community-based education and popular education more generally.

Meanwhile, Chapter 2 also raised issues around democracy, not only as a goal but as a potential challenge, too, within anti-capitalist globalization movements themselves. Democratization has been placed on the agenda, globally as well as locally, with potentially enhanced scope for citizen involvement and community participation, internationally. Democratization has also emerged as an inherently problematic process, however. Whatever the limitations of representative forms, direct – including participatory – forms of democracy also emerged as inherently problematic. Despite inspiring examples of direct democracy in practice, there are examples, too, where such initiatives have been more contentious. Those with the greatest initial advantages, including the greatest advantages in terms of income, social class, race/ethnicity and education, may well turn out to be the most effective participants (Hirst 1990). And programmes to promote democratization via community participation, capacity-building and empowerment may have the effect of reinforcing these patterns (Berry et al. 1993; Anastacio et al 2000). Those individuals and groups with the least social capital, initially, tend to be those who benefit least from such programmes, while those with the most social capital, initially, may be best placed to increase this still further. Through community participation, particular representatives can become transformed, turned into 'community stars', the acceptable faces of the NGO/community sectors (not that this is necessarily a particularly comfortable role, in practice). Community stars tend to experience competing pressures from all sides, 'seen by other parts of the community as part of the problem rather than as part of this solution', as participants described these processes in the context of urban regeneration in Britain (Anastacio et al. 2000: 24).

There would seem to be two major implications, here, for global social movements. First, the case for increasing democratization through direct and/or participatory forms and/or enhanced roles for civil society more generally needs to be set within the context of strategies to tackle structural inequalities, promoting economic and social rights as well as political rights. Otherwise political spaces tend to be dominated by those with most power, economically and socially.

In addition, global social movements, like social movement organizations more generally, need to address issues of democratic representation and accountability *within* their own structures as well as beyond them, in the wider society. While emphasizing the significance of the contributions of the anarchists to grass-roots organizing, based on libertarian socialist approaches to democracy, Klein has commented, in contrast, on the fact that many of the key NGOs involved in anti-globalization campaigns, 'though they may share the anarchists' ideas about democracy in theory, are themselves organized as traditional hierarchies. They are run by charismatic leaders and executive boards, while their members send them money and cheer from the sidelines' (Klein 2002: 272). These issues around democratic representation and accountability run through anti-globalization movements more generally, within and between organizations and groupings, from South to North (and perhaps more typically from Northern spokespeople to their Southern supporters). As the experiences of the new community-based trade union organizing in the USA illustrated, in Chapter 4, however, organizations and movements *can* find ways of renewing themselves, reversing even long-standing tendencies towards bureaucratization and elitism.

Chapter 3 provided illustrations of some of these dilemmas, in practice, as social movement organizations grappled with the tensions between managing effective organizations, devising high-profile 'surprise' tactics and delivering immediate gains for their supporters, while keeping them actively engaged, mobilizing for more transformational goals for the longer term. Social movement organizations were attempting to manage the 'insider' and 'outsider' roles, making an impact via lobbying at international policy levels while retaining their independence, avoiding becoming protest businesses while operating within and between competing pressures from the market as well as from the state, globally as well as locally.

The discussion of social movement theorists in Chapter 3 identified themes of particular relevance here. First, as Della Porta and Diani pointed out, the 'shared beliefs', which constitute one of the defining characteristics of social movements, are not fixed in time (Della Porta and Diani 1999). On the contrary, in fact, there are two-way processes at work, as individuals and groups join on the basis of shared beliefs – which can then be strengthened through shared activities, and through shared reflections on these experiences. While demonstrations may raise public awareness of particular issues, for example, they may have just as much, if not more, impact in terms of promoting solidarity among their own participants. As Chapter 3 also pointed out, however, participants may draw widely differing conclusions from the same experiences, becoming inspired to further commitment, or increasingly demoralized in the face of apparently insuperable resistance. Experiential learning needs the backing of critical theoretical analysis, if social movements are to build solidarity and commitment to shared goals for social transformation.

Second, debates on 'resource mobilization' provide insights into ways of developing strategies for collective action, maximizing opportunities to organize and making the most effective use of external resources such as the time, the money and the access to specialist expertise that liberal Left elites may be prepared to inject into 'good causes' (Crossley 2002: 82). Conversely, these debates have also highlighted the risks inherent in becoming effectively 'patronised from above', and the potential that elite sponsorship 'may also divide social movements, defining their acceptable and non-acceptable faces, the former to be supported, the latter to be marginalised and if possible discredited' (Piven and Cloward 1992).

External resources are not the only sources of support, however. As McAdam and others have emphasized, social movements need to build upon their own resources, too, including the resources of their own networks and organizational experiences (McAdam 1988). The relevance of this has already emerged in the context of trade union and community organizers building upon previous experiences of organizing in the USA against the Vietnam War. Organizational skills can be passed on from one cycle of protest to another and networks can be revived, when movements re-emerge, after periods of relative quiescence.

These key organizational skills have included the ability to 'frame' effectively, to define issues and pose demands in ways that focus attention and maximize support. 'Framing' featured in the 'political process' approach discussed in Chapter 3, along with the discussion of 'repertoires of contention', the ability to develop effective tactics, including the ability to innovate and to surprise the opposition, to embarrass the powerful through the use of humour as well as pressurizing them through more conventional campaigning.

'Students Against Sweatshops': a case in point

'Students Against Sweatshops' illustrates these organizational issues in practice, mobilizing resources, building on networks and maximizing contextual opportunities more generally. 'United Students Against Sweatshops' (USAS) was founded in 1998, based on a network of campus anti-sweatshop groups. USAS developed out of campaigns in the USA and elsewhere, in the early 1990s, focusing on the appalling labour conditions of workers in the clothing industry, both in the USA itself and in the South. The campaign started to gain momentum through developing links with the trade unions, via the AFL-CIO's provision of summer jobs for college students in 1996 (as part of the AFL-CIO's organizing agenda). This provided the background opportunities and resources for mobilization.

The campaign really began to take off as 'some students began to research and challenge their universities' connections to apparel companies' (Featherstone 2002: 11). Until then, the issue had been discussed in terms of humanitarian concern. As a US high school activist had reflected in 1998, young Americans empathized 'because these workers are our age. If they lived here (in the US), they'd be in school' (Krasner, quoted in ibid.: 9).

Through connections with the trade unions, students came to see that the issue was also closer to home by far. Providing college 'apparel' (e.g. college sweatshirts and trainers) was a $2.5 billion dollar industry, an industry in which key players included major multinationals such as Nike and Reebok. The college students working in the trade unions began to research their own colleges and found that 'administrations were doing next to nothing to ensure that clothing bearing their logos was made under half-decent conditions' (ibid.: 11). In this way, then, the issue was 'framed', defined in terms that gave it immediacy and focus, generating demands that could be pursued with particular college administrations.

The students deployed a number of well-tested tactics. In 2000, for example, there was a sit-in, with students occupying the university president's office, accompanied by 'folk-singing, acoustic guitar, recorders, tambourines and ringing cellphones as well as a flurry of international news coverage' (ibid.: 20), which persuaded the university to shift its position. This was followed by sit-ins in other universities.

In addition, a number of more novel tactics were developed. For example, the University of California's anti-sweatshop group held a nude-optional party titled 'I'd Rather Go Naked Than Wear Sweatshop Clothes'. In similar vein, twelve Syracuse students biked across campus, 100 per cent garment-free. Through such tactics, students gained maximum publicity for the campaign, focusing upon the university itself as a corporate actor in the global economy. This led to a series of teach-ins to educate students about the underlying issues, showing how WTO policies were affecting higher education. 'USAS activists – and the wider student movement they have so galvanized,' concluded Featherstone, 'are teaching themselves and their fellow students to question facts of social and economic life that they have been taught to take for granted all their lives' (ibid.: 33).

Like other movements, USAS has also had to address a number of issues associated with social movement organization. Questions have been raised, for example, about whose voices are most effectively represented. Some students of colour recognized the ways in which black and ethnic minority groups were particularly vulnerable to sweatshop labour practices, but questioned the extent to which they were being represented in the campaign. White students, it was argued, were likely to receive more media coverage and anti-sweatshop organizing has been described as cliquish, with a close-knit, white hippie activist culture that 'is not welcoming to people of color' (ibid.: 64).

Like other movements, USAS has debated issues of structure and internal democracy more generally: how to campaign effectively, internationally, linking with workers in the South, without becoming so tightly organized that they might be compared with the hierarchically structured corporations against which they were campaigning. As one student summarized these debates: 'What is a leader? How should we be treating each other? If we don't ask those questions,' she continued, 'we create organizations that no one wants to be part of' (ibid.: 57).

Drawing from community development and community education debates

The concept of 'community' has been contested, just as the concepts of 'development' and 'globalization' have been (Crow and Allen 1994). As Stacey, the British sociologist, commented some thirty years ago, 'It is doubtful whether the concept "community" refers to a useful abstraction' (Stacey 1969: 134); the word bears so many meanings, depending upon users' perspectives, as to render it effectively meaningless, in her view. Far from discouraging further usage, however, this conceptual ambiguity has, if anything, increased, as the NGO and community sectors have acquired enhanced roles, in more recent years. Unsurprisingly then, 'community development' and 'community education' have been conceptualized and practised in widely differing ways too (Mayo 1994; Mayo 1997). Rather than attempting to explore these varying perspectives and approaches in detail, in the limited space available, this chapter concludes by summarizing those aspects with particular relevance for global social movements. There are parallels with the preceding discussion of immediate objectives and longer-term aims, and there are potential implications for the development of organizational strategies and tactics.

Community development has been defined as being about 'the involvement of people in the issues which affect their lives', offering a method through which people can 'develop their knowledge, skills and motivation, identify the common threads of problems which they experience in their lives, and work collectively to tackle these problems' (AMA 1989: 9). This involvement can take place in communities based on shared neighbourhoods or in communities based on shared identities or interests. Community development is seen as a collective process, based on the importance of people acting together 'to influence or assert control over social, economic and political issues that affect them' with an emphasis upon confronting attitudes and the practices of institutions which discriminate against disadvantaged groups (ibid.: 10). Without suggesting that this is the most generally agreed definition, it has characterized the pattern of a number of subsequent approaches. The UK Standing Conference for Community Development, for example, produced a working statement on community development that included each of the above elements, emphasizing that this is about enabling people to act together more effectively 'to influence the social, economic, political and environmental issues which affect them' (SCCD 1992).

At this level of generality, community development could be, and has been, supported and promoted from a wide range of perspectives, associated with the centre as well as with the Left of the political spectrum. 'It is radical', it has been argued, 'to the extent that, in calling for greater citizen participation, it creates new groupings and patterns of decision-makers', but it can also be seen as conservative, by keeping issues defined, in local terms, within broadly existing social arrangements (Cary 1970: 5). Self-help can, of course, be promoted via community development, too, attempting to bridge the widening gap between communities' needs and the resources available to meet them (in the context of public expenditure cuts and the increasing marketization of services). In summary then, community development work can be undertaken to meet short-term needs, providing technical support to individuals and groups in communities, to enable them to meet some of their own needs, and to press for improved service provision, within the context of current social arrangements. Transformational community development work, in contrast, aims to take this process further, promoting community empowerment and contributing towards working for social transformation (Mayo 2002).

Whatever the differences in their perspectives, however, community development workers and activists need to share an increasingly sophisticated common core of knowledge and skills. To build community groups and develop community-based alliances, they need to be skilled in using participatory action research to analyse the issues, alongside their communities, identifying potential allies and opponents and developing effective strategies accordingly. In addition, they need to be excellent communicators – to communicate with the range of diverse groupings within communities as well as with the relevant professionals and decision-makers beyond. And they need to be skilled group workers, if they are to facilitate the development of strong democratic organizations, with the ability to work constructively with differences, coping with internal as well as external conflicts.

Key texts on community development work provide analyses of relevant approaches, together with case studies of how these approaches can be applied effectively in practice, how to identify the key issues, for example, how to help people set up and run groups to address these, groups both democratic and effective, achieving short-term winnable gains without losing sight of longer-term goals. How to work in situations of conflict and how to deal with prejudice and discrimination – within groups as well as outside them, in the wider community and the wider society. How to enable groups to avoid becoming dominated by particular cliques, widening their support inclusively, and sharing power democratically. How to pass on knowledge and skills, adapting activists' learning from previous experiences – without supposing that one size necessarily fits all, in organizational terms. In addition, they provide illustrations of more practical skills in practice, skills such as how to work with the media and information technologies, how to manage resources and how to monitor and evaluate progress towards agreed aims and objectives (Twelvetrees 2002; Henderson and Thomas 2002). Finally, these texts explore the need for organizational death and decent burial – when groups or campaigns have achieved their aims, or simply run their course. Successful endings are those celebrating past achievements, leaving participants empowered for the future rather than demoralized, if groups disintegrate – or even embittered, if there are wrangles over any remaining assets.

Community development texts provide no 'magic bullets'. If there were simple formulas for building effective, socially inclusive and democratically accountable social movement organizations, then these formulas would presumably have been marketed already. As has already been argued in previous chapters, human beings are not simply the product of social structures, they have the capacity to act upon their social environments, whether rationally or irrationally, whether as individuals or as members of groups and organizations. Rather than searching for simple answers, then, it would seem more realistic to explore common questions. What issues have been identified as key factors in the success of community groups and community-based organizations, and how might their experiences be interrogated by others, in global social movements, to identify possible ways forward, taking account of the differences as well as the similarities?

The very fact of identifying common issues can mark the first steps towards working for solutions. When organizers recognize, for example, that a movement is failing to attract new members and/or members from particular minority communities, or that rank-and-file members are becoming alienated, as decision-making seems increasingly concentrated in a small clique, that recognition can spark off the search for collective ways forward. New members can be attracted through a range of activities, drawing upon the experiences of successful campaigning elsewhere, from petitioning outside supermarkets to public demonstrations – forming a human chain around an entire city where international talks were being held, a tactic very successfully deployed by Jubilee 2000, as Chapter 9 explains – from media endorsement by sports celebrities and rock stars to community festivals on village greens. Similarly, when organizers and activists recognize that their movement is ossifying – becoming part of the problem rather than part of the solution – they can develop strategies to tackle bureaucratization, as the trade unionists who embarked on the revitalization of the labour movement set out to do, with support from the top as well as from the bottom, in the case study in Chapter 4.

In general, texts that set out to pose strategic questions might be expected to be more useful than texts claiming to provide one-size-fits-all answers. There have been notable exceptions, however, when it comes to texts that explore tactics in practice. For example, one of the most controversial North American community activists, Saul Alinsky, produced a much-quoted organizers' handbook, *Rules for Radicals* (Alinsky 1971). These were based upon his own experiences, community organizing in Chicago, where he established the Industrial Areas Foundation (IAF) in 1940 to promote his particular approach more widely.

Alinsky was rather less concerned with the strategic issues surrounding movements' internal democracy, being more focused upon developing indigenous leadership to build coalitions of people's organizations in neighbourhoods. Despite a formal democratic structure, the IAF itself has been described as operating in ways that favour authoritarian methods in practice, methods that do not, it has been argued, 'sit easily with democratic values' (Henderson and Salmon 1995: 29). Alinsky had much to say, however, about the tactics needed to build these people's organizations. In *Rules for Radicals* he presented thirteen tactical rules, controversial perhaps, and often confrontational, but effective, he argued, on the basis of his own extensive organizational experiences.

'Tactics' – the relevant chapter – started by explaining that tactics 'means doing what you can with what you have' (Alinsky 1971: 126). If you have numbers on your side, Alinsky explained, you can parade them publicly. If you do not, then 'raise a din and clamor that will make the listener believe that your organization numbers many more than it does' (ibid.). Power, he argued, *'is not only what you have but what the enemy thinks you have'* (ibid.: 127).

The second rule was *'never go outside the experience of your people'* (ibid.) (which leads to confusion, fear and retreat) but, as the third rule explained, *'Wherever possible go outside of the experience of the enemy'* (to cause them confusion, fear and retreat). And use tactics that people enjoy (the sixth rule). The students organizing against sweatshops, for example, demonstrated the relevance of this particular maxim.

Alinsky's fourth rule was: *'Make the enemy live up to their own book of rules'*. In other words, hoist opponents on their own petards. The powerful can be publicly embarrassed when they are caught failing to live up to their own principles, such as formal commitments to tackling global poverty or promoting the rights of the child. Ridicule is also a potent weapon, to embarrass the opposition (the fifth rule) when caught breaking their own rules.

Time, Alinsky pointed out, is also a key factor. *'A tactic that drags on too long becomes a drag'* as the seventh rule explained (ibid.: 128). *'Keep the pressure on'* as the eight rule argued, 'with different tactics and actions' (ibid.). Constant pressure was essential (the tenth rule). Threats may be effective here, and may be more terrifying that the reality (the ninth rule).

Here Alinsky provided illustrations of the use of threats, threatening tactics that would have created ridicule and embarrassment to the public authorities concerned. When commitments to the Woodlawn ghetto organization were not being met by the City of Chicago, for example, O'Hare Airport became the target of just such a threat. Alinsky developed this threatening tactic on the basis of his observation of the fact that, on landing, many airport passengers make a 'beeline for the men's or the ladies' room'. Community activists surveyed the airport, calculating the number of men and women who would be required to occupy the toilets all day, whether sitting or standing (in the case of the urinals), working in teams on a rotating basis.

The threat of the nation's first 'shit-in' was 'leaked' to the administration. Within forty-eight hours, the Woodlawn organization was invited to meet the relevant authorities. At this meeting, the authorities emphasized that 'they were certainly going to live up to their commitments and they could never understand where anyone got the idea that a promise made by Chicago's City Hall would not be observed. At no point, then or since,' Alinsky concluded, 'has there ever been any open mention of the threat of the O'Hare tactic' (ibid.: 143–4).

Alinsky's twelfth rule was that 'The price of a successful attack is a constructive alternative' (ibid.: 130). In other words, campaigns, to be credible, need to be able to argue for convincing solutions. Some of the dilemmas inherent in this approach, its potential dangers as well as its strengths, have already emerged, in the context of debates about the incorporation of protest.

The final rule, the thirteenth, was to 'Pick the target, freeze it, personalize it, and polarize it' (ibid.). As Alinsky explained, in a complex urban society, it is all too easy for blame to be shifted, and responsibility evaded. It is difficult to maintain the momentum of campaigning if the targets are constantly moving. There are parallels here with earlier discussions of the importance of 'framing', posing issues in terms that resonate with potential participants.

This thirteenth rule has also been contentious, however. Personalizing targets might sharpen the campaign's focus, but this might also depoliticize the underlying issues, scapegoating individuals rather than unravelling the structural causes of social problems. As has already been suggested, Alinsky's style of community organizing has had its critics, including some from the Left of the political spectrum (uncomfortable with his populism) as well as critics from the Right (uncomfortable with his use of conflict).

In Britain, in recent years, there has been growing interest in Alinsky's style of community organizing. As Henderson and Salmon explained, in their account, this 'enthusiasm for a method of working which was first developed on the other side of the Atlantic more than fifty years ago' came out of concerns over 'the growing powerlessness of ordinary people, anger because of the growth of inequalities in society, combined with frustration induced by the ineffectiveness of traditional community work responses' (Henderson and Salmon 1995: 1). This prompted 'an urgent search for ways in which citizens can begin to fight back' (ibid.).

It was, as Henderson and Salmon explained, 'against this background that a number of concerned people – most of them with experience of community work in the UK – began to look to America for inspiration' (ibid.: 2). A number of community workers, charitable fund administrators and church leaders accordingly went to the USA, and some went on to train in Alinsky's methods at IAF. The first UK initiative – to build more effective people's organizations in deprived areas – was launched in Bristol in 1990. Since then 'broad-based community organizing' has been developed in other cities too (often with the support of churches and other faith-based organizations), taking up economic as well as social problems. This has included campaigning on jobs and low pay, working, in some cases, alongside trade union organizations.

While Alinsky-style organizing developed the use of militant conflict tactics, however, Alinsky's own political analysis was most definitely not rooted in a Marxist analysis of structural conflicts in capitalist societies. Alinsky did identify the power differentials between the 'haves' and the 'have-nots', just as he identified the need to challenge racial discrimination. But he also argued for building people's organizations across class boundaries, remaining deeply sceptical about political ideologies in general and about Marxist approaches to class politics in particular. In *Rules for Radicals* and *Reveille for Radicals*, Alinsky affirmed his own commitment to working for the great American dream – the dream of the American Revolution – for a democratic, free (market) society based upon 'all those rights and values propounded by Judeo-Christianity and democratic tradition' (Alinsky 1989: xiv). As Henderson and Salmon pointed out, the IAF has 'drawn upon a tradition of "populism" in the USA, going back to the late nineteenth century when the Alliancemen formed the short-lived People's Party. The "populists" advocated policies that stemmed from notions of mutuality, the common good and co-operation, and these values continue to survive in a society where there is also a strong attachment to a "shoestring-to-riches" philosophy' (Henderson and Salmon 1995: 8).

This brings the argument back to the importance of theoretical clarity about differing perspectives and the need for *more* rather than *less* theoretical debate. So how might this theoretical clarity be achieved? Participating in social movements can be an educative process, in itself, and social movements have been analysed in terms of their educative potential. 'Cognitive praxis', according to Eyerman and Jamison, is defined in terms of social movements' capacity for combining theory and practice, providing a 'social laboratory for the testing of new social roles' (Eyerman and Jamison 1991: 166), opening up cognitive space, new opportunities for thought and the transformation of social consciousness.

There is, in fact, a growing body of evidence to demonstrate the varying ways in which people can and do learn from their participation in social movements, in practice. Foley's study of learning through social action, for example, provides powerful illustrations of the ways in which people learn through such experiences, from women's campaigns for service provision and an environmental campaign to save a rainforest in Australia to workplace struggles in the USA, from women's struggles under military rule in Brazil to liberation struggles against colonial rule in pre-independence Zimbabwe (Foley 1999).

As has already been suggested, however, there is nothing automatically or necessarily transformative about the process. Foley concluded by emphasizing the 'complex, ambiguous and contradictory character of particular movements and struggles', arguing for the importance of analysing these as the 'necessary basis for future strategies' (ibid.: 143). As Eyerman and Jamison also recognized, there is a key role for movement intellectuals here. They can draw upon intellectual analyses that can be applied, within the movement, as part of a continuing process of dialogue between theory and practice, action and reflection, followed by further action and further reflection.

How might all this relate to debates within community education? Like community development, community education itself is a contested notion, with varying meanings, depending upon the perspective of the user. As Edwards has pointed out, not all of these meanings are equal, either, and 'the power embedded within them also seeks to construct certain discourses as more valid, "truer" than others' (Edwards 1997: 13). Unsurprisingly, then, in the current global context, the dominant paradigm in the literature on adult education and training (including the literature on adult education and training in community-based settings) has, as Walters has pointed out, 'a human-capital, free-market perspective' (Walters 1997: 6). Lifelong learning is advocated, from this neoliberal perspective, as a means for increasing the productivity of labour and enhancing its flexibility, enabling adults to take responsibility for their own employability in an increasingly precarious labour market. Community-based learning is included in this ideological package for its potential to reach those parts of the labour force that are not being reached in other ways – the redundant and the long-term unemployed, people with physical and/or mental illnesses or disabilities, women seeking to return to paid employment, people defined, for whatever reason, as needing to be reintegrated into the world of work, in the 'learning society'.

From this perspective, community education can also contribute via capacity-building programmes to facilitate participation and partnership working. Learning may be advocated, in addition, for its potential contribution to the promotion of active citizenship. Here too, however, the model may be one that emphasizes learners' deficits, their lack of the relevant knowledge and skills – knowledge and skills the capacity-building programmes set out to provide.

As an approach to community-based learning, the deficit model has been subjected to fundamental criticisms. In contrast, the humanistic school has been concerned with a more democratic, holistic approach.

While recognizing that people may indeed need to acquire key areas of knowledge and skills, the starting point has to be people's own situation, and their own definitions of their needs, social, political and cultural as well as economic – both individually and collectively. This provides the basis for an educational process rooted in dialogue and mutual respect.

There is a long tradition of such approaches to adult education in general and community-based education more specifically. Earlier in the twentieth century, for example, the progressive writer and educationalist, R. H. Tawney, put the case for social engagement, linking education and social movements, developing knowledge to meet social needs. If you want education, he argued, 'you must not cut it off from the social interests in which it has its living and perennial sources' (Tawney 1926: 22).

Rather than attempt to summarize these progressive traditions in Britain and elsewhere, this chapter concludes with a brief review of one particular approach: 'popular education'. This has drawn on the work of Latin American educationalists as well as taking theoretical insights from the Marxist theorist, Gramsci, among others. Popular education has strong resonances, then, with European as well as Latin American progressive political thinking more generally, in addition to building on radical traditions in adult and community-based education more specifically. In recent years, popular education has been applied and theorized in European contexts, including Scotland and Spain, while continuing to be practised in the countries of its origins, in Latin America, as the Brazilian Landless People's Movement (Movimento dos Trabalhadores Rurais Sem Terra or MST) illustrates.

Popular education has been defined as 'popular' (from the the Portuguese and Spanish, meaning 'of the people', the people being the working class, the poor, the unemployed and the peasants), as distinct from populist, in the sense that:

- it is rooted in the real interests and struggles of ordinary people
- it is overtly political and critical of the status quo
- it is committed to progressive social and political change (in the interests of a fairer and more egalitarian society)
- its pedagogy is collective, focused primarily on the group as distinct from individual learning and development
- it attempts, wherever possible, to forge a direct link between education and social action (Martin 1999: 4–5).

The emergence of popular education in Latin America has been linked to the development of struggles for democracy and radical social change, from the 1960s and 1970s through to the 1980s (Kane 2001). One of the key figures was Paulo Freire, a Brazilian educationalist whose ideas have had major influence not only in Latin America but worldwide.

Freire developed his approach through reflecting on his own experiences of witnessing (and to some extent suffering from) poverty and deprivation in north-east Brazil, in the Depression between the two world wars. Drawing upon liberation theology (and subsequently drawing upon the work of Gramsci and other Marxist thinkers), he developed strategies for literacy teaching designed to enable the oppressed to break out of the 'culture of silence' – the resignation preventing them from challenging the sources of their oppression. Through processes of dialogue between learners and teachers, individuals and communities would become critically conscious of their own realities, and this 'conscientization' would represent the first step towards enabling them to work for social transformation, as conscious subjects rather than passive objects of change.

Freire's theoretical work was rooted in his own practical experiences, teaching workers who had come to internalize negative self-images of themselves as they had been stereotyped, as people incapable of learning, rather than as inherently capable and creative human beings. Rather than providing education of the 'banking' type, depositing knowledge into the supposedly empty vessels of learners' heads, Freire started from the opposite, a problem-posing approach. Learners needed to be active rather than passive, engaged in critical dialogue, working democratically in partnership with the educator (Freire 1972). The starting point was the learners' reality – instead of learning how to write about 'cats sitting on mats' or 'John and Jane', learners would start by developing images selected to represent key issues for local people – to trigger debate and critical reflection. Working together on the basis of problem-posing, learners and educators would 'become jointly responsible for a process in which all grow' (ibid.: 53).

Freire continued to develop his thinking after he left Brazil, during the military dictatorship that took power in 1964. He worked abroad, spending many years in Geneva, as special consultant to the World Council of Churches, before returning to Brazil in 1980, a founder member of the Workers' Party (Partido dos Trabalhadores or PT), becoming minister for education in São Paulo in 1989, as well as being actively involved in the Workers' University of São Paulo, firmly committed to developing learning for social transformation. He died in 1997.

Freire's approach has been criticized for being too idealistic and too vague, capable of being understood in widely differing ways, with humanist as well as Marxist interpretations (Youngman 1986). He has also been criticized for failing to take sufficient account of gender as well as social class (Coben 1998). And his methods have been applied – and misapplied in what has been described as 'pseudo-Freirian' ways – by an extraordinary range of educators. These have ranged from those providing business education for multinational corporations to those working for social transformation via projects such as REFLECT (Regenerated Freirian Literacy through Empowering Community Techniques – a worldwide community education initiative developed by ActionAid building upon Freire's work) (Kane 2001).

'The amount of critical review Freire attracted', it has been argued, 'was essentially a measure of his stature; it took place, mostly, within a framework of general support and though the length of criticisms is lengthy – and illuminating – it does not detract from the significance of his contribution' (ibid.: 50). 'There is no doubt,' Kane concluded, 'that the educational principles elaborated in *Pedagogy of the Oppressed* remain central to discussions on popular education today' (ibid.: 51). In his later life, Freire himself reflected on these criticisms of his approach, recognizing the importance of addressing inequalities in the material world – including inequalities in terms of gender in addition to social class – as well as the importance of changing people's consciousness. As he commented himself, 'I grew more aware of education's limits in the political transformation of society [...] education per se is not the lever of revolutionary transformation' (Freire and Schor 1987: 33). While maintaining his commitment to dialogue as the basis for educational processes, he also recognized that educators could not necessarily move straight into such alternative styles, especially when working with learners used to the 'banking' approach. Nor should the learner's increasingly active involvement in any way imply the educator's redundancy. On the contrary, in fact, Freire's concept of praxis emphasized the continuing importance of theory, reflexive action linking theory and practice.

There are parallels here with Gramsci's approach. Freire himself acknowledged his debt to Gramsci, whose works he discovered after he had already been grappling with similar ideas. 'I discovered that I had been greatly influenced by Gramsci,' he commented, 'long before I read him' (Freire 1995: 64). Gramsci had also emphasized the importance of dialogue between educators and learners, intellectuals and activists, while remaining convinced that movements required theory as well as practice, praxis or critical reflection. And this needed to be rooted in a Marxist analysis of the structural causes of exploitation and oppression in capitalist societies, including a critical understanding of the dominant ideologies that worked to legitimize the status quo. As Brookfield has argued more recently, 'a critical theory of adult learning should have at its core an understanding of how adults learn to recognize the predominance of ideology in their everyday thoughts and actions and in the institutions of civil society. It should also illuminate how adults learn to challenge ideology that serves the interests of the few against the well-being of the many' (Brookfield 2001: 20).

Popular education in practice: the Landless People's Movement in Brazil

The Brazilian Landless People's Movement (MST) developed out of spontaneous land occupations, carried out by peasants in the late 1970s, with the demise of the dictatorship (Kane 2001). These groupings came together in 1984, to fight for land, land reform and social justice for all marginalized and oppressed groups more generally. MST is an independent social movement, although many activists have been influenced by liberation theology, and by other religious beliefs. The movement also has general support from the Workers' Party. Their tactics include campaigning and direct action, occupying land and setting up encampments, which then become settlements, with an emphasis on co-operation and participatory democracy.

When he visited an encampment in Viamo, Kane found that the 1,400 people there had organized themselves into groups, with teams to look after issues such as food supplies, health and sanitation, as well as education. By 2001, MST was catering, altogether, for 150,000 children in schools (Bransford and Rocha 2002), as well as organizing popular adult education, typically based on Freirian approaches to education for social transformation (Kane 2001). From 1996, MST had organized a campaign to train literacy workers to tackle the problem of adult illiteracy, persuading the Ministry of Education to provide support (although this lasted only until 2000). In addition, MST has organized training courses for activists, including programmes organized jointly with the left-wing trade union confederation Central Unica dos Trabalhadores (CUT) (Bransford and Rocha 2002).

'All education', Kane argued, 'is considered political and whether it happens to be campaigning, organising co-operatives, tackling illiteracy or running specialist courses, every aspect of MST practice is underpinned by the desire to politicise, raise critical awareness and encourage the emergence of "subjects" of change' (Kane 2001: 104). The MST alphabet, for example, has *acampamento* (camp) for A, *marcha* (march) for M, *reforma agraria* (agrarian reform) for R, *seca* (drought) for S, *terra* (land) for T, *uniao* (union) for U and *vitoria* (victory) for V (Bransford and Rocha 2002). The predominant ideology has been influenced by Marxism, it has been argued, mixed with popular religiosity and rural communitarian practices, with a strong emphasis upon self-liberation. The MST, Kane concluded, 'is a good example of how in Latin America a "movement" is considered the "school" in which popular education takes place' (Kane 2001: 105).

MST's approach to education has been criticized for being more dogmatic and less democratic than its activists claim. Bransford and Rocha conclude, however, that 'for all that' the grass-roots democratic structure is 'not a sham'. And the occupations themselves are 'seen as a unique "school of life" where men and women discover their own worth, acquire self-assurance and knowledge, and become citizens' (Bransford and Rocha 2002: 125).

MST's experiences have been the subject of much interest globally. 'Contrary to much *fin-de-siècle* preaching on the demise of radical alternatives,' Kane concluded, 'the MST shows that the vision of a radically better world continues to be a great motivator for change and that the role of popular education is as important as ever' (Kane 2001: 108). Praxis, reflective action, starts from the immediate, the concrete, conscious human subjects taking collective action, then critically reflecting, developing theoretical analyses of the underlying social relations that need to be challenged before embarking upon further action.

6 | People to people exchanges: sharing local experiences in a global context

The previous chapter concluded by pointing to the contributions of popular education, rooted in the analyses developed by Freire, and Gramsci before him, earlier in the twentieth century. Movements such as the Landless People's Movement in Brazil developed their own approaches to learning, starting from the concrete experiences of men and women in their collective struggles for social transformation. Through analysing the structural causes of their problems and critically reflecting upon their experiences of collective action to tackle these, activists linked theory and practice, developing more reflective action for social change.

This chapter takes up the theme of learning from experience, with a specific focus upon sharing learning from collective experiences and reflecting upon these, globally. Critics of some of the more populist versions of participatory development have pointed to the inherent limitations of local knowledge, and the importance of supplementing this with external and analytical knowledge – the contributions of outsiders (Mosse 2001). While recognizing the potential importance of the contributions of outside experts, however, this chapter focuses upon the possibilities for local people to become the experts for each other internationally as well as locally – 'the communicators and the instigators of a participatory development process' (Patel and Mitlin 2002: 128) through 'people to people' exchanges on a global scale.

The first section of this chapter summarizes debates on the relative contributions of local knowledge and wider knowledge, the contributions of insiders as well as outsiders, learning through critically reflecting upon experiences in collective action. In the global context, this learning can be shared in novel ways, electronically via e-mail and the worldwide web as well as via video, fax and phone. While the globalization of the means of communication opens up new mechanisms for exchanging experiences and networking across national boundaries, however, these supplement rather than replace more traditional 'face-to-face' mechanisms, it will be argued.

The second section of the chapter illustrates these arguments through a case study of people-to-people exchanges, focusing upon the experiences of homeless people's organizations, internationally. Through these international community exchanges, it has been argued, home-less people, especially women who have traditionally been particularly disadvantaged, have been enabled to develop wider knowledge and organizational capacities, including enhanced technical capacities. In addition, those involved with the case study argued, people, including poor homeless people, have gained confidence and skills in impacting upon the policy process, building new relationships nationally and networking more effectively internationally (ibid.).

Insiders as well as outsiders as experts, learning from sharing experiences and networking internationally

Previous chapters have pointed to some of the limitations as well as the strengths of populist approaches to participatory development and social change. Participation in social movements can be an educative process in itself, opening up cognitive space and providing a 'social laboratory for the testing of new social roles' (Eyerman and Jamison 1991: 166). But these learning experiences can be complex, ambiguous and contradictory (Foley 1999), requiring critical analysis, whether from inside or outside the movement in question, or both. The assumption that 'the articulation of people's knowledge can transform top-down bureaucratic planning systems' has similarly been questioned. The reality, is has been argued, is more complex. Local knowledge does not simply exist in some social vacuum, as a fixed commodity. People's knowledge is itself 'constructed in the context of planning and reflects the social relationships that planning systems entail' (Mosse 2001: 17). Local knowledge, like any other type of knowledge, 'reflects local power', including power and authority relationships according to gender (ibid.: 19), power relationships that can be effectively reinforced, rather than challenged via participative development projects. The most powerful elements within local communities tend to be the ones whose voices predominate. Their perspectives may be further skewed, in any case, as they attempt to 'second guess' external donors' own agendas for develop-ment – tell them what you think that they expect to hear about your needs, if you want to be successful in bidding for development funds, focus upon soil erosion problems if the donor is into tackling that, water conservation if that is a priority for the donor in question.

Local knowledge is inherently limited, too, by the scope of locally available information about the impact of wider policies, nationally and internationally. Local people may – or may not – be aware of the effects of structural adjustment policies or unpayable debts, for example, at least until they become involved in wider campaigns on these issues as internationally is not simply facilitated by the Web. The *logic* of the computer is one of feedback' (ibid.: 24).

The potential contribution of new information technologies has already emerged as a key factor in facilitating exchanges of experiences, developing analyses and building networks and alliances, globally. The Internet has 'introduced a more interactive and immediate way to share experience', it has been pointed out, with signs that 'South–South inter-ctions increasingly take place using electronic means' (Singh 2001: 181). hile celebrating this potential, however (even if access is still biased wards those based in the North), there remain questions as to how the web can continue to be so relatively free from control from the down. As the next example also illustrates, even some of those who been most enthusiastic about the potential role of the Internet have his as complementing rather than replacing networking, and the ges of experiences and analyses, face-to-face.

Zapatista struggle, which 'burst onto the world stage on January (Callahan 2001: 37) in the southern Mexican state of Chiapas, characterized, from one perspective, as a postmodern rebel-odying 'a new approach to revolutionary struggle, one based nsformation of civil society, not on the simple seizure of state indigenous ethnic movement with 'a progressive, internation-with links to the ecological and feminist movements and to s of the left in the first and third worlds' (Burbach 2001: 13). have best captured 'the paradoxes and hopes of the post-ith the slogan "one world with room for many worlds" ' e Zapatistas did not, as some pundits feared they might, le and mountain strongholds to storm Seattle', a number ions active in planning the direct action, protests and ttle did have solidarity links with them (Callahan 2001: Callahan's account, the Zapatistas did not co-ordinate f action and protests that disrupted the ministerial WTO and IMF in London, Seattle, Washington DC, But they did contribute in their own ways, inspiring gan, one simple word: 'Enough' (or 'Y Basta' in the ugh of neoliberalism, globally (ibid.).

nched their campaigns in response to the nega-e rapid penetration of capitalist social relations, iated effects of neoliberalism via privatization e spread of free trade (via the North American he Zapatista rebellion focused on the effects of utset this has been described as more than a

they affect them, locally as well as globally. Rather than simply taking local knowledge as unproblematic, then, outside professionals could contribute wider analysis, as well as technical expertise, engaging in processes of dialogue as reflective practitioners (ibid.).

Freire reached similar conclusions in his later reflections on the role of the educator. Having emphasized the importance of starting from people's concrete experiences in their own social contexts, he came to realize that the educator's role included 'the duty to challenge' as well as the duty to respect local people and their culture (Freire 1990: 133). 'My respect for the soul of the culture does not prevent me from trying, with the people, to change some conditions that appear to me as obviously against the beauty of being human,' he argued (ibid.: 133), going on to illustrate his point with the example of the Latin American cultural tradition that women cook for men. This was widely taken for granted, the common-sense view; as one man explained to him, 'it is determined historically that all men have the right to eat what women cook' (ibid.: 132). This did not mean that change was not possible, however. On the contrary, Freire argued, if this was cultural and historical, it could be changed and the possibility of change could and should be posed.

Gramsci had argued in parallel that rigorous theoretical work was essential, if the common-sense assumptions that underpinned unequal social relations in capitalist society were to be challenged. Intellectuals had a key role to play here, engaging in critical dialogues with activists, although he did also argue for the importance of what he termed 'organic' intellectuals' commitment to the movement, as insiders rather than outside experts. While Gramsci emphasized the importance of intellectuals' potential contributions, however, he did also point out that everyone could develop the critical awareness to question dominant ideas and to envisage alternatives for social transformation (Gramsci 1968). By implication, then, social movement activists could – and indeed should – become their own experts too, sharing their learning with social movement activists elsewhere, as they reflect upon their experiences of challenging dominant approaches and working towards developing alternatives. As will be suggested subsequently, the process of sharing these experiences has the potential to promote further action as well as further reflection, building networks of solidarity as well as critical understanding, globally.

The importance of sharing experiences and analyses has been valued in widely varying contexts. Writing of the action-research project 'Women Building Bridges' – boundary-crossing on terrains of conflict – Cockburn reflected on the potential for developing shared purposes and alliance-building, identifying commonalities while taking account of difference and inequality (Cockburn 2000). This action-research set out to explore ways of developing 'transversal politics', promoting dialogues across boundaries, taking account of differences within and across national borders in three contexts characterized by conflict, Northern Ireland, Israel/Palestine and Bosnia-Hercegovina.

Having participated in the life and work of the three projects and gained an understanding of these in depth, the researcher saw that the women were interested in meeting each other to share experiences and strategies. A workshop was therefore organized in Mijas, southern Spain, in 1996, for representatives of the three projects, including representation across the local divides. From the evaluation, the researcher concluded that the women valued the opportunity to identify the

> similarities in the sufferings of people in very different countries and finding a shared analysis of such troubles as having their origins in politics more than prejudice, and as much outside the region as inside, as much in the international agency of big imperialist nations as in the domestic hatred of little ones. It reinforced the sense already present in the projects that women have something to say to each other, not only about a shared positioning in conflict but about their potential contribution to community development, the restoration of justice, the reduction of violence and eventual peace. (ibid.: 54)

As Cockburn pointed out, however, despite provision for reporting back, those who were not there could not readily share the workshop experience. 'It may even have given rise, on return,' she suggested, 'to a certain distance between the travellers (who talked animatedly about the experience) and those who had not been picked to go' (ibid.: 55). This issue was addressed via the organizing of exchange visits, with women travelling in each direction for visits of two weeks – with videos of the visits to show and discuss with those not able to travel. Through these visits there were opportunities for sharing experiences and learning in greater depth, opportunities that were also more challenging in some ways than the more controlled process in Spain. This more open-ended, exploratory approach did not in any way invalidate the exchange programme, Cockburn concluded. On the contrary, in fact, as one of the women from Northern Ireland commented in Bosnia, 'in trying to make sense of your situation, we're really making sense of our own' (ibid.: 57).

Cockburn concluded by reflecting upon the benefits of international feminist networking more generally, whether via exchanges or via

e-mail, fax and phone. In contexts of war and civil strife, network[ing] across national boundaries enabled women to look beyond their div[ided] communities. The same skills and sensitivities to difference and in[equal]ity, the tools of transversal politics, were relevant too, she ar[gued] 'encounters between women of the rich North and those of [the poor] South, or in co-operation between women of the capitalis[t West and] the ex-communist East' (ibid.: 61).

Realistically, this did not, in itself, point to the exister[ce of a] women's movement. Women, 'even when they identify [as women, are as] politically diverse as men, and the cohesion of "wome[n" as a] movement cannot be taken for granted' (ibid.: 46). In[ternational] networking could not, of itself, eradicate wome[n's suffering, she] concluded, although when new abuses come to lig[ht it enables women] to support each other in exposing and resistin[g them.

Mutual support has been key to the tra[dition of solidarity] both within and across national boundarie[s. From the workers] from the first Internationals in the ninete[enth century to the] new organizing agendas of social move[ments in the twenty-] first century, solidarity has been conce[ived in both global] as local terms. In the context of car[...] solidarity has been seen as more vi[...] argued, 'a complex (even disorga[nized)] internationalism' (Munck 2002[...] taking account of gender and [...] issues as well as workers' ri[ghts, needs to be re-] conceived. If trade unions [...] has argued in similar vein[...] to develop multi-scalar [...] arena' (Wills 2002: 6).

Solidarity has tr[...] analyses, providing [...] The new interna[...] drawing upon th[...] cording to Wa[...] worker self-a[...] an alternat[...] hierarchy [...] the pra[...] netwo[...] flexib[...] the worldwi[...]

backward-looking peasant response to capitalist development (although the movement has been criticized on precisely such grounds). The Zapatistas were concerned more broadly with their notion of 'dignity', a notion that has been defined in terms of their fight for a radical transformation of civil society and culture – with a particular emphasis upon communications, globally as well as locally. 'An on-going dialogue with local, national and international civil society is central to the Zapatista revolution' (Jeffries 2001: 130). 'In the Zapatista mirror, solidarity is the building of alternative resistance networks around the world through the practice of radical democracy, liberty and social justice with a related emphasis on localism, autonomy and horizontal relationships among all the participating groups and organizations' (ibid.: 136).

Global electronic networks were key here, including the People's Global Action Network. The Zapatistas were promoting a 'network of voices that not only speak but also struggle and resist for humanity and against neoliberalism' (ibid.: 141). As Harry Cleaver – an American activist who has been credited with having done 'more than any single other person to promote the Internet as a medium for activists' (Paulson 2000: 283) – has pointed out, new information technologies were the electronic fabric of struggle, facilitating the free flow of democratic communication and co-operation. According to a US military report, in fact, the Zapatistas had waged a war of the flea, a war which, thanks to the Internet and global networking, had turned into a war of the swarm (quoted in Klein 2001: 8).

Cleaver has written of the contribution of the Internet in terms of providing access to information, when there was very little coverage in the press. The speeches and reports of their 1994 convention, for example, were made available via the web. In addition, 'cyberspace provided forums for informal discussion and debate' (Cleaver 1998: 86). While celebrating the contributions of electronic networks, however, Cleaver himself was also aware of their limitations. The Internet was, of course, limited to those who had access to it. In any case, electronic networks were complementary to, rather than substitutes for, the 'more familiar tactics of solidarity movements: teach-ins, articles in the alternative press, demonstrations, the occupation of Mexican government consulates and so on' (ibid.: 82). The role of face-to-face contacts was key, too, in that the observers in Chiapas areas, by their very presence, curtailed some of the worst government abuses of human rights. International gatherings such as the International Meeting for Humanity and against Neoliberalism in 1996 (attended by some three thousand representatives from forty-three countries) similarly provided support and added impetus.

Meanwhile, governments in the North began to fight back by trying to gain more control over cyberspace, via the enforcement of intellectual property rights, for example. Cleaver quoted Jose Angel Gurria, the Mexican Secretary of State, who told a gathering of business people at the World Trade Center in April 1995 that the conflict in Chiapas was 'a war of ink, of the written word and a war of the Internet' (ibid.: 93). At the time of writing, he suggested, the available evidence suggested that 'the efforts by the state to counter these networks inside the Net have been limited and ineffective. The initiative continues in the hands of the solidarity networks providing support to the Zapatistas' (ibid.: 95). Meanwhile, there were powerful pressures on the Zapatistas to become a regular political party and/or to become incorporated into a 'domesticated, neutralised and all too "civil" society' (ibid.: 97). The problems in Chiapas and in the Internet, Cleaver concluded, were similar: 'how to continue the elaboration of new kinds of cooperation and self-determination while preventing the imposition of centralised control' (ibid.: 98).

Such accounts of the Zapatistas and their cyber solidarity networks have been the subject of contestation and vigorous debate. Hellman, for example, has put forward fundamental criticisms of what she has described as the 'narrow range of progressive opinion available to those who can only follow events in Chiapas electronically' (Hellman 2000: 292). In an earlier article she referred to 'Internet junkies' who fetishized new technologies.

In his response to this article, while differing with some points of her interpretation, Paulson agreed that 'vicarious participation in an Internet "community" does not substitute for real community (or real activism)' (Paulson 2000: 276). Both emphasized that international solidarity with movements such as the Zapatistas needed to be seen within the context of organizing against neoliberalism and capitalist globalization – including struggles at home as well as struggles abroad. This link between developing solidarity globally and enhancing struggles locally emerges in the following case study.

People-to-people exchanges for urban transformation

Despite greater emphasis upon people's participation, globally as well as locally, much of the teaching, it has been argued, 'remains in the hands of professionals' (Patel et al. 2001: 231). To tackle this imbalance, people-to-people exchanges have been promoted, to enable local people to become experts themselves, developing their own alternatives and presenting these to their neighbours and to communities elsewhere. 'The argument is not that community exchanges avoid power in knowledge but rather that the emerging knowledge is owned by the poor and more likely to serve their interests' (Patel and Mitlin 2002: 134). This particular case study focuses upon initiatives developed by NGOs in Asia and South Africa, from 1990, supporting international exchanges between urban communities.

'From those exchanges', it has been concluded, 'has emerged a people's movement, now linking more than 650,000 members in eleven countries. The links within this movement lie not in formal constitutions or e-mail circulars but in one group of visitors sharing their stories around a fire in someone's shack or mapping a settlement with the local residents' (Patel et al. 2001: 232). While this is a global movement, in the sense that its activities are global in scope, the focus is not on international lobbying or monitoring the World Bank, for example, per se. 'At the heart of this movement is a network of people-to-people exchanges. The squatters in one settlement share their hopes and frustrations, their successes and their problems with others; in so doing, they understand and analyze their situations, gain new insights and strategies, mobilize other residents, and secure the confidence and support they need to move forward' (ibid.: 232).

Organizing global networks of squatters and homeless people might seem to be one of the most challenging projects imaginable. From the perspective of those engaged in community development with homeless people in Northern cities such as London, there are negative stereotypes to counteract from the start, including stereotypes about homeless people's assumed transience and dependency. Such characteristics might be considered the polar opposites of those associated with a well-organized community. As this case study illustrates, however, homeless people and urban squatters in Southern cities can and do develop their own grass-roots organizations and networks and their experiences can and do have relevance for homeless people and their organizations in the different context of Northern cities.

The impetus for this particular set of initiatives came from groups of pavement dwellers, mainly women, in Mumbai, India, in the late 1980s. These pavement dwellers began to develop strategies to meet their needs and to share these with their neighbours. 'Through this sharing, the capacity to teach, disseminate new ideas, explore current events, and analyze settlement and city development options has become embedded in these communities' (ibid.). The women pavement dwellers went on to form a network of women's savings collectives, Mahila Milan, and joined with an existing federation of grass-roots organizations, the National

Slum Dwellers' Federation. This had been set up earlier, in 1974, by community leaders from informal settlements around India to secure land tenure and basic amenities for its members. (There are parallels here with the development of the self-organization and development of co-operatives among women workers, the Indian Self Employed Women's Association, SEWA, outlined in Chapter 4.)

It was through the National Slum Dwellers' Federation that the international links were developed and the exchanges planned and co-ordinated. The Indian women's visits proved dynamic in their impact. As they talked about their approach, more and more savings collectives grew and so did federations, in other countries too. In 1996, these federations agreed to formalize their links via the Shack/Slum Dwellers International (SDI) (ibid.).

While the emphasis was firmly upon self-organization, with local people clearly taking the lead, these exchanges – especially the international exchanges – did draw upon external support, including support with transport and other basic costs. The Society for the Promotion of Area Resource Centres (SPARC) is an Indian NGO that started work in Mumbai in 1984. From the start, SPARC had a particular focus upon supporting women pavement dwellers who represented the most vulnerable people in the city. While providing support, however, SPARC worked with local communities rather than working for them.

Having won respect for the manner in which SPARC engaged with communities of pavement dwellers in Mumbai, the NGO was invited to explore the development of a partnership with the National Slum Dwellers' Federation (NSDF). SPARC, as an NGO, was able to provide the interface with formal development authorities, and to mobilize resources, while the NSDF focused on organizing communities at the grass roots. Working together, they were able to develop 'precedents', models of alternative approaches developed by communities themselves, 'precedents' that could be accompanied by mass demonstrations of support.

'Community exchanges for local learning and for mobilization played a key role in this process' of developing alternative models and policies and pressurizing the relevant authorities to support these (ibid.: 235). SPARC's view was that although squatters and pavement dwellers knew how to survive in the city (almost certainly better than did outside experts), the development of alternative strategies would require professional involvement, and most importantly, it would require community reflection, analysis and learning.

The exchange process builds upon the logic of 'doing is knowing'. Exchanges lead to good sharing of experience and, therefore, a new set of people learning new skills ... They draw large numbers of people into a process of change ... They help to create personalised and strong bonds between communities who share common problems, presenting them with a wide range of options to choose from and negotiate for, and ensuring that they are not alone in their struggles. (ibid.: 236)

'Do you know how many people use a watering place? Or a toilet?' asked Sona, a pavement dweller and 'barefoot housing-planner', working with people in a township community in Natal, South Africa (Wichterich 2000: 148). Because 'you have to know, if you are to demand water pipes from the town council'. With her help, the township residents conducted their own survey in a matter of hours, providing the evidence that supported the case for their negotiations with the town council. The women from India had more experience of struggling to obtain a share of municipal housing, land and infrastructure, including more experience of this type of research. The South Africans, hardened as they had been by their struggles in the apartheid era, had some lead, Wichterich commented, 'in terms of organization, solidarity and resistance' (ibid.: 149–50) – although new political strategies were needed subsequently, she went on to suggest, since 'the political strategies that worked in the liberation struggle are not suited to conflicts with the democratically elected government'. Both groups, then, had vital contributions to make to the other. As Wichterich concluded, this regular shuttle between Mumbai and South Africa had greatly facilitated the exchange of ideas as well as experiences – without implying that there were ready-made solutions to be passed around globally. 'The workers call their cooperation simply "the Alliance" – a grass roots network from slum to slum, from pavement to pavement' (ibid.: 148). Exchanges between communities could facilitate the development of alliances; they could also build the communities' political presence, both locally and beyond.

This last point was particularly marked in the case of international exchanges, when local people gained the status of 'international experts'. 'With an international exchange,' Patel et al. argued, 'community leaders from another country are invited to receptions with senior politicians and to media interviews.' And as 'the international guests are drawn into local activities, political opportunities arise for the host community' (Patel et al. 240). Clearly there is nothing automatically transformative about the outcomes, as the discussion of the potential limitations as well as the potential benefits of external resources illustrated in Chapter 3.

The point that was being emphasized by SPARC here was simply that such exchanges could open political spaces and mobilize resources as well as providing opportunities for the development of solidarity, both locally and beyond. International community exchanges, it has been argued, 'have grown into a movement of solidarity and mutual understanding between the urban poor' (Patel and Mitlin 2002: 129).

In 1988 SPARC became one of the founding NGOs of the Asian Coalition for Housing Rights (ACHR) and it was through this coalition that 'SPARC began to share the methodology of exchanges with other NGOs and community-based organisations in Asia' (Patel et al. 2001: 237). By the 1990s, SPARC had also begun a programme of exchanges with communities working with a South African NGO, People's Dialogue on Land and Shelter, set up to support networking among squatter communities and people living in informal settlements. This was the basis for the development of the Shack/Slum Dwellers International in 1996.

As *Face-to-face*, an ACHR publication, commented,

> Until a few years ago, these kinds of exchanges between poor people were rare. There are now increasing numbers of poor community groups moving around visiting each other – in their own cities and countries and in other countries. And an increasing number of support organisations are hustling to make this possible. In some circles, eyebrows go up at this penetration into privileges that have traditionally been the preserve of professionals. But more and more development activists are welcoming this newly expanding and increasingly systematic horizontal exchange process as a new development tool – *a poor people's pedagogy*. (*Face-to-face* 2000: 10)

Successful exchanges required careful planning, setting out to explore key questions that had already emerged on the basis of action on the ground. 'Exchange is based on a foundation of activism on the ground' (ibid.: 10) if it is to be genuinely valuable, rather than a more general fact-finding mission, before anything has been happening on the ground. It was essential to send a balanced group, with women as well as men, more experienced activists as well as 'first-timers', to avoid creating a hierarchy of those with international experiences. While people needed time to adapt to new cultures, ten days was plenty long enough – two weeks maximum. Otherwise fatigue would set in – and activists would be diverted too long, away from local action. Finally, *Face-to-face* concluded, 'exchanges should be an extension of the ongoing process' if they were to strengthen the ongoing work. 'Participants must take exchange for what it is – no more and no less an exposure to new things, from which each individual and each community must themselves decide what to use' (ibid.: 10).

The main focus of the SDI has been upon supporting local action and struggles for land and infrastructure, and for co-operative development initiatives, including savings groups. While much of the focus has been local, however, there has been a global dimension, it has been argued. These exchanges had strengthened groups' capacities 'to deal with what is oppressive and exploitative within their local environment' and also contributed to wider learning and the creation of knowledge about the possibilities of alternative approaches (Patel et al. 2001: 239). In addition, Patel et al. suggested, through international exchanges, local communities could develop the knowledge and skills to argue for policy changes, whether within their national contexts or beyond, internationally. International travel as well as the development of electronic communications have 'enabled a movement of autonomous savings groups to define themselves and help their predominantly female members to secure housing, land, improved incomes and better lives for their children' (ibid.: 245).

While much of the focus has been upon South–South exchanges, people-to-people exchanges have not been confined to the South. Patel et al. quoted Gaventa's conclusion, based upon exchanges between workers in the South and in the United States: '[We] increasingly found an inter-relationship between issues upon which we worked and those of other countries' (Gaventa, quoted in ibid.: 244). In 2000, the Department for International Development in London hosted an 'urban community exchange' meeting, which shared reflections on the benefits of community exchanges, with contributions from India and southern Africa, illustrating the benefits of people-to-people exchanges.

In addition to a range of donors (invited to adjust their policies to take account of these lessons), the meeting was also attended by representatives from UK organizations, plus interested individuals, including the author. Following this up, I pursued materials on the experiences of UK organizations and groups that had been involved in these processes of international exchanges, collecting reports on their visits and speaking with individuals involved. The Groundswell Project, based in London, was a case in point.

As the Groundswell Project explained, in a publication, *Learning for Social Change: Sharing Information and Experience*, the project had been established in 1996 'to promote practical solutions that involve homeless people for tackling homelessness and social exclusion. Groundswell is a loose network of groups with diverse interests coming together around a common set of values' (*Learning for Social Change* n.d.: 73). Since 1996 Groundswell had developed partnerships with community activists and educators from a number of countries, including India, South Africa, Pakistan, Zimbabwe and Thailand. 'Inspiration from India and South Africa came through stories of community processes in practice,' Groundswell commented – quoting from visitors from SPARC, India and from People's Dialogue, South Africa – while recognizing that what works in one place could not simply be transplanted, wholesale, to another (ibid.: 74).

In January 2000, Groundswell hosted a three-day exchange meeting between sixty-four homeless and ex-homeless people from the Ground-swell UK network and leading community members from the National Slum Dwellers' Federation in India, the South African Homeless People's Federation and the Zimbabwe Homeless People's Federation (organizations also represented at the donors' meeting). The report described the initial discussions as inspiring, as the international visitors told their stories. Over the course of the meetings, new ideas were explored (including ideas about the relevance of developing a UK Homeless People's Federation too). The process was challenging for all involved, the report concluded, leading people 'to question what, why and how they are doing what they are doing' (ibid.: 6). Finally, the participants prepared for their meeting with government representatives, which was opened with a statement reflecting their enhanced collective confidence, putting across the common position they had managed to negotiate, despite the range of views involved. On the basis of their subsequent reflections, Groundswell prepared a resource pack, to facilitate such exchanges and campaigning elsewhere in the UK.

The following January (2001) Groundswell organized for a group of homeless and ex-homeless people from the UK to visit SPARC, Mahila Milan and the NSDF in India. One of the most powerful elements of our trip, they concluded, was the sharing of people's stories and experiences with the slum dwellers, pointing to their enhanced understanding of the similarities in the causes of homelessness, despite the more immediately obvious differences in basic conditions.

> For the UK group, the work of the NSDF and Mahila Milan had been extremely inspiring, and it was surprising and exciting for participants both from the UK and India to discover that they shared many common experiences ... We learned not only about the NSDF and Mahila Milan, but also about ourselves and our strengths and to have confidence in our ability to lead by example. (ibid.: 10)

The Indian trip was described as mind-blowing. The Indians seemed to take the view that since government could not be relied on, people had to get on with it themselves – whether that involved collecting statistics to counter official statistics, which understated the problems, or taking direct action to solve the problems – building facilities or organizing co-operative credit schemes, for example. The Indians' spirit was described as amazing. Organizing the ten-day trip had been challenging, from getting the group together and dealing with practical issues such as obtaining passports and visas, to organizing the feedback process afterwards. But this had all been worthwhile, participants concluded.

Reflecting on the whole experience, one of the participants began by commenting on the differences between Mumbai and the other Indian settlements they visited, in contrast with British cities. Indian slums and informal settlements tended to have their own forms of social organization (often based upon migrants' areas of origin and/or occupation). Co-operative savings schemes took off, in these contexts, where there were histories of trust. This contrasted with the situation in Britain, where homeless people had found it harder to organize in this way, although there had been some developments in this direction, perhaps, in places like 'Cardboard City', Waterloo, or Lincoln's Inn Fields (two informal settlements in London which had both been subsequently forcibly cleared).

While the context was very different, however, there had been some exploration of the common causes of homelessness. They had identified common structural factors, such as the lack of work in the home base of origin, which drove people to migrate to cities in search of a livelihood, and there were comparable issues relating to land and property development processes. In addition, both UK and Indian groups identified common causes of a more personal kind, problems such as domestic violence, drugs and alcohol abuse, problems also linked with poverty, unemployment and personal despair.

The context in Mumbai was particularly relevant though, not only in relation to the factors involved in homelessness, but also in terms of the specific factors that made for the spaces that could be opened up, politically and in relation to the development of alternative policies. In the past, this participant commented, the dominant policy had simply been to bulldoze informal settlements (as described in the novel *A Fine Balance* by Rohan Mistry, set in the 1970s, he explained). Subsequent political regimes might have been more fundamentalist, but the Hindi Party had more favourable attitudes towards slum dwellers, who included traditional peoples as well as migrants to the city, it was suggested. By the mid-1980s, then, there had been some shift in policy, and this opened up more space for slum dwellers and pavement dwellers to press for their needs to be met. And there was, in addition, a history of co-operative savings schemes among women, a history that could be built upon. This was very different, he pointed out, from the situation in Britain.

Sharing experiences and telling stories had been a very powerful experience, he felt. Through the trip, the participants had come together as a group. People found they had a great deal in common. These experiences were being shared subsequently, through report-backs and follow-up events in other British cities. The wider structural issues, including the issues relating to land and property development markets, were also being explored – although some groups (including travellers) found these easier to grapple with than others did. More generally, though, involvement in one type of issue or campaign tended to lead to involvement in others. Most of those who went to India had already been involved in some of the wider issues and debates, he thought. But the process of the exchange had stimulated further interest in wider networking and campaigning. 'It's a process, not a one-off event,' he concluded.

Finally, he added some reflections about the roles of professionals. Professionals had tended to monopolize such opportunities for exchange visits in the past, and 'people at the bottom also need space to do it'. While emphasizing the importance of involving local community activists, however, he was clear that professional support was key. The issue was how to work with professionals without professionals taking over. SPARC was a positive model here, he reflected, because they did work *with* people rather than *for* them, enabling and facilitating rather than controlling the process.

Towards new ways of sharing insider and outsider learning

SPARC developed people-to-people exchanges as a strategy – opening up spaces for learning and critical reflection, spaces that had tended to be dominated by professionals rather than community activists. This had been identified as a problem in local contexts – and an even greater problem at the global level. 'When professionals are agents of change, the locus of learning is taken away from the community, or is never invested within it,' it was argued (Patel et al. 2001: 236). Through people-to-people exchanges, in contrast, local people could develop their own knowledge and analytical skills, together with the confidence to challenge professional experts and consultants and begin to hold them accountable, developing 'a movement of solidarity and mutual understanding' internationally (Patel and Mitlin 2002: 129).

The point was absolutely not to reject professional expertise per se, or to assume that all relevant knowledge and critical understanding was already present in communities of squatters and pavement dwellers. Rather, 'SPARC has sought to explore how professionals might work in partnership with the urban poor to support community driven processes of change' (ibid.: 133). Mosse's emphasis upon the need for an 'understanding of social relationships and social processes' was reinforced by the experiences of SPARC, they argued (ibid.: 134).

Clearly no methodology was automatically empowering, they concluded. Some of the potential hazards have already been raised, including the potential distance that could arise between the travellers and those who had not had the opportunity to travel (Cockburn 2000). But Patel and Mitlin concluded that the evidence was positive overall. The use of community exchanges through a loose federation of local organizations appeared 'to have offered something tangible to thousands of local communities across southern Africa and Asia' (Patel and Mitlin 2002: 135).

In addition, homeless people's organizations have succeeded in having an increasing impact on the policy process internationally. As the movement has developed, their networking has become increasingly effective both in gaining recognition via international forums and in building on this recognition to pressure governments in parallel. Homeless International's website includes evidence of precisely such developments. For example, SDI, participated in the inaugural meeting of the United Nations Committee on Human Settlements (UNCHS) as UN-Habitat, a full UN programme launched in Nairobi in 2002. SDI attended with seventy representatives from all over Asia, Africa and Latin America, giving as well as attending workshops. As the website explained, like Homeless International, SDI have been part of UN processes since the start of UNCHS, attending the 'five years on' meeting in New York in 2001, reminding practitioners from all over the world, by their presence, that those directly concerned must be involved in order that solutions might work.

There are potential implications here for professionals and their learning as well as for community activists and the organizations that support them, locally and internationally. Professionals also need to be supported in learning to work in new ways, in the global context, including learning via international exchanges. For instance, the Turning Point Education, Training and Consultancy Organization (based at Goldsmiths, University of London) is a voluntary organization that provides education and training in community and youth work, enabling community activists and volunteers to gain professional qualifications. International exchange visits are a key component – and ten study visits have been organized since Turning Point was established in 1978 – to Morocco, Greece, Tunisia, Egypt, the Dominican Republic, Cuba, Mexico, South Africa, the Philippines and Brazil.

As the report on the tenth visit to Brazil explained, the theme, as agreed with the Brazilian hosts, was 'understanding the lives and aspirations of the peoples in Brazil and establishing links to the international communities' (Turning Point 2001: i). The aim was a two-week programme 'that focused on mutual learning through dialogue with our various counterparts and partners in Brazil' (ibid.: ii), including the objective of exchanging 'ideas and experiences to enrich their own and colleagues' work practices' to work for 'equality and empowerment, and development; capacity building, economic growth and civil society'. Community development and youth workers should be enabled to gain greater understanding of 'the needs of people from an international [perspective]', including understanding issues such as structural adjustment and debt (ibid.).

The group from Turning Point – a culturally diverse group, twenty-four in total – included students, together with experienced community and youth workers, tutors and members of the organization's management board. Their hosts were non-profit organizations in Salvador, Brazil, an arrangement resulting from careful preparation, to ensure a match, mirroring work in the UK. Key themes in both countries included challenging racism and sexism and working with young people, responding to their love of art, music and dance.

The evaluation was very positive, overall. Group members emphasized their learning, including their learning about the political context as well as their learning about community and youth work in Brazil. There were comments, too, about the lessons in terms of 'inspiration and solidarity' with particular appreciation of the strength and determination of Afro-Brazilians on race and community issues. While all the projects visited were appreciated, however, time was identified as a problem – trying to pack so much into two weeks was difficult. And some participants felt that they would have liked to have contributed more in return. The projects' preparation was praised, but some felt: 'we should have done more practical things with some of the projects … Sometimes we just took not gave' (ibid.: Appendix i).

The Brazilian hosts agreed that although there had been an important exchange around the nature of community work in Brazil and the UK, there could have been a more detailed exchange. In future, it was suggested, an 'ambassador' could go first, to brief the hosts about their guests. This would, it was hoped, result in fuller and more meaning-ful exchanges of information when the full group arrived. For a 'true exchange to occur', the hosts concluded, 'it would be important for host organisations here to have the chance to visit your community, see your everyday reality, and personally see the places where you do your work'. More practically, the hosts also commented on their interest in developing possible partnerships in the North. 'The extreme difficulties which we face whilst carrying out our work makes it difficult not to look to organisations arriving from the "First World" as having some possibility of helping us or make contact with organisations that could provide funding, otherwise open up possible partnerships' (ibid.: Appendix v).

The following year a group from Salvador, Brazil, did visit London, on a return exchange, a visit also very much appreciated by hosts as well as guests. The Brazilians commented in particular on the value of visiting communities with shared roots, and learning about black community arts in London.

Reflecting on some of the lessons overall, colleagues emphasized the importance of the intensive preparatory work that went on beforehand as well as the importance of the post-trip discussions. This exchange had been carefully integrated into the students' overall learning, providing stimulating opportunities for exchanging views on competing theories as well as for exchanging views on practical working methods in the different contexts. There are parallels here with the conclusions of the homeless people's exchanges, similarly emphasizing the importance of careful preparation and debriefing. There are parallels, too, with their conclusions about the potential value of these exchanges in terms of raising profiles locally. Similar conclusions were drawn about the assistance of the visit in raising the host's profile within Brazilian society.

Meanwhile, the same year, there was also a study visit from one of the hosts from the previous visit to the Philippines, a visitor from a network of NGOs responding to the conflict in Mindanao, the second largest island in the Philippines, by working to build linkages and solidarity, both in Mindanao and abroad. As this visit demonstrated, community-to-community exchanges can facilitate political understanding and promote solidarity internationally, as well as locally, providing lessons for professionals as well as for community activists.

7 | Globalization and gender: new threats, new strategies

Through people-to-people exchanges, social movements were strengthened locally and pressures developed for wider policy changes, internationally. This chapter focuses upon the complementary ingredient for the development of social movements, the essential contribution of analysis and critical reflection. Whether locally or globally, as Weeks, Hoatson and Dixon have argued, on the basis of Australian experiences, social movements need to engage in these, if they are to challenge the dominant economic or social boundaries, the 'almost totalising mantra' of the World Bank and the OECD (Weeks et al. 2003).

This chapter starts by summarizing debates on women and development and strategies to challenge gender inequalities in the context of globalization. Feminism has a history of campaigning for women's rights across national borders, providing support and inspiration through international connections, as the campaign for women's right to vote demonstrated in the nineteenth and early twentieth centuries (Keck and Sikkink 1998). More recently, in the last decades of the twentieth century second-wave feminists succeeded in getting women's issues on to international agendas, symbolized and taken forward via the Decade for Women (1976–85) following the UN Women's Conference in 1975. Discrimination against women was officially challenged, internationally (Young 1993), and this potentially strengthened the position of feminists campaigning at the national level.

While there have been significant achievements, however, there are continuing dilemmas for feminists. Women are not necessarily in a position to benefit from enhanced legal rights if they lack the economic means, or the access to key services such as education, to enable them to benefit in practice (Molyneux and Razavi 2002). Meanwhile, more recently, there have been potential challenges, attempts to reduce even these hard-won gains, with increasing pressure from extreme social conservatives and fundamentalists in the current global scenario.

There have also been efforts to promote mainstreaming within the context of neoliberal policy agendas more generally. But mainstreaming does not necessarily guarantee that women benefit, effectively, from mainstream services. On the contrary, if mainstream social services are being reduced, as part of wider strategies to roll back the state, women may experience additional pressures to provide social care themselves – unpaid. Targeting mainstream services – another characteristic feature of neoliberal policy agendas – focuses on meeting the needs of the poorest. Since many of the world's poorest people are female, targeting has been presented as being of benefit to women. But not all women are located within the poorest households and women may be treated unequally in less poor households, too (Pearson 1998; Elson 2002), just as they may suffer from rape, domestic violence, bride burning or lack of reproductive choice (Sen 1997). Tackling gender inequality is not only a matter of tackling poverty, globally (Jackson 1998) – although gender inequality does need to be addressed in the context of campaigning for justice on a global scale.

Having set out these debates on gender justice internationally, in the context of globalization, this chapter focuses on the case of Development Alternatives for Women for a New Era (DAWN). DAWN is a feminist network of women activists, scholars, researchers and policy-makers from the South, committed to alternative approaches to economic development based upon social justice, peace and freedom from all forms of oppression by gender and by class, race and nation (Taylor 2000). The network brings together shared theoretical analyses rooted in political economy. In addition, DAWN analyses and shares experiences of policies in practice, country by country and region by region. On the basis of these theoretical analyses and detailed policy research DAWN challenges global policies and campaigns for alternatives.

DAWN's approach complements the approaches explored in the previous chapter. Both approaches have contributed to campaigns for policy changes internationally, with varying ways of linking theory and practice, critical analysis rooted in experiential learning on the ground. DAWN combines the local with the global, too, illustrating the continuing relevance of local and national policies in the global context.

Women, development and globalization: differing approaches

Globalization and the accompanying spatial reorganization of economic activities have created new gender hierarchies, it has been argued, hierarchies 'which are intensified through class, ethnic and national membership' (Young 2001: 33). Women have been identified among the most exploited labour of the sweatshops of the global factories, prime victims of the processes of capitalist globalization. And neoliberal economic policies have been held responsible for transforming the public policy environment in ways detrimental to women (Elson 2002).

On the other hand, capitalist globalization has opened opportunities for paid labour (however poorly paid). Although employment cannot simply be equated with empowerment, these opportunities have, in some contexts, increased the scope for women to challenge patriarchal social relations (Pearson and Jackson 1998: 11). The processes of capitalist globalization have not been entirely negative or beyond contestation. It is not theoretically helpful, nor does it promote political action by or for women, it has been argued, 'to turn into frightened rabbits when confronting the "snake" of globalization' (Young 2001: 46). Far from remaining passive victims, women have been actively developing strategies to defend their interests both as women and as workers (Pearson 1998) and to challenge their oppression, globally as well as locally.

The nature of this oppression has been the subject of varying interpretations, however. The facts might seem relatively clear. As the *Human Development Report* of the United Nations Development Programme pointed out in 1999, no country treated its women as well as its men, according to measures of factors such as life expectancy, wealth and education (UNDP 1999). As Nussbaum has summarized women's position: 'women in much of the world lack support for fundamental functions of a human life. They are less well nourished than men, less healthy, more vulnerable to physical violence and sexual abuse. They are much less likely than men to be literate, and still less likely to have pre-professional or technical education' let alone enjoy full and effectively enforceable legal and political rights (Nussbaum 2002: 45).

But facts are not necessarily clear – nor do they speak for themselves. It has been widely assumed, for instance, that 70 per cent of the world's poor are women. Once such a statistic has been quoted, it may be quoted again and again, whether or not the figure was soundly based in the first place (Momsen 2002). Similar points have been made about the assumption that a third of the world's households are headed by women, typically poor women, or that this proportion is necessarily increasing – the reality being more complex, it has been argued, with increases in some places but not in others (ibid.).

If the facts have been in dispute, so have the varying theoretical assumptions drawn upon for their interpretation. There is not the space here to develop the discussion of differing perspectives within feminism, from concepts of male dominance and patriarchy – with overtones of universality, across differing social and cultural contexts – to postmodernist approaches that emphasize cultural relativism – suggesting Western/Northern feminism is at best irrelevant, if not actually damaging, a form of cultural imperialism, imposing white middle-class women's individualistic demands on women with very different priorities and values in the South. Traditionally, Marxist feminists emphasized economic factors, recognizing the significance of class as well as gender, and stressing the importance of women's access to paid employment, while liberal feminists placed greater emphasis upon the importance of women's legal and political rights. And post-structuralist feminists have debated varying approaches to the analysis of power and domination, exploring the different ways in which women, as active agents rather than passive victims, have bargained and carved out spaces in the household sphere (Kandiyoti 1998). While these approaches have refined our understanding of household dynamics and gender relations, however, there seems no obvious way, in Kandiyoti's view, 'to bridge the gap between theories of gender and feminist social practice, especially in the field of gender and development. A suspension of judgement about our most central assumption, renewed each time we encounter a new social context, may be salutary' (ibid.: 147).

This conclusion reinforces the continuing importance of critical reflection and theoretical analysis. As the following summary illustrates, women's issues have been raised in recent decades with varying implications for policies in practice. As Thandika Mkandawire, Director of the United Nations Research Institute of Social Developmen, commented, in 2002, the 1980s and 1990s saw revitalized debate over democratic and participatory governance, a context in which

> women's movements flourished as strong advocates of women's rights and attained a considerable number of legal and institutional advances. And yet the last two decades of the twentieth century also saw the ascendance of neoliberal agendas in many parts of the world, with regressive social and economic consequences. This has placed significant constraints on the substantiation of human rights in general, and women's rights in particular. (Mkandawire: Preface v)

As the following summary also illustrates, it has not only been liberal feminist agendas that have been taken up, to a greater or lesser extent, within neoliberal development strategies. Populist concerns have also been met with neoliberal policy responses, with increasing emphasis upon participation and self-help. But this has effectively meant that women's unpaid labour has been required to compensate for the mainstream services that have been reduced, as a result of these same neoliberal strategies.

From 'Women in Development' to 'Gender and Development'

In summary, the resurgence of second-wave feminism in the North began to impact upon development debates in the 1970s. There was pressure on particular governments (including the USA) and there was increasing pressure on the United Nations system, including pressure from Scandinavian NGOs. It was in response to these pressures that the UN designated 1975 as the International Year of Women, with a Women's Conference on the themes of Equality, Development and Peace, followed by the UN Decade for Women, from 1976–85 (Young 1993). While much of the impetus was to rest with national governments, to set up structures to address women's issues, this was to be within the broad framework of international support and the growth of a number of international women's NGOs and networks. As Young concluded, even if the development industry was not significantly changed, 'the UN's promotion of the issue gave a considerable fillip to the women involved' (ibid.: 29).

Then as now, feminists had varying perspectives, and differing priorities for policy agendas. There was a predominant emphasis at this period, however: that of Women in Development (Moser 1993; Young 1993). Women in Development has been described as an 'add-on' to mainstream policy and planning practice. The broad aim was to 'bring' or 'integrate' women into the planning process (Moser 1993: 4). Planners and policy-makers had been affected by gender blindness, it was argued, failing to understand that women had key roles as farmers as well as wives and mothers, or failing to recognize that development projects that involved women's input could actually increase the burdens on already overworked women.

Women in both North and South engaged in research and publications, as well as lobbying to challenge these gender-blind assumptions and to provide the evidence to argue for more positive policy responses. But these responses tended to be limited to 'add-on' initiatives such as support for small-scale income-generating activities, with a particular focus on projects to help poor women to provide more effectively for their families, as part of the wider focus on tackling poverty. Although women were raising demands for gender-equity as well as gender-awareness and meeting basic needs (Moser 1993), most donors and more traditional NGOs preferred not to engage directly with more challenging aspects of women's oppression, unequal relations between women and men and the ways in which these relationships were being affected by structural processes of change, internationally as well as locally (ibid.). Many Third World governments were similarly uninterested in addressing these more challenging aspects, believing that Western-exported feminism was ethnocentric and irrelevant if not actually divisive, labelling Third World socialists and feminists as 'bourgeois imperialist sympathizers' (Moser 1993: 67).

Mainstream Women in Development has been categorized as lying 'squarely within the framework of what has been called liberal feminist theory' (Young 1993: 129). The underlying premise was that women are rational individuals seeking to maximize their interests – but are disadvantaged in doing so as a result of their restricted access to economic, social and political life. The policy implications of liberal feminism have been characterized as focusing on the removal of such legal and institutional barriers for women, making the economic and social system more 'user-friendly' for women. Meanwhile, liberal feminists hoped that economic development and modernization would widen opportunities and dissolve some of the grosser forms of patriarchal belief systems more generally.

Critics of Women in Development have pointed to its failure to challenge the underlying processes of development in a more fundamental way, or indeed to challenge gender relations more fundamentally either. In contrast, Gender and Development was developed as an approach that questioned the view that the basic problem was how to integrate women into existing structures. On the contrary, it was precisely these structures and processes that were giving rise to women's disadvantage – and so were in need of fundamental change.

Gender and Development attempted to be holistic, addressing social, political and cultural dimensions as well as exploring the ways in which the development of a (global) market economy was impacting upon women of different classes, colours and creeds. While recognizing the contribution of socialist development theories, as an approach, Gender and Development was critical of what was seen as the lack of value given to reproductive work in socialist approaches and the absence of structures allowing for challenge and dissent (ibid.).

In terms of their policy implications, Women in Development and Gender and Development have shared many objectives. Both have emphasized the importance of breaking down the barriers that prevent women from gaining an adequate income, for example, and both have emphasized the importance of challenging institutional arrangements and attitudes that disadvantage women. But Gender and Development has differed from Women in Development in its emphasis upon empowering women to challenge the structural causes of their oppression, including the structures of unequal gender relationships. Whether or not this has made Gender and Development less acceptable to mainstream development in practice has been more questionable, perhaps.

From the 1980s, as neoliberal strategies for development became more predominant, there was increasing emphasis upon efficiency. Women in Development approaches could contribute to these agendas, it emerged. Particularly since the 1980s debt crisis, women's economic contribution was highlighted. In addition to increasing their economic contribution, women were also seen 'primarily in terms of their capacity to compensate for declining social services by extending their working day' (Moser 1993: 70), increasing their triple burden as producers, wives, mothers and carers and community volunteers. As Moser concluded, this has been very popular as an approach with organizations such as the World Bank, although these assumptions have also been widely criticized from feminist perspectives. The efficiency approach, she concluded, 'relies heavily on the elasticity of women's labour in both their reproductive and community managing roles. It only meets practical gender needs at the cost of longer working hours and increased unpaid work' and 'because of the reductions in resource allocations, it also results in a serious reduction in the practical gender needs met' (i.e. via mainstream services) (ibid.: 73).

Gender and Development approaches, with their emphasis upon empowering women to challenge the causes as well as the symptoms of their oppression, would seem generally less adaptable to the requirements of neoliberal policy agendas. Gender and Development approaches were taking a more positive view of the state, too, seeing this as a potential locus of support for women, providing essential health and welfare services (Young 1993). In practice, however, although Gender and Development approaches have been, at least to some extent, mainstreamed, no approach has been beyond the scope of pressures from neoliberal policy agendas overall.

The logic of Gender and Development approaches was to address male–female power relations rather than just adding women's projects on to existing development agendas. This implied mainstreaming, or indeed 'menstreaming', recognizing the central importance of men and masculinities. Projects to tackle issues of reproductive health, including projects to promote safer sex, for example, require men as well as women to change their behaviour. As women themselves have commented, 'It's not just enough to change women. We need to change men as well, and analyse masculinity and change it' (Chant and Gutmann 2000: 39). Women are not always the losers, it has been argued, either, and projects that focus upon meeting women's needs risk producing a backlash from men (Chant and Gutmann 2002).

Key agencies, including the World Bank as well as NGOs, have been convinced by these types of argument. The extent to which these commitments have been implemented in practice has been more questionable, however. The reality, at the turn of the century, according to a former funder of the Oxfam Gender Unit, was that Gender and Development was still 'peripheral not core' (Chant and Gutmann 2000: 10). Key agencies like the World Bank were espousing Gender and Development objectives in principle while slipping back, in practice, to targeting projects for women, more reminiscent of Women in Development approaches. Unless women are empowered to move beyond this 'project-trap', feminists have argued, 'and to take part in the making of policy where key decisions about resource allocation are taken, they will always be a residual category in development' (Kabeer 1999: 43).

As Pearson has pointed out, feminists face a series of paradoxes here. The enthusiasm for 'gender rather than women in development approaches signals not just a change in language or a depoliticising of the field' (Pearson 1998: 5). Development policy and practice had become 'infused with gender' (ibid.) – even if the rhetoric was stronger than the reality. Meanwhile, in contrast, neoliberal strategies were resulting in the reduction and reorganization of social services and increasing pressures on women to provide alternatives – unpaid. Pearson concluded that these paradoxes and uncertainties provided 'an opportunity for, rather than a failure of, gender analysis' (ibid.). Theoretical analysis was more essential than ever, at the turn of the century, if feminists were to campaign effectively in this complex and contradictory global context.

Development Alternatives with Women for a New Era (DAWN): critical feminist perspectives from the South

DAWN has been credited with having made the best articulation of the empowerment approach (Moser 1993). This network of women from the South – actively engaged in feminist research and working for equitable, gender-just and sustainable development – was launched at the United Nations Third World Conference of Women in Nairobi in 1985 (Bunch et al. 2001). This was a timely intervention, and one that attracted enormous interest – some 2,000 women attended the DAWN workshops in Nairobi (Stienstra 2000). This was a period in which there were increasing criticisms of the approaches that had been predominant in the previous decade, focusing as these did upon integrating women into existing structures and processes of development. By 1984, when the DAWN network was forming and planning its input to the Nairobi conference, the inadequacies of such approaches had become increasingly apparent.

'We are now more aware of the need to question in a more fundamental way the underlying processes of development into which we have been attempting to integrate women,' they argued (Sen and Grown 1987, quoted in Young 1993: 133).

> Throughout the Decade (The UN Decade for Women) it has been implicit that women's main problem in the Third World has been insufficient participation in an otherwise benevolent process of growth and development. Increasing women's participation and improving their shares in resources, land, employment and income relative to men were seen as both necessary and sufficient to effect dramatic changes in their economic and social position. Our experiences now lead us to challenge this belief. (ibid.)

DAWN set out to analyse the conditions of the world's women and to formulate a vision of an alternative future, a world where inequality based on class, gender and race is absent from every country and from relationships among countries.

> We want a world where basic needs become basic rights and where poverty and all forms of violence are eliminated. Each person will have the opportunity to develop her or his full potential and creativity, and women's values of nurturance and solidarity will characterize human relationships. In such a world women's reproductive role will be redefined: childcare will be shared by men, women and society as a whole. (DAWN 1985, quoted in Moser 1993: 75)

This was a vision of an alternative future informed by political economy, drawing upon socialist approaches as well as feminist concerns.

Although DAWN was independent of any particular political party or parties, the collapse of the former USSR and Eastern and Central European socialist states at the turn of the 1990s presented challenges. Implicitly, if not explicitly, socialism had been seen to represent an alternative development future (providing that previous inadequacies, especially inadequacies in relation to feminist agendas, could be remedied). The 'new world order' of the post-1989 situation required some rethinking.

The outcome of DAWN's analysis of this 'new world order' was to focus upon the international economic system, globalization and the impact of the neoliberal strategies that were now being presented as the only way forward, globally. DAWN decided to tackle the predominance of neoliberal agendas head on. The strategy that DAWN developed from the 1990s centred upon contributing to key international events such as the International Conference on Population and Development in Cairo, in 1994, the World Summit on Social Development in Copenhagen in 1995 (including the recall conference in Geneva in 2000) and the Fourth World Women's Conference in Beijing in 1995. DAWN focused on researching and critically analysing capitalist globalization as neoliberal strategies have been impacting upon women in different countries – and relating this analysis to the specific policy concerns of the international event in question. DAWN has researched the impact of the debt crisis on women, for example, as well as focusing on environmental sustainability, militarism, reproductive health and rights (including HIV/AIDS) and political restructuring in the context of the increasing marketization of governance.

DAWN does plan ahead, taking account of key events coming up internationally and preparing evidence to put to these. But the approach is also flexible and organic. If an important unexpected event comes up, then DAWN will respond, if it can, even if this was not previously in the work schedule.

Although DAWN's analysis has been developed by academics and researchers, this has been rooted in the experiences of poor women in the South. By introducing this analysis that 'related the daily experiences of women to colonial relations between countries and the macroeconomic policy framework', it has been argued, 'DAWN gave women a new way of viewing global processes and development issues' (Bunch et al. 2001: 224). DAWN has specifically focused upon linking the micro and the macro, holistically, highlighting the connections between women's daily lives and the wider economic, social, cultural and political framework. This approach, it has been suggested, has transformed debates on women in development, and helped to mobilize women worldwide into a political constituency (ibid.).

DAWN has developed this global role from relatively small beginnings, organizationally. Following the successful launch in Nairobi, DAWN's founders organized a meeting in Rio to launch an ongoing programme of research and advocacy. A steering committee was established with a secretariat based first in Bangalore, India, then in Rio de Janeiro, Brazil, next at the University of the West Indies and more recently, from 1998, at the University of the South Pacific in Fiji. This rotation of the secretariat's base has been explained as having been set up to ensure that 'different regions of the South will benefit from its analysis and advocacy work and that DAWN will eventually earn a profile in each of these regions' (ibid.: 226).

The steering committee has members from the different regions of the South and regional co-ordinators have responsibility for ensuring that there is a strong and effective regional dimension to DAWN's work – a particular feature of DAWN's work programme at the beginning of the twenty-first century. As DAWN's 2001 publicity brochure has explained, 'DAWN is emphasising work at the regional level in an effort to extend its reach and influence, connect more closely with the priorities of women's civil society organisations in each region, and help strengthen capacity to deal with issues arising from the impacts of globalisation'. The steering committee meets once a year. This has been supported financially with funding from varying sources such as the Ford Foundation, HIVOS (Humanist Institute for Co-operation with Developing Countries), the John D. and Christine T. MacArthur Foundation, the Swedish International Development Co-operation Agency and the United Nations Development Programme. This funding has also enabled DAWN to employ a co-ordinator with support in the office. Having more than one source of funding has been important for DAWN, not relying on any one funder making it easier to remain independent.

In addition, research co-ordinators facilitate research and analysis and advocacy work on the key themes of the environment, reproductive rights and population and alternative economic frameworks in the context of globalization (Bunch et al. 2001). Activists attend regional meetings so that the analysis is informed by and linked to advocacy and campaigning. These connections between consistent analysis and effective organizing have been central to DAWN's approach – although members of DAWN themselves have also reflected on the difficulties of developing and sustaining these links between researchers and women working at the grass-roots (DAWN 1990; Stienstra 2000).

Since the mid-1990s, in addition to strengthening its own regional links, DAWN has also strengthened its links with other progressive networks. From 1996, for instance, DAWN worked with the Structural Adjustment Program Review Initiative, an NGO initiative involving a wide range of civil society groups in evaluating World Bank structural adjustment programmes (Bunch et al. 2001). DAWN has been credited with playing a key role here, 'at the forefront of signalling the harmful effects of structural adjustment on women', alerting women in the North that 'this was not simply a Southern's women's problem, but one that would also reshape the lives of women in the North' (Stienstra 2000: 79).

In addition to collaborating on research and critical analysis, DAWN has also collaborated in organizing panels at international events. At the World Social Forum in Porto Alegre, Brazil, in 2001, for example,

DAWN joined with Latin American feminists to ensure that there were feminists in the main forum, in addition to taking part in two discussion panels, including the panel on 'Transparency and Accountability: Gender Budgets'. This was organized with REPEM (Red de Educacion Popular Entre Mujeres de America Latina y el Caribe) and the United Nations Development Fund for Women, to discuss women's economic rights, the invisibility of non-paid women's work and an analysis and study of national and local budgets (DAWNInforms 2002).

Similarly, in preparation for the UN World Conference Against Racism, Racial Discrimination, Xenophobia and Related Intolerance (held in South Africa in 2001), DAWN drew on the analysis that the Women's International Coalition for Economic Justice was developing, as well as referring to UNIFEM's background paper, exploring the ways in which gender subordination may be informed and heightened by racism and xenophobia (ibid.). These wider networks and partnerships have been important in maximizing the effectiveness of DAWN's international advocacy work, building a broad alliance to work for the reform of international institutions and international policies. While maintaining its critical feminist stance, DAWN has been working from the inside, working with international organizations and agencies as well as national governments to make an impact in the here and now. In addition, networking has been important in strengthening pressures on governments to ensure that they live up to whatever commitments they are encouraged to make at these international conferences.

In developing this range of networks, regionally and internationally, DAWN has been strategic. There have been issues on which it has been possible to work with Northern governments, for example, just as there have been issues on which it has been possible to work with Southern governments. But DAWN has been mindful of the need to hold on to its own progressive feminist agenda. So, for example, while DAWN has been extremely critical of neoliberal global agendas, DAWN's research also drew attention to the fact that 'everywhere in the South, anti-feminist reactionaries draw strength from the opposition to neoliberalism. If the anti-globalisation movement fails to recognise the twin dangers of neoliberalism on the one side and fundamentalism on the other,' the DAWN website DAWNInforms continued, 'it will not address the concerns of half of humanity. If the choice were between the Republican Party in the U.S.', this article continued, 'and Afghanistan's Taliban, as a woman, I would take my chances with the Republicans' (DAWN 2002). (DAWN has, of course, also been concerned to critique Christian fundamentalism – as DAWNInforms explained, one of the highlights of the

World Social Forum meeting in Porto Alegre in 2001 was the surprise demonstration against the conservative Republican Bush administration's then expected attack on abortion rights which would also impact upon overseas reproductive health programmes.)

DAWN has been similarly strategic in building alliances with feminists and working with anti-global campaigners in the North as well as in the South. At the World Social Summit in Copenhagen, for instance, DAWN organized a hugely successful and massively well-attended event, with a panel that included poor women from the North. Some men from Southern delegations were overheard expressing some surprise when they heard about this. What could women from the North possibly know about poverty and why on earth were they being given a platform? Also overheard were the most lucid explanations from Southern women who had actually attended the event, explaining the common underlying causes, rooted in the processes of globalization, dominated as these were by neoliberal policy agendas.

DAWN has been clear about maintaining feminist perspectives within campaigns around globalization. For example, while DAWN was actively involved in the Women's Caucus, and there were public events running all day, during the 'Battle of Seattle', the daily newspaper that was produced by a group of NGOs failed to provide adequate cover. So DAWN's webpage included some critical reflections on the ways in which North/South women's activities were generally marginalized by the male-commanded NGO and social movement resistance in Seattle.

Commenting on the paradoxes of working for gender justice with social movements, more generally, DAWN's Southeast Asia co-ordinator reflected: 'Post-Beijing, DAWN has been active in inter-linking with social movements and male-led NGOs in what we refer to as negotiating gender in the male-stream.' DAWN was involved in a range of global groupings and networks including the International Council of the World Social Forum. There were increasing intersections, it was argued, both of analysis and collaboration among the movements for economic justice, people-centred social development, and recently for peace, civil liberties and democracy. But DAWN was also clear that 'we are at the same time opposing the marking and disciplining of women's bodies and agencies by fundamentalist communitarian ideologies and resistance struggles that, just like the state, turn women into motherhood idols and icons' (DAWNInforms 2002).

On the issue of partnerships with the private sector, particularly transnational corporations (TNCs), or with international trade and financial institutions, DAWN has been even more cautious. An article on 'Perilous Partnerships – with Whom, for Whom' drew attention to some of the questions that needed to be addressed, in response to proposals for partnership initiatives around the World Summit on Sustainable Development in 2002. The type of partnerships that were to be recommended, it had been suggested in contrast, were bottom-up, participatory and democratic partnerships/initiatives based on principles of gender justice and human rights. Partnerships locked NGOs into a very difficult position, it was argued. 'On the one hand, they provide opportunity to engage in dialogue, which is important. On the other hand, they represent a strategy of control and deliberately gloss over the inequalities in power and capacity of different actors (NGOs and TNCs), and use NGO participation to legitimize the claims to democracy in the neo-liberal models of governance' (DAWNInforms 2002).

Marketisation of Governance: an example of a DAWN publication, presenting critical feminist perspectives from the South

DAWN developed its own critical analysis of these paradoxes facing social movements, in the context of political restructuring, with the publication *Marketisation of Governance: Critical Feminist Perspectives from the South* (Taylor 2000). This publication illustrates DAWN's approach theoretically, applying the insights derived from political economy to expose the political dimensions of economic globalization. In addition, the publication illustrates the ways in which DAWN works, building upon collective analyses and debates regionally and then disseminating the shared conclusions internationally.

The book was launched at the recall World Social Summit on Social Development in Geneva in 2000 to expand the global debate on governance, democracy and social development. The Chair of the United Nations Commission on Social Development, Dr Zola Skweyiya, who spoke at the launch, commented that DAWN could not have chosen a more relevant topic, or a more appropriate venue than Geneva 2000 for this (DAWNInforms 2002). Explaining the reasons for entering these debates, the report co-ordinator pointed out that 'DAWN and women of the South noticed trends after the collapse of the Eastern bloc: the changed political landscape, the rise of fundamentalism, the discrediting of state-led development, and the ascendancy of neo-liberal economics' (ibid.). Faced with the resultant fractures and contradictions within global institutions, DAWN decided that women of the South needed 'to articulate a vision that would recast the analytic frameworks that influence political restructuring' through a collective process of reflection, rooted in 'the lived experiences of women from the South' (ibid.).

'How. do we move beyond this mantra of efficiency, marketisation of governance and marketisation of social justice objectives so that we can reclaim the space within global and regional and national arenas that will actually be used to bring people who have been marginalised back into the centre of governance?' (ibid.).

As a subsequent article on the DAWN website commented, echoing some of the concerns raised by Molyneux and others, one of the key lessons of recent years was that

> while we were busy putting in place de jure rights, formal programmes and mechanisms for women (including participatory programmes and mechanisms such as participatory Poverty Reduction Strategy Papers) we failed to adequately take stock of how new trends of marketisation and backlash arising from the tensions and ruptures created by globalisation had systematically eroded the opportunities that allow women, especially the poor, to enjoy those de jure rights and freedoms. (DAWN-Informs 2002)

'The only answer to globalisation', one panellist at Geneva 2000 had already concluded, 'is the globalisation of solidarity' (ibid.) based on an alternative critical analysis rooted in the experiences of women in the South.

DAWN had set to work to develop this alternative analysis of political restructuring back in 1996 after intense and rigorous debates around the World Social Summit in Copenhagen and the World Conference on Women in Beijing. 'Were we really looking at how to engage within a global space that expanded the framework for the attainment of rights of those people who were previously excluded?' (Taylor 2000: 3). What was the impact of global governance, in reality, including agreements made in the boardroom of the WTO, and how was all this affecting the legitimacy of the nation-state? 'While new spaces were opening up for critical engagement we had to ensure also that our engagement did not diffuse our objectives as a feminist network from the South or lead to co-option' (ibid.).

DAWN obtained funding (from the Heinrich Boll Foundation, Germany) to develop the Political Restructuring and Social Transformation (PR and ST) research project. Seminars were organized in the different regions in 1999, to debate papers from contributors in that region. The outcomes of these regional debates were then brought together in an inter-regional meeting, held in South Africa in February 2000. On the basis of this collective process of research and critical analysis, the final publication, *Marketisation of Governance* (ibid.), was produced and launched in Geneva that summer, presenting the experiences as well as the analyses of feminists in the South.

This publication began by unpacking key contradictions in feminists' relationships with the state. The state was being critiqued from the neo-liberal Right as well as from the Left and by feminists for state failures to meet people's needs. While the neoliberals concluded that the market was the best allocator of goods and services, however, DAWN argued that whatever the critique 'the state is seen as the arbiter of democracy and therefore its role in public policy and action cannot be abolished. Neither can it be left to the NGO sector (as if this is an independent sector), nor can it be left to what is glibly seen as a unified homogenous civil society sector' (ibid.: 13). There was particular concern that pre-occupations with economic growth through the market were eroding the state's capacity, 'while at the same time development directions are discussed in terms of governance and efficient management. The debate has shifted from issues of distribution to efficiency and management' (ibid.) – in the interests of multinational capital rather than those of poor women in the South.

DAWN's analysis of the nation-state recognized the inherent biases in terms of race, class, ethnicity and religion as well as in terms of gender. States were not entirely monolithic organizations, however. Women had succeeded in finding political spaces and making some – albeit limited – gains. The international recognition of women's rights as human rights at the Vienna Conference on Human Rights in 1993 had been a step forward, in this respect, as had the achievements of the Beijing and Copenhagen gatherings in 1995. Although the percentage of women in formal positions of power (as politicians and/or bureaucrats – or 'femocrats') was low, still women's issues were at least being articulated and placed on official agendas. The African contributions provided ex-amples, for instance, to illustrate the importance of even limited gains for women – together with dire warnings about the consequences for women in contexts where the state had been destroyed, as in Rwanda, Liberia and Sierra Leone.

A noticeable shift had been occurring, however, a shift from 'parlia-mentary democracy and the public interest role of the state through to the shifts in how to secure faster gains for the private sector to promote economic growth' (ibid.: 17). There was a 'compact of power' between state-led institutions and transnational corporations (ibid.). Develop-ment tended to be tied through aid to 'a commitment to western style democracy/pluralism and in the post cold war, post modern period, this has led to a greater acceptance of political and economic liberalisation

[...] the impacts of which have been varied, affected by both complementary and contradictory pressures', it was argued. 'There is internal and external pressure to have open competition for power and civil liberties and then there is economic liberalisation (one dollar one vote) where decision-making is removed from the majority' (ibid.: 43).

DAWN's analysis explored the links between these processes of liberalization, democratization and globalization. The state was under increasing pressure, some were arguing, to reorganize to serve market interests more effectively. The increasing prominence of multinational financial institutions was identified as key here, institutions such as the World Bank, the IMF and the WTO. Structural adjustment programmes and agreements to promote trade liberalization were promoted by these institutions, together with the agreement on Trade Related Intellectual Property Rights (TRIPs) – described as 'the effective and extensive monopolisation of scientific knowledge and technical capacities within the most advanced economies' (ibid.: 52). The General Agreement on Trade in Services (GATS), promoting the outsourcing of services, including public services, was identified as another example of a contentious policy with particular implications for women, children and the poorest people in the South.

'The rolling back of the state in the form of deregulation from public interest to regulation in terms of private interests is a major cause for concern,' DAWN concluded (ibid.: 59). In post-apartheid South Africa, for example, rigorous public-sector rationalization had been prescribed by external policy advisers in line with structural adjustment programmes. Ironically, far from state spending being redirected to the most deprived, resources had been directed towards paying foreign consultants to write policy documents. 'These documents were being given legitimacy and national content and flavour,' it was argued, 'by incorporating mainstream NGOs and academic institutions as secondary partners in the process' (ibid.). While NGOs were identified as increasingly at risk of becoming part of the problem, however, there were also examples of situations, such as in the Caribbean, where NGOs were credited with contributing to the critique of 'the market and trade agreements that undermine people' (ibid.: 77).

Meanwhile, in India, for example, rolling back the state's caring role was being accompanied by increasing its controlling role. Special units of Indian police were being trained by Western security experts to protect the life and property of foreign investors, the privatization of security to contain and stamp out resistance 'to the economic violence inherent in the market' (ibid.: 60).

Unsurprisingly perhaps, then, in this context, many of the gains from Beijing and Copenhagen were being institutionalized in ways that were reducing the actual benefits for women. In South Asia, there had been women heads of state (although this phenomenon had also been described as the 'over the dead body' syndrome whereby widows or daughters of dead charismatic male leaders acquired the legitimacy to take over the mantle in a culture of dynastic politics). Women were also leading the way in terms of development initiatives to benefit women such as the renowned Grameen Bank. All South Asian states had state agencies, in the wake of the UN Decade for Women, with the high point being identified as being around preparations for and follow up to the Beijing Conference in 1995. But there were powerful pressures leading in the opposite direction.

One of the possible exceptions that was quoted in the South Asian context was the Panchayat Raj in India, which reserved seats for women in local government. As a result, over a million women were members of Panchayat Raj, local government structures, by the turn of the twenty-first century, an experience described as unique in the process of political restructuring and social transformation in the region. Even in this case, however, DAWN concluded that, 'in terms of genuine participation of women, the experience is very mixed and difficult to generalise in a country as vast as India with Panchayat Raj functioning in 22 states' (ibid.: 99).

Women and Development 'add-on' approaches were seen as particularly prone to increasing marginalization. On the other hand, the shift towards Gender and Development approaches to gender mainstreaming was also seen to have its own inherent limitations. The African contributions reflected that the abolition of 'women's desks' and departments in the institutions of governance had been justified by officialdom as part of attempts to promote mainstreaming – bringing women's issues in from the periphery to the core. But concerns were expressed. Would women's issues simply sink without trace, or would male project officers in male-dominated organizations have the knowledge, experience or skills to ensure positive effects for women? The conclusion drawn from this discussion was that women clearly needed both: women-specific and integrated activities and organizations.

Meanwhile, post-Beijing, with the deteriorating economic and political situation in many contexts in South Asia, for example, some momentum was being dissipated. This was impacting on civil society and the NGO sector as states became more repressive and authoritarian, it was argued. And the failures of governments were leading to the hardening of identities and the intensification of conflicts. As the state withdrew from its role of provider of services and protector of rights, in addition, 'various community-based organisations have no option but to step in to provide basic services, which carries the danger of becoming part of the system and losing the capacity to remain autonomous and critical' (ibid.: 132) – not to mention potentially adding to women's existing burdens.

As the contributions from Africa also pointed out, the replacement of state functions with privatized/international development NGOs was not necessarily gender-neutral, regardless of their progressive content. The assumption that civil society could offer a panacea for all the weaknesses and failings of the state was not necessarily realistic. On the contrary, in fact, 'the majority of community associations, non-governmental organisations and social movements in Africa have entrenched gender inequality in their institutional cultures and practices', it was argued (ibid.: 151).

The book concluded by summarizing the dilemmas for feminists committed to bringing about social transformation. DAWN's analysis provided the basis for developing strategies to make the most of the opportunities that had been opening up in the global arena. The objectives were for feminist women's movements to engage with different forms of power, forming alliances nationally, regionally and globally while retaining their autonomy from the state. Strategies also needed to include an emphasis upon building grass-roots democracy as well as a human rights culture, at every level. And this in turn needed to include strategies to hold global economic institutions of governance such as the WTO to account.

DAWN's particular contribution

DAWN has been considered unusual, if not unique, in being a progressive feminist network which is so effective in international arenas – without being dominated by groups of white women from the North, who have often been seen as tending to play leading roles at this level (Stienstra 2000). DAWN's research has benefited from the particular expertise of academics who have been committed to promoting processes of dialogue, rooting their analyses in the experiences of women in a wide range of different situations in the South. These specialists have brought their professional skills as academics and researchers, together with their skills and contacts in policy arenas, nationally and internationally. DAWN has been highly proficient in operating at this global level, preparing policy papers, collecting evidence from different contexts to support their arguments and then presenting these at preparatory commission meetings and full international gatherings.

DAWN has clearly been recognized as making strategic impacts, including impacts at global events such as Cairo, Vienna, Rio, Copenhagen, Geneva and Beijing. *Marketisation of Governance* went on to provide a critical analysis of the ways in which the very processes of globalization themselves have been pressing in alternative directions. In addition to providing this research and analysis, DAWN has also worked to strengthen progressive feminist movements and social movements more generally.

The author was personally involved in one specific example that illustrates DAWN's contributions to international solidarity. This was when DAWN effectively acted as informal mentor to another international NGO – an NGO concerned with community development, preparing for the recall Social Summit in Geneva in 2000. DAWN shared a platform at a joint event – providing a briefing beforehand about how to assemble the case to be put, involving the organization's membership by gathering examples from member organizations in different member-states. This enabled the NGO's case to be put effectively, supported with the evidence, locally, nationally and regionally, to demonstrate achievements and shortcomings, where governments had so far failed to live up to previous commitments on the issues in question. DAWN also shared contacts and specific knowledge and skills about the practicalities of organizing such events internationally.

Operating at the global level poses particular challenges. As if the challenges of taking on global institutions were not enough, there are also formidable logistical problems to be addressed. The spread of e-mail has been recognized as a key factor which has been of assistance to DAWN in overcoming these logistical problems, facilitating the exchange of information and views on the drafting of papers, for instance. But DAWN has also benefited from its expertise in attracting funding to support face-to-face meetings and attendance at international events.

Operating at the global level poses challenges too, in relation to issues of representation and democratic accountability. After the success of DAWN's first interventions at Nairobi, there were expressions of interest from others who wanted to join the group. After careful reflection, however, DAWN decided not to become a membership organization. Setting up a formal organization would have been a huge task in itself, with its own organizational logic and requirements. Even if they had decided to pursue this option, having a formal organization would not, of itself, have resolved the dilemmas inherent in ensuring democratic representation internationally. On balance, then, DAWN opted to focus on providing research and analysis as a think tank of progressive feminist lobbyists from the South, albeit closely informed by the experiences of women at the grass-roots. Some of these issues and dilemmas around representation and accountability emerge in other contexts, however, including the chapter below on Jubilee 2000.

8 | Rights to public services: the Global Campaign for Education

'Millions of parents, teachers and children around the world are calling on their governments to provide free, good quality, basic education for all the world's children. They are part of the Global Campaign for Education; we add our voice to their call' (Nelson Mandela and Graca Machel, April 2002)

Education has already been identified as one of the key services, if not *the* key service for human rights and social justice agendas. As the *Oxfam Education Report* pointed out, 'mass education creates the skills needed to assess and monitor government actions. It also creates the demand to be heard. Constitutions, legislation, and international treaties may provide the judicial backing for civil and political rights, but it is education that creates the "voice" through which rights can be claimed and protected' (Watkins 2000: 63). Without education and healthcare, as the previous chapter argued, human beings are unable to benefit from human rights effectively, in practice (UNESCO 2002) – lacking the capability – the 'actual ability to achieve valuable functionings as a part of living' (Sen 1993: 30).

While education has been advocated as essential for the implementation of rights and justice agendas, however, this has not been the only focus of contemporary debates. Education has also been prioritized for somewhat different reasons, with particular emphasis on its contribution to improving productivity through the development of human capital (Fine and Rose 2001). Neoliberal strategies have focused upon these economic purposes, as well as emphasizing the role of the market in the delivery of educational services. The dominant global approach, it has been argued, 'culminates in the progressive liberalization of trade in education services instead of progressive realization of the right to education' (Tomasevski 2003: 2).

Like DAWN, the Global Campaign for Education has undertaken research and policy analysis in order to tackle these paradoxes, building a movement to challenge governments and international agencies' policies and pressurizing them to make – and most importantly to implement – commitments on education as a human right. While the Convention on the Rights of the Child (1989) and the 1990 Jomtien Conference on

'Education for All' were key events, in this respect, together with the World Education Forum, known as the Dakar Conference, ten years later, educational commitments have also been debated in other gatherings, including the fourth Women's Conference in Beijing, the Social Summit in Copenhagen in 1995 and the recall Social Summit in Geneva in 2000. Like DAWN, too, educational campaigners have demonstrated their particular expertise in advocacy at such international events, and the negotiations that precede these gatherings. And they have similarly supported their arguments with carefully documented evidence, drawing upon the knowledge, skills and experience already developed from working at local, national and regional levels.

A broad range of educational issues have been included in the campaign, from pre-schooling to primary schooling, from secondary schooling to university education, adult literacy and lifelong learning. While education itself has been the focus, the Global Campaign for Education has also addressed a number of related issues that impact upon children's chances of benefiting from educational opportunities, including the problems associated with child labour and with early marriages and pregnancies. The quality of education has been central to campaigning, as well as the amount of education provided, recognizing the damage that can be caused by inadequate or inappropriate provision. Shortages of basic materials, including books, have been major concerns, for example, together with problems arising from inadequate training provision for teachers. As Tomasevski has also pointed out, when children are indoctrinated – subjected, for example, to racism, or sexism, or war propaganda – this represents an abuse rather than a furthering of human rights (ibid.).

This breadth has been reflected in the breadth of participants in the Global Campaign for Education. Teachers and their trade unions have taken part – as well as NGOs and other groupings concerned with the range of issues involved. Drawing upon their experiences working in local contexts, trade union organizations and NGOs have also brought strong commitments to ensuring that the campaign is genuinely democratic and accountable, building on national as well as regional networks.

This chapter starts by summarizing the context within which the Global Campaign for Education developed, working for the effective implementation of official commitments to 'Education for All' as agreed at Jomtien – despite conflicting pressures from neoliberal agendas, globally. This sets the framework for the discussion of the campaign itself, and the particular contributions of different constituent organizations and groupings. The chapter concludes by raising some of the potential implications for global campaigning around the provision of services more generally.

The international context

Children's rights emerged in the late 1980s and 1990s within the context of more general debates on human rights. The 1989 UN Convention on the Rights of the Child applied this approach, giving renewed emphasis to the Universal Declaration of Human Rights' commitment to making primary education compulsory and freely available to all. In addition to this right to education, children were to enjoy rights to healthcare, play and leisure and the right to special assistance if disabled. Children were to be protected from economic exploitation and sexual exploitation and abuse. And the Convention also recognized children's rights to influence decisions made on their behalf, to express their views and to form associations. In other words, children were to be defined as active participants whose voices were to be heard. This emphasis upon children's rights to participate, to have some say in shaping the decisions and the provision of services devised for their benefit, predated the Convention, dating back to child participation projects from the 1970s, if not earlier (Ennew 1998). One of the key proponents of children's participation was the Save the Children Fund UK, an NGO which went on to become an active member of the Global Campaign for Education in 1999.

Meanwhile, back in 1990, the World Conference on Education for All in Jomtien, Thailand, reaffirmed the importance of education as a priority for development. The emphasis upon education as a human right was not so clear, and the World Conference on Education for All has also been criticized for failing to commit governments to provide free compulsory education for all – at least at primary level (Tomasevski 2003). But despite these limitations there was considerable optimism that the World Conference would result in renewed commitment to education, both from international donors and from national governments. More specifically, the Jomtien Declaration included targets for achieving six core goals:

- the expansion of early childhood care and development, especially for the poor and disadvantaged
- universal access to (and universal completion of) primary education by the year 2000
- the reduction of adult illiteracy rates to one-half of the 1990 levels by the year 2000, with particular emphasis on female literacy

- improved learning achievements (emphasizing quality outcomes)
- expansion of basic education and training for adults and young people
- improvements in the dissemination of knowledge, skills and values required for sustainable development (Watkins 2000)

As the *Oxfam Education Report* pointed out, 'none of the basic ideas adopted at Jomtien was new; but at a time when progress towards education for all had stalled in many regions, when North–South co-operation was at a low ebb, and when the education systems of developing countries were collapsing under the burden of debt, economic stagnation and rapid population growth, the conference appeared to set a new course' for the 1990s (ibid.: 73).

The commitments adopted at Jomtien represented a potentially significant step forward then, providing standards that could become the focus for future campaigning. Governments and international organizations and agencies could be held to account, pressurized and publicly embarrassed if they failed to live up to their promises. There are parallels here with the strategies adopted by feminists campaigning for the implementation of commitments towards gender equality. Like DAWN, international campaigns for 'Education for All' collected evidence, building up the cases to apply such pressures locally, nationally and regionally as well as internationally.

Far from having emerged in a policy vacuum, the benchmarks agreed at Jomtien themselves represented responses to previous lobbies and campaigns. In addition, the climate of opinion was influenced by the practical achievements of NGOs and others, demonstrating ways of improving the quality as well as the sheer quantity of educational provision, actively involving parents as well as children themselves. As has already been suggested, participative approaches to educational work with children as well as adults dated back at least to the 1970s, if not earlier (Johnson et al. 1998).

Educational expansion had been rapid in the first decades after the Second World War, and universal primary education had been planned to be attained by 1980. Governments were committed and international agencies were pledged to assist those unable to afford these commitments. Educational spending represented the largest single item in many governments' expenditures (although not as large as military spending in all too many cases, including Britain and the USA) (Tomasevski 2003).

The outcomes, however, turned out very differently. The 1980s have been described as the 'lost decade' in terms of development (Young

1993). Neoliberal development strategies compounded the problems they were supposed to be resolving as public spending was reduced and structural adjustment progammes pressurized debtor governments to charge for basic services, including health and educational provision. Women and children were identified as being particularly vulnerable as a result, especially the poorest women and girls in the world's poorest countries (Cornia et al. 1987). Girls have accounted for the majority of children not enrolled in primary school (Watkins 2000).

Malawi's experiences illustrate these negative effects of neoliberal policies in practice. In 1981 a World Bank report argued that to improve the quality of education the government of Malawi should increase school fees in both primary and secondary schools. The view was that increasing fees need not be a problem in terms of undermining equity goals, as long as resources were put into 'selective subsidies for the poor, or to increase educational provision for disadvantaged groups' (Psacharopoulos and Woodhall 1985). So the government of Malawi raised school fees in 1982.

This resulted in what have been described as plummeting school enrolment figures (Tomasevski 2003). Contrary to World Bank expectations, equity goals were seriously undermined. Poor parents were simply unable to pay. This has been the pattern across a range of countries where the costs of education have been increased. In Malawi, as elsewhere, school fees present major obstacles for poor households, as do charges for books and school uniforms. Meanwhile, poor families may depend upon their children's labour, and girls may also be required for domestic labour and the care of younger children. Given that the quality of education is often very low in any case, education has been described as 'an expensive and often unrewarding gamble' from the perspective of poor families (ActionAid 2002: 9).

There were clear contradictions here – between formal commitments to education as a human right, and neoliberal policies for the marketization of services in practice – policies that came to be increasingly challenged, internationally, as the decade wore on. As previous chapters have already demonstrated, policies softened, partly if not wholly in response to these global challenges, with increasing emphasis upon protecting the world's poorest peoples and ensuring them access to key basic services. This, then, was the international context for the development of campaigning. Meanwhile, in Malawi, when fees were eliminated in 1994, following a change of government, enrolments apparently doubled (Tomasevski 2003).

As previous chapters have also pointed out, however, the softer lines of the 'post-Washington consensus' that emerged in the mid- to late 1990s did not necessarily imply the end of neoliberalism in practice. On the contrary, educational spending has been advocated as a form of investment in human capital, its purpose defined in terms of its contribution to economic growth and competitiveness in the market economy. For individuals, from this perspective, education is similarly defined in terms of its potential as an investment, its value to be calculated in terms of the additional earnings to be anticipated.

In the decade following Jomtien, the World Bank's increasing concern with poverty reduction was not incompatible with this 'human capital' focus. On the contrary in fact, as Fine and Rose have argued, education was given top priority. But this was in the framework of strategies for investing in human capital – making women more productive as well as men, 'utilising women's resources in development' and increasing the future productivity of their children (Fine and Rose 2001: 179). Education was being seen as something of a panacea – a fuzzy notion with very varied meanings, depending upon the differing perspectives of the users, advocated for its supposed contributions to the development of human capital and economic growth, while helping to reduce poverty, promote gender equality, facilitate social inclusion and encourage active citizenship. There are parallels here with the 'third way' approach to 'education, education, education' in New Labour's Britain, the supposed panacea for such a range of socio-economic, political and cultural problems.

Meanwhile, governments in the poorest countries were spending scarce resources on debt repayments – at least until the latter part of the decade, when debt relief began to be linked to the reallocation of resources to education and health in heavily indebted countries (issues discussed in more detail in the following chapter). While there was some increasing recognition of the key role of the state as provider, and less emphasis upon fees, in the latter part of the 1990s, marketization remained a key theme. There were, in addition, continuing concerns about the quality and relevance of education, together with concerns about approaches that in some instances constituted abuses rather than contributions to human rights. These concerns were voiced in Action-Aid's review, which concluded

> the quality of education is very low in most cases (in the poorest
> areas where ActionAid was working at the turn of the Millennium)
> with inadequate infrastructure, large classes, demoralised and under-
> trained teachers, uninspiring methods and overburdened curricula. A
> key determinant of demand for primary education is not so much the

absence of schools but the fact that those which do exist do not function properly. In some cases schools have become the worst violators of children's rights, containing, suppressing, intimidating and silencing children. (ActionAid 2002: 9)

By the latter part of the 1990s, it was becoming increasingly clear that the targets agreed at Jomtien were not going to be achieved then, either in terms of the quantity or the quality of provision. It has been estimated that some 855 million people – or one in six of the world's population – were functionally illiterate at this time, and the problem of illiteracy was being reproduced in the next generation. More than 125 million children of primary school age – one in five of the total number in developing countries – were not in school and another 150 million were at risk of dropping out, mostly before they acquired basic literacy or numeracy (Watkins 2000). Classes of up to eighty children were not uncommon, while textbooks and pencils were luxury items.

In the run-up to the follow-on conference in Dakar, scheduled for 2000, NGOs and trade union organizations representing teachers were meeting regularly, preparing their contributions to these international debates. They identified a number of reasons for the fact that progress with these targets was proving so disappointing. And they argued that education was to be defended as a public service and a right, not as a privilege. In addition to the lack of financial resources, they identified the failure to involve teachers in improving the quality of education as a key factor in the probable failure to meet the Jomtien targets, together with the lack of democratic participation more generally (UNESCO 2001). Accountability and transparency were needed at all levels 'so that the school is genuinely in the public sphere and the government's record in providing education is open to public scrutiny' (ActionAid 2002b: 6).

This active involvement of NGOs and trade unionists was seen as a very encouraging feature of the preparations for Dakar in 2000. The Global Campaign for Education that emerged in this context, bringing NGOs and education trade unions together with other campaigning organizations, was warmly welcomed in many quarters, including by the UN Secretary-General Kofi Annan. In April 2000 at Dakar he affirmed the fact that 'Individual NGOs have made remarkable contributions towards education in many countries, and they have now joined in a Global Campaign for Education. Today, I say to the NGO community: we cannot win the battle ... without your expertise, your energy, and your capacity for action' (Global Campaign for Education website).

The context in terms of debates within NGOs and trade union organizations

Meanwhile NGOs and trade union organizations had themselves been undergoing processes of reflection, rethinking their own roles in the context of the 1990s, globally. During the 1980s, as Watkins argued, 'the relationship between NGOs and States underwent a significant change' as governments strapped for resources were increasingly looking to the NGO sector to provide services at lower costs (Watkins 2000: 310). Were NGOs getting drawn into dubious ground here, letting governments off the hook, providing short-term projects rather than addressing longer-term policy dilemmas? And were NGOs being used to spearhead neoliberal strategies for increasing privatization, legitimizing retreats from the public provision of services – with NGOs as the acceptable face of more market-orientated alternatives? As the report on behalf of the Collective Consultation of NGOs concluded, 'At best, their [NGOs'] educational activities are complementary to and integrated with government education programmes; at worst, they may duplicate or undermine government services' (ActionAid 2000: 7).

By the mid-1990s, NGOs such as ActionAid were beginning to question the extent to which their strategies were compatible with a human rights approach to education, education as a right rather than a privilege or an act of charity, geared towards participation and community as well as individual empowerment. ActionAid undertook reviews of their programmes in particular countries, starting with the Kenyan programme's review of its work – and had the courage to make their findings public. This willingness to make public forthright criticisms of its own work was heralded as being as 'rare among NGOs as among major donors' (Watkins 2000: 310–11). As a result of this commendable openness, ActionAid was able to contribute to a wider shift in policy, Watkins concluded.

In summary, it was concluded that programmes such as school-building initiatives had not been entirely positive in terms of the impact on school enrolment or school achievements. On the contrary, in fact, there were cases where school fees had been increased once the buildings had been improved (in line with policies on cost sharing, actively supported by the World Bank at that time). As a result poor children were more systematically excluded than before (ActionAid 2002a). On the provision of access or non-formal education programmes ActionAid was similarly self-critical. 'Unintentionally we were absolving governments of responsibility and becoming agents of the privatisation of education for poor children [...] The real challenge,' the ActionAid report continued, 'lay in reforming the government system' (ibid.: 38) and that, in turn, involved addressing governments' resource problems and the problems arising from macro-policies such as structural adjustment.

ActionAid brought in advice from Greenpeace, an organization with a proven track record of campaigning globally as well as locally, to assist in rethinking their educational strategy. The emphasis shifted towards a more fluid and flexible approach, working closely with those directly concerned in the South – 'a sailing boat', taking account of different forces, rather than 'a steamboat', charging ahead regardless, as one person expressed this shift. This greater emphasis upon process and active participation fitted very readily into the approaches that ActionAid had already developed, through the REFLECT programmes (see Chapter 5), for example, and through ActionAid's support for parental participation.

ActionAid was committed to ensuring that grass-roots involvement was strengthened through the process of campaigning for education as a human right, building capacity and facilitating empowerment rather than leading from the front, from the North. As the Global Education Review reflected, 'one of the classic problems for NGOs developing policy and advocacy work in recent years (to tackle the causes rather than simply alleviating the symptoms of poverty) is the divorce that exists between their grassroots programme work and the policy work undertaken in capital cities' or via jetting to Geneva (ibid.: 49). In contrast, Action-Aid set out to develop an approach that promoted self-advocacy for education as a human right, based around a strong Southern coalition, strengthening existing networks and building new ones where there was none. Comparisons were drawn with the experiences of the Landless People's Movement (MST) in Brazil, working with mobilizations of the people directly concerned.

This strategic rethink – and ActionAid's willingness to discuss this openly – has been identified as a key factor in the development of macro-level strategies in the NGO sector, more generally, in the run-up to the Dakar Conference. In addition, ActionAid developed the Elimu campaign (*elimu* being Swahili for 'education'), launched in Harare, Zimbabwe, in 1999. The aim was to mobilize for the achievement of the goals of 'Education for All', with the immediate focus upon the forthcoming Dakar event. And the process was to be participatory, with the widest participation of poor parents, civil society organizations and governments in the South. National coalitions in some fifteen countries across Africa, Asia and Latin America brought together 'diverse international and national NGOs, trade unions (especially teachers' unions), parents' associations, women's movements, child labour or debt campaigners, social movements etc' (ibid.: 45).

Building the Elimu campaign was a major step forward. As the Mozambique group reflected early in 2000, despite their passion and commitment to education, civil society organizations had lacked awareness about national education strategies, let alone the capacity to engage in sophisticated debates with the World Bank and donor experts. Through Elimu, ActionAid facilitated the development of strong national coalitions that gained the respect of other civil society organizations as well as governments and donors.

The process of building Elimu had itself been a participative one. As one senior manager from an ActionAid country programme commented, when the campaign was launched, the expectation was that this would involve more scholarships and more school building – plus more REFLECT programmes.

> But as the thing unfolded we realised that the more fundamental issue was not what ActionAid could do but what government should do and wasn't doing. If we had been told from the start that we must go and demand the rights of the poor for education, we would have rejected the whole thing. Instead the Elimu approach is to let people develop this analysis themselves, but all the time raising new questions, new perspectives for us like the report cards and budget tracking (techniques to promote active, participative monitoring). (ibid.: 47)

This meant that Elimu built firm roots. National alliances developed the capacity to pressurize their own governments and to lobby key donors and UN agencies, together, more effectively.

The development of Elimu – and the thinking behind this – was a major contribution, laying the groundwork that facilitated the emergence of the Global Campaign for Education. Other NGOs have recognized this, pointing to the strength of the Southern coalitions that were developed and supported, just as they have valued ActionAid's readiness to be open about sharing the process of rethinking earlier approaches (Watkins 2000). In addition, tribute has been paid to ActionAid for its willingness to put the interests of the wider campaign first, before their own organizational self-interests or concerns about their own organizational profile. It was to ActionAid's credit, it was pointed out, that Elimu was eventually ended as a separate campaign. This was to strengthen the global campaign itself, by ending the separate 'branding' of the Elimu campaign, thereby avoiding any competition for 'space, time and recognition' (ActionAid 2002a: 76).

While debates within NGOs were a significant aspect of the context within which the global campaign developed, debates within the trade union movement, nationally and internationally, were also relevant. In summary, in many national contexts, the 1980s represented something of a 'lost decade' for trade unionism as well as for development more generally. This was also a hard time for trade unions. Economic restructuring coupled with privatization and public expenditure cuts impacted upon jobs, and particularly upon jobs in previously well-organized sectors. As Chapter 4 argued, neoliberal policies specifically aimed to promote labour 'flexibility' and casualization make life more difficult, undermining the strength of organized labour. In response, trade union organizations developed new approaches to organizing, including the organizing agendas and the social movement unionism initiatives that emerged in Australia, Britain, Canada, the USA and elsewhere. Trade unionists defending public sector jobs in key services similarly developed new approaches, recognizing the importance of building alliances between service providers and service users, based upon their shared interests in the quality as well as the quantity of the services in question. There was increasing recognition of the importance of making an impact on policy agendas for the longer term, as well as defending members' immediate interests in the here and now.

Ironically, as Chapter 4 also pointed out, in the aftermath of the Cold War, following the demise of the former USSR in 1989, trade union organizations found new spaces within which to mobilize internationally. Freed from some of the constraints of the previous era, international trade union organizations began to take on the challenges posed by neoliberalism. And this, in turn, implied the need to develop new alliances, working with civil society organizations as well as working with previously less organized sectors of the workforce. In the case of education trade unions, organized via Education International, this involved bringing non-teaching staff into membership, along with teachers, spanning both formal and informal sectors. And it involved building links with civil society movements concerned with adult education as well as with schools. In this sense, then, the trade union movement was as ready as a number of NGOs and civil society organizations were to come together in the Global Campaign for Education, bringing with them the strength of organized labour, rooted in the South as well as the North. These Southern roots were significant, too, in encouraging Southern NGOs to participate.

The Global Campaign for Education is launched

The Global Campaign for Education (GCE) was officially launched in 1999 in the run-up to the World Conference on Education in Dakar in 2000 to influence the agenda. The campaign brought together 'representatives of the world-wide movement to end child labour, non-governmental organisations working with landless people in Brazil, disabled people in India and rural communities in China. It includes the world's largest confederation of teachers' unions – Education International (representing 23 million teachers) – and international development agencies' (Watkins 2000: 13), including ActionAid and Oxfam. By this time it was clear that the targets set at Jomtien were not going to be achieved by 2000. The global campaign aimed to raise awareness of the 'scale of the challenge facing the government representatives heading for the Dakar conference – and their lamentable record of achievement over the past ten years' (ibid.: 335). Through careful preparatory work, backed by lobbying and demonstrations (including a march by ten thousand schoolchildren) during the conference itself, GCE set out to pressurize donors to agree a global action plan to support national governments to achieve their commitments to 'Education for All'.

Each of the constituent members brought a specialist contribution to the campaign. Education International brought the breadth of its 23 million (now 25 million)-strong membership, its roots and democratic structures, firmly established in the South as well as the North, its resources (both financial and organizational) and its stability as an independent self-financing organization. Oxfam brought its particular expertise in research and policy analysis, including its particular expertise and lobbying skills around international financial issues such as structural adjustment and the debt issue. ActionAid brought its own particular experiences of working in participative ways around the quality as well as the quantity of education, including the reputation and trust that had been developed internationally through REFLECT. And ActionAid brought the experiences and contacts developed through Elimu, which were also key to the development of GCE's legitimate democratic roots. The Global March against Child Labour was similarly firmly rooted, with a particularly powerful reputation for successful campaigning on children's rights in South Asia. Save the Children Fund (SCF), which joined later in 1999, brought its own very practical experiences of working on quality issues in the South, as well as its expertise in participation and children's rights more generally. (SCF has been informally nicknamed the 'thoughtful NGO' because of this particular expertise.) As a number of commentators reflected, each partner brought its own particular knowledge and skills and its own connections.

Initially, the focus was on making a big push for the Dakar event. The campaign worked at different levels. GCE partners collaborated on research, policy analysis and policy development – to lobby donors to guarantee the resources for 'Education for All'. There were regular meetings with relevant government departments, for example. Meanwhile GCE partners were also facilitating grass-roots mobilizations, with public protests, for example, in India, Brazil, Tanzania, Britain, Spain and more than twenty other countries. This preparatory work, in the run-up to Dakar, took place over a mere six to eight months or so. But even in this short space of time, GCE had built up a formidable reputation, with a high profile in terms of its lobbying work and the legitimacy of being so firmly rooted, internationally, South as well as North. This was a formidable achievement, and particularly so given that the partners did not even have the opportunity to meet together before Dakar (which was the first time that they all met up in person).

The actual process of compiling the submission for the Dakar Conference was seen as having been vitally important in terms of capacity-building. Each government's performance was compared and contrasted with its previous targets, so that the GCE's global analysis was firmly supported with evidence compiled at national level (like DAWN's approach to compiling submissions for international events). Through this process, the constituent members owned the final report in a way that might have been less likely if they had simply been invited to comment on a penultimate version, compiled by a small drafting committee.

There were two-way processes at work here. The fact that the report so evidently represented the findings and the demands of such a wide range of interests in the South as well as the North gave it legitimacy with governments and donors. And the process of being involved strengthened the national coalitions, giving them greater access to their own governments, strengthening their profile with the media and enhancing their credibility more generally. Far from being in competition with each other, local and national approaches were complementing the work at the international level. Several commentators suggested that this had not been fully appreciated initially. As the campaign's potential for contributing to capacity-building became more clearly recognized, however, this became more explicitly built into GCE's working priorities.

Predictably perhaps, when the constituents came together first, there had been some tensions. There had been fears, for example, that Northern NGOs, with their greater resources, might expect to dominate, simply using their Southern counterparts to legitimize the campaign – without actually listening to their concerns or taking account of their priorities. As one of the commentators pointed out, people needed time and space to build up trust. The campaign had the advantage of being able to build on the trust that had already been developed through previous initiatives, however, including the trust that had been developed through Elimu and through REFLECT programmes. There seemed widespread agreement that these previously existing relationships of trust had been a key factor, assisting the campaign in working through these initial tensions – going on to develop their genuinely shared position.

In addition to the potential tensions between North and South, there were potential tensions between the NGOs and the trade union organizations. As both sides recognized, there are different ways of working here, with different organizational styles and approaches to democratic representation and accountability. Chapter 4 explored some of the criticisms of trade unions, as insufficiently flexible and narrowly focused on the 'bread and butter' issues affecting their members in the here and now. Conversely, NGOs had been criticized for being insufficiently representative or accountable, prone to involve themselves in initiatives that effectively facilitated the marketization of services and the casualization of labour.

Here too, however, both sides confirmed that they had developed more effective ways of working together, as a result of their experiences in GCE. NGOs referred to their enhanced understanding of trade union organizations' ways of working, recognizing that trade unions need to refer back to their members before taking key decisions. Even if trade union organizations seem less flexible as a result, there has been increasing recognition that their procedures do actually facilitate democratic accountability. Similarly, trade unionists referred to the advantages of NGOs' abilities to respond more flexibly. Trust had been built up too, as NGOs had demonstrated their commitment to public service provision and their opposition to marketization (Save the Children Fund 2002). Both sides emphasized that trade unions and NGOs had developed greater mutual understanding and both sides emphasized the importance of building these alliances for the longer term.

GCE's achievements at Dakar and beyond

In addition to being welcomed by the UN Secretary-General, GCE's contributions to the Dakar Conference were welcomed by the heads of other UN agencies and by the representatives of a number of Southern governments. GCE sharpened the focus on issues of quality as well as on the scale of educational provision and the resources required from donors to reach the goals of 'Education for All' in the world's poorest countries. The importance of involving teachers and their trade unions in improving the quality of education was emphasized – and recognized, along with the importance of involving civil society organizations at the grass-roots – including parents and children themselves. Three barriers to achieving 'Education for All' had been identified in the report on behalf of the Collective Consultation of NGOs – the resource deficit, the quality deficit and the democratic deficit – closely related problems, all of which needed to be addressed.

The final communiqué adopted by governments at Dakar included a number of GCE's demands. There was commitment to free and compulsory primary education of good quality – as a human right – by the year 2015. And there was commitment to the principle that no country committed to 'Education for All' should be allowed to fail for lack of resources. Neither of these commitments would have been made, it has been argued, in the absence of the GCE (Watkins 2000: 335). The role of civil society organizations was affirmed and Southern governments were called upon to involve civil society in the preparation of 'Education for All' action plans by 2002. As the Elimu newsletter concluded, 'NGOs and trade unions walked away from the World Education Forum in a much stronger position than when they arrived – having won recognition as legitimate policy actors and having carved out space for civil society participation in a time-bound process of developing national action plans' (Elimu 2000: 1).

While these were key achievements in principle, it was another matter to ensure that they were carried out in practice, however. Watkins concluded:

> The challenge facing the GCE's members now is to build on what was achieved there. That means engaging with Southern governments as they develop their national education strategies – and it means holding Northern governments to account for the commitment they have made. In his final address to the Forum at Dakar, the Global Campaign's Tom Bediako put the governments and institutions on notice: 'In the last few months we have seen a flowering of a world-wide movement of civil society dedicated to the fight for quality education for all … I want to tell you we will not go away. We will continue to campaign at local, national, and international levels. (Watkins 2000: 336)

Following Dakar, the GCE reflected on the implications of this commitment to continuing campaigning. The focus needed to shift towards pressurizing governments and donors to turn these promises into reality – starting right away, rather than waiting for the run-up to 2015. UNESCO has had responsibility for ensuring independent monitoring, bringing out reports on different aspects of progress, each year. These annual reports have provided additional focus for continuing campaigning, as the GCE responds to their conclusions on progress to date and the likelihood – or otherwise – of achieving the Dakar goals by 2015.

The campaign's overall focus had been seen as potentially problematic in some quarters. Given that there was such widespread agreement about education's importance in general, how could the campaign move beyond the level of platitudes? How can you campaign for something as apparently desirable as motherhood and apple pie? Education has suffered from a rather bizarre curse, it has been argued: the curse of consensus. 'Everyone agrees that education is a good thing. Everyone agrees that we should be spending more, improving quality. No-one will argue vigorously against investment in education' (Gopal and Archer 2002: 6). By focusing upon implementation, target by target, the GCE has moved beyond the level of platitudes, building a campaign with support at the grass-roots as well as credibility among donors.

In addition to its other campaigning activities at national and international levels, the GCE currently organizes a Global Action Week every April, around the anniversary of the Dakar Conference in 2000. These Global Action Weeks maintain and develop the campaign's momentum, focusing upon particular aspects of 'Education for All' goals. Increasingly, the emphasis has been upon Southern priorities, with activities planned to maximize people's involvement. In 2003, for example, the Global Action Week focused upon girls' access to education and the specific targets on gender parity by 2005 (more of an issue still in the South). Plans for this included activities such as songwriting and celebrity concerts, as well as the more traditional campaigning activities such as petitions, rallies, marches of girls and women to parliament and associated media mobilizations. Some 1.8 million people participated in what has been described as the world's largest lesson.

Resources have been made available to support these initiatives, including resources from Northern NGOs, providing grants to facilitate campaigning in the South as well as the North. This emphasis on facilitating participation has been a continuing theme, across NGOs and trade union organizations. Education International has encouraged partnerships, for example, so that better-resourced Northern national organizations can support their less-resourced Southern counterparts.

The structure the GCE has developed reflects these concerns. Following the Dakar Conference, as it became clear that this was going to be a long-term campaign, the GCE met in New Delhi, India, in 2001. As the report of this meeting pointed out, 'after Dakar, it was clear that the work of GCE was only just beginning' (GCE 2001: 1). In addition to planning and agreeing advocacy goals, including inputs to the formulation of national action plans and lobbying at key international events, GCE reviewed its own governance structures. The relatively loose network that had served, in the pre-Dakar period, needed to become more formalized.

A full-time secretariat was established, initially based in the North in offices provided by Education International, but subsequently to be transferred to an African base – in recognition of the importance of the campaign's Southern roots. Overall, there were to be more Southern representatives on the board than Northerners, a clear statement about the campaign's priorities and focus. Everyone was agreed, it seemed, on the importance of having a strong Southern voice.

Different members would contribute in cash and in kind in terms of their specific areas of expertise. 'Whoever can get the job done does it,' as one commentator put it. But there would be continuing commitment to ensuring that policy papers genuinely represented the views and experiences of all sections, as well as including contributions from those with specialist expertise.

Overall priorities for the coming three years were to be agreed at the world congresses. This would set the framework for campaigning in the coming period, with broad agreement about the focus, from year to year. Prioritization might have been expected to involve considerable negotiation, given the range of interests involved, from trade union organizations to NGOs, from North to South. This did not seem to have been problematic in practice, however. Commentators pointed out that the campaign had succeeded in keeping a broad focus around their common interests – without becoming fuzzy. Neither NGOs nor trade union organizations could think of examples of issues that had actually been divisive, publicly, although both recognized that there might have been such differences. It was also pointed out that issues were discussed at regional meetings, first, which helped to ensure that agreements could be negotiated satisfactorily, subsequently.

Similarly, there seemed to be broad agreement about the balance to be struck between keeping to agreed priorities, on the one hand, and having the flexibility to take up immediate issues as they arose, on the other. Some issues (such as the Iraq war) were potentially hot to handle, though. And other issues were left aside because they were already the subject of existing campaigns. The issue of the General Agreements on Trade in Services (GATS), for example, was not prioritized, although opening educational provision up to the global market would have major negative implications – because other international organizations were already focusing upon this. GCE's work on GATS is therefore linked with these other campaigns.

The achievement of the goals of 'Education for All' is potentially affected by a wide range of issues, from HIV/AIDS (which has been having a drastic impact on teachers as well as children, particularly in sub-Saharan Africa) to the debt and poverty reduction strategies (the subject of the following chapter). GCE has clearly recognized the significance of these issues, without being in a position to focus on them all – except as part of related campaigns. In this sense, then, GCE can be seen as part of a wider movement, campaigning for one of the services essential for the pursuit of human rights agendas and social justice more generally.

Wider implications?

The Global Campaign for Education has its own particular history, rooted in the networks that had already been developed by its constituent members, both NGOs and trade union organizations in the South as well as the North. Campaigns around other service areas have their own histories and their own reflections on these. The GCE is not being offered as any type of blueprint – although aspects of GCE's experiences might well be transferable to other campaigning contexts.

Part of the GCE's success in building an effective campaign would seem to be attributable to the strength of its roots. There seemed to be widespread recognition, at Dakar, that GCE represented far more than the 'usual suspect' lobbyists, however expert. The campaign's proposals were clearly based upon local evidence about the quality as well as the quantity of educational provision, and local experiences of building alternatives from the base. Together in GCE, trade union organizations and NGOs could demonstrate their legitimacy, representing teachers and other education workers as well as service users, children as well as parents, civil society organizations and national coalitions in the South as well as the North. The trust that was so essential to building such an alliance could not have been established, participants pointed out, had it not been for the work that had already been undertaken and the networks that had been developed, as a result – linking civil society organizations and trade unions, across as well as within national boundaries.

The long-term success of GCE, it has been suggested by participants, depends upon the way in which it has been building really strong national alliances and campaigns across the South, and linking these via regional alliances. ActionAid, Oxfam and SCF now jointly manage the Commonwealth Education Fund, providing resources to invest in further strengthening these campaigns and alliances – the first time that they have been able to devote significant resources to this key aspect of the GCE's work.

Another distinctive feature of the GCE has been the way in which participants have been contributing according to their own particular abilities and areas of expertise. The differences between the NGOs and trade union organizations involved, from North to South, might have proved barriers to effective collaboration. But the GCE seemed to turn these differences into positives, with each party contributing in complementary fashion. There was recognition of the importance of the fact that an international NGO was prepared to put the interests of the wider campaign before its own organizational interests. And there was also recognition of the importance of ensuring that the process itself was empowering for Southern participants. This enabled them to develop their own capacities 'to sit round the table with government and donors as equals and really hold their own' (ActionAid 2002a) rather than relying on Northern NGOs to negotiate on their behalf.

The GCE succeeded too in 'framing' the issue of 'Education for All' effectively, turning the 'curse' of consensus and complacency around, generating anger and outrage about the state of education and educational inequities globally (Gopal and Archer 2002: 6). The importance of the 'framing' process has already emerged in previous chapters, in the context of social movement theorists' debates. The ability to 'frame' issues in ways that resonate with participants and focus their campaigning was identified as a key ingredient in successful mobilizations.

When GCE took off as a continuing campaign, after Dakar, strategies were developed for the longer term, with the focus upon achieving the targets for 2015. But this was not at the expense of organizing for the here and now. Momentum was maintained through initiatives such as the Global Action Weeks, initiatives that engaged the energy and enthusiasm of children and their parents as well as involving the organizations of civil society and the trade union movement, nationally and internationally. There are echoes here of discussions in previous chapters – debates about the balance to be struck between the short term and the longer term, working for achievable gains, nationally as well as internationally, without losing sight of longer-term strategies, operating effectively at the different policy-making levels while building sustainable movements and alliances for social change from the grass-roots.

9 | Learning from Jubilee 2000: mobilizing for debt relief

'Debt relief is today fairly and squarely on the global agenda,' supporters claimed, pointing to the achievements of Jubilee 2000, challenging the negative effects of globalization through citizen action both South and North (Dent and Peters 1999: 1). Jubilee 2000 had mobilized people of all faiths and people of no faith, academics, pop stars, trade unionists and businessmen, sportspeople and artists, young and old, black and white, organizing together on a global scale (Jubilee 2000 Coalition 2000). 'Jubilee 2000 is a weird thing,' reflected Bono of U2, 'a mixed bag of economists, pop stars, popes and people on the streets. We have swarmed together to force politicians into realising that there is only one way to give the millennium year meaning – by cancelling those debts which steal the future from the world's poorest countries' (ibid.: 11). In the space of four years, Jubilee 2000's campaign for the remission of unpayable Third World debt made a remarkable impact, raising the issue's profile internationally as well as locally, within communities. This was the context in which the Director of the UK Coalition concluded that 'The World will never be the same again ... because of Jubilee 2000' (ibid.: 3).

While debt continues to represent one of the major barriers to poverty reduction globally, Jubilee 2000 did succeed in contributing to the achievement of immediate improvements in some of the poorest countries, enabling resources to be diverted from debt repayment to spending on education, health and housing. School fees were abolished in Uganda, Zambia and Tanzania, for example, and Mozambique used the savings to provide free immunization for children (Denny and Elliott 2003: 20). Progress on debt relief has been held up in other cases, however, and countries continue to stack up new debts as a result of factors such as reduced export earnings due to falling commodity prices. So although Jubilee 2000 wound itself up in its existing form, with the millennium that was its immediate focus, campaigning has had to carry on. This has been backed with research from Jubilee Research, one of the successor bodies, addressing the continuing issue of debt as well as contributing to campaigning on related aspects of economic and social justice.

The experiences of Jubilee 2000 illustrate a number of themes that have emerged already in previous chapters. There are parallels, in terms of the campaign's theoretical analysis of the underlying issues, and there are similarities as well as differences in terms of organizational approaches, strategies and tactics. Taken together, these experiences illustrate a number of factors that have been central to the achievements of global social movements. And they point to ways of addressing the challenges that face individuals, groups and organizations aiming to build genuinely representative, democratically accountable, socially inclusive and sustainable movements for human rights and social justice, at the global level.

This chapter starts by summarizing the history and achievements of Jubilee 2000 before exploring the lessons participants themselves have drawn from their experiences. The evidence for these reflections comes from published sources, discussion papers and from interviews with individuals involved as staff and activists in Jubilee 2000 itself and its constituent organizations, together with some reflections from a decision-maker who experienced Jubilee 2000 from the receiving end (working on responding to the lobbying). In addition, the author had the opportunity to attend three meetings and participated in one of the major public events.

Having examined a range of views on the lessons to be drawn from these experiences, the chapter concludes by returning to the differing theoretical perspectives on global social movements explored in Chapter 3 and their varying contributions to the analysis of global social movements in the twenty-first century.

Jubilee 2000 Coalition

What precisely was the Jubilee 2000 Coalition and what might it mean to describe it as part of a global social movement? Jubilee 2000 has been described as a broad coalition, 'one of the biggest global campaigns ever' in the words of the *Guardian* journalist who summarized its achievements at the end of 2000 (Bunting 2000: 15). This was an ad hoc coalition, launched in 1997 to focus on achieving relief on unpayable debt of the world's poorest countries by the end of the year 2000, to celebrate the millennium. The title 'Jubilee 2000' referred to the biblical concept of 'jubilee' as the freeing of slaves, the redress of past injustices and the writing off of debts. The campaign's symbol was a chain, referring to international campaigning against the slave trade in the nineteenth century, representing the enslaving nature of the debt burden – and conversely, coming more positively to represent the human links, the chain of activists linking hands in solidarity.

Although the campaign was intentionally short-lived, an organizational decision that will be explored in more detail below, it built upon previous campaigning, including previous campaigning by NGOs concerned with development issues. Other key constituents included a range of faith-based organizations as well as trade unions, many of whom have continued to be concerned with debt and related development issues such as trade. In this sense then, Jubilee 2000 has been part of a longer-term movement for global justice.

At the time of the millennium, in 2000, the UK Jubilee Coalition had 110 organizations as members and there were, in addition, sixty-nine coalitions worldwide, including seventeen in Central and Latin America, fifteen in Africa and ten in Asia. Supporters were actively involved through their membership of constituent organizations and as individuals, signing the record-breaking petition (signed by 24 million from over sixty countries by June 1999), wearing the lapel badge, attending meetings and writing to politicians. In addition, supporters took part in major events such as the 70,000-strong human chain around the centre of Birmingham, UK, in 1998, to lobby the G7 meeting of the wealthier and relatively more powerful nations who were major creditors in their own right as well as being majority shareholders in the key international organizations, the IMF and the World Bank.

The contested definitions of what constitutes a social movement and varying perspectives on why and how social movements develop have already been explored in Chapter 3. In summary, in European debates, there has been some emphasis on analysing the underlying causes that give rise to social movements, together with new social movement theorists' emphasis on issues of cultures and identities. Feminism's questioning of traditional gender roles and identities provides an illustration of this latter point. In North American debates, in contrast, there has been more focus upon questions of resource mobilization – organizing to gain resources and to impact upon decision-making processes – together with questions of political processes, the structures of political opportunity and the ways in which social movements use these spaces to mobilize effectively. Both approaches have been seen to have relevance for the study of social movements in general (Crossley 2002) and both have been seen to have more – or less – relevance for the study of global social movements, mobilizations with social movement and social movement organizations (Dalton 1994; Jordan and Maloney 1997).

Both approaches have aspects of relevance for Jubilee 2000. The campaign challenged predominant constructions of indebtedness and questioned neoliberal development strategies more generally. In addition,

Jubilee 2000 challenged negative images of the poor in the South as passive 'victims' of capitalist globalization. The most prevalent images of developing countries, it has been argued, remain Live Aid-type images of starving children with flies around their eyes, too weak to brush them off, dependent upon the resources and knowledge of the industrialized countries of the North to progress (VSO 2002). In contrast, Jubilee 2000 provided an example of a mobilization to promote change through solidarity rather than through charity, however well-meaning.

Jubilee 2000 was, in addition, committed to making effective impacts upon decision-making processes, allying with more traditional organizations and movements to work for immediate and practical gains at both national and international levels. The coalition aimed to work through lobbying and negotiation with decision-makers as well as via mass mobilization at the grass-roots (Dent and Peters 1999). These aspects were less compatible with new social movement approaches. As will be suggested below, this was not an approach that related to Jubilee 2000 that closely. Participants themselves emphasized the campaign's goals and achievements on both counts, for the longer term as well as for the shorter term – although both have also been the subject of continuing debate.

Jubilee 2000 did, however, exemplify the four social movement themes that were identified by Della Porta and Diani, the themes of *informal interaction networks* (as well as more formal ones, because formal organizations such as churches and trade unions also participated) *based upon shared beliefs and solidarity and engaging in collective action focusing upon conflicts, including the use of protest* (Della Porta and Diani 1999). As Della Porta and Diani also recognized, shared beliefs and solidarity are not simply to be taken as givens in social movements. There are two-way processes at work, as individuals and groups join on the basis of shared beliefs, convictions that may then be strengthened through participation in collective action. There was evidence of the ways in which participants' beliefs were being enhanced through their experiences of collective action and collective reflection, just as there was evidence of participants' knowledge and understanding of the underlying issues being strengthened.

Finally, how might Jubilee 2000 be described as being part of a social movement that was genuinely global? It was not only that Jubilee 2000 was an international campaign – although the campaign's supporters certainly did span five continents. Jubilee 2000 was global too in the sense that the target was the issue of unpayable debt and its underlying causes, rooted in processes of capitalist globalization. While the focus was global, however, there were differing views on how far capitalist globalization itself was to be challenged. The campaign included those who argued that neoliberal agendas were inherently inimical to the interests of the poor, as well as those who argued that a genuine global movement could 'reform these agendas and make globalization work for poor people around the world' (Collins et al. 2001: 148).

Although Jubilee 2000 represented a critical response to economic aspects of globalization, however, like so many of the mobilizations already discussed in previous chapters, the campaign was also the beneficiary of the global transformation of communications. As a number of commentators reflected, the spread of e-mail and access to the Internet were key factors facilitating effective campaigning. Global celebrities played their part too, bringing the issues to a wider audience (although the involvement of celebrities such as pop stars also provoked controversy).

Jubilee 2000 was part of a global movement in a third sense too. Herman has described globalization as 'an active process of corporate expansion across borders' and as 'an ideology, whose function is to reduce any resistance to the process by making it seem both highly beneficial and unstoppable' (Herman 1999: 40). There are parallels here with the mantra of Britain's neoliberal prime minister, Margaret Thatcher, in the 1980s, that 'there is no alternative' – a recipe for resignation, alienation and disempowerment. Jubilee 2000, in contrast, represented a fundamental challenge to the notion that there were no alternatives.

The emergence of Jubilee 2000 was seen to have represented a creative response to the more favourable political climate in Britain and the USA, under Blair and Clinton, potentially offering more space for the development of alternative agendas after the Thatcher/Reagan years. After a period of pragmatism and cynicism there was a renewed sense of purpose, participants suggested: 'putting things on the agenda – coming out after years of Thatcherism', 'a sense that you can achieve objectives'. The very emergence of Jubilee 2000 demonstrated encouraging possibilities for developing citizen action at the global as well as the local and national levels.

Paradoxically, it has been argued, globalization has the potential for increasing individuals' self-reflexivity and choice as they develop creative responses to the increasing power of transnational actors and organizations (Giddens 1990). As Cohen and Kennedy have also argued, the implications of globalization, for the reflexive citizen everywhere, include enhanced possibilities for challenging 'the truth claims put forward by governments' (Cohen and Kennedy 2000: 36). 'Consequently,' they continued, with greater self-consciousness and knowledge and greater awareness of our growing transnational interdependency, 'ordinary citizens everywhere are challenging state power and forging links with their counterparts in other countries' (ibid.: 37). The experiences of Jubilee 2000 provide illustrations of some of the possibilities as well as the challenges of social action based upon solidarity in this global context.

Participants' perspectives on Jubilee 2000

Given the breadth of the coalition, a plurality of views on the achievements of Jubilee 2000 might have been anticipated, together with a range of views on the strengths and weaknesses of the campaign. Clearly there *were* differences of view on how much had been achieved, depending on the extent of the goals in question, beyond the agreed aim of the cancellation of unpayable debt. Was the aim very specifically to make some progress on debt relief for the poorest countries? This was perceived as the most that could realistically be achieved by some Northern campaigners, quoted by Collins, Gariyo and Burdon, for example, quoted many US activists who initially 'saw this as the most that could be gained by the US campaign' (Collins et al. 2001). Or was the aim to replace rather than to reform existing debt relief programmes, processes and institutions (a view more prevalent among Southern campaigns)?

This latter position was put very clearly by Jubilee South, an international movement constituted at a South–South Summit in 1999. Jubilee South took the position that creditors were using these debts as 'an instrument of exploitation and control of our people's resources and countries'. This alone was sufficient, Jubilee South argued, to render the so-called debts of the South illegitimate. Far from owing these debts, it was argued, the peoples of the South repudiated them, demanding total debt cancellation without conditionalities: 'Don't Owe – Won't Pay.' (Jubilee South website).

These demands were rooted in a political perspective that was explicitly anti-capitalist, calling for the transformation of the global capitalist economic system – a perspective not necessarily shared by participants across the South, let alone across the campaign as a whole. The notion of conditionality was particularly controversial. Making debt relief conditional on resources being redirected towards social development was seen as reasonable by some. These types of conditions were about ensuring accountability, for the benefit of people in the South, it was argued, rather than using conditions to enforce free-market dogmas, for the benefit of donors (Dent and Peters 1999). Others, in contrast, saw these conditions as a way of reimposing structural adjustment, by another name, reinforcing external control of Southern economies to serve the strategic aims of neoliberal global agendas.

Although these were important differences, however, relating as they did to underlying differences of overall political perspective, they did not seem to fit neatly into North vs South positions. On the basis of the interviews, in fact, the ability to work together emerged as striking, especially in view of these underlying differences. There was considerable agreement about the key issues and themes, in fact – although there were, of course, differences of emphasis about how these were to be evaluated.

First, there seems to have been broad agreement about the importance of Jubilee 2000's roots. As one commentator reflected, 'it certainly did not spring from nowhere'. Far from being spontaneous, this was a well-grounded campaign. It emerged from a history of research and campaigning in the 1980s among what might loosely be termed a movement concerned with development and human rights issues when debt became identified as a key issue. A number of NGOs, including Christian Aid, Tear Fund, Friends of the Earth, Oxfam and the World Development Movement, for example, had already done considerable groundwork, in terms of researching the impact of neoliberal economic agendas, including the impact of the structural adjustment programmes the World Bank and the IMF were promoting as conditions for lending to indebted countries. The question of debt itself was identified as centrally important, along with related questions, such as the need for fairer trade. The Debt Crisis Network came together in 1988, on the basis of these NGO concerns, and the concerns of their Southern NGO partners, with the negative impact of debt and structural adjustment.

These NGOs brought different strengths and areas of expertise. Christian Aid and Tear Fund, for example, brought the strength of their broad roots in the churches, while the World Development Movement brought the energy and enthusiasm of its active membership (having been set up by Oxfam and Christian Aid to campaign at a time when NGOs, as charities bound by charitable legal requirements, had tended to be less involved in active campaigning). Oxfam's particular contribution, it has been suggested, was its expertise in research and policy analysis and the respect this expertise commanded with governments and international organizations. Having well-founded facts and figures was seen by a number of commentators as having been an important factor in Jubilee 2000's credibility.

There was also broad agreement that Jubilee 2000 had roots in the

South as well as in the North. As one participant explained, 'lots of homework on the debt issue had already been done and there were debt groups around the world'. There were debt groups, for example, in Uganda and Mozambique with similar groupings in Honduras and Nicaragua. This set the scene for the emergence of Jubilee 2000 as a genuinely global initiative when this came together in the mid-1990s as a campaigning network. The coalition was based initially in Christian Aid's offices.

When Jubilee 2000 started, there had been considerable scepticism in some quarters about the possibility of developing a broadly based global campaign on such a relatively abstract issue. Economics tends to be seen as a complex subject in the North, even among relatively highly educated professionals, so how could a broad coalition of peoples spanning the South as well as the North be expected to be attracted to a campaign on the debt? Several participants commented that they had initially had their doubts too.

The very specific emphasis on the forgiveness of debt for the forthcoming millennium was identified as having been a key factor in the campaign's success in finding an effective and clearly communicable focus. 'The message was simple and compelling,' in the words of one participant, explaining how he came to become involved. The millennium gave the debt issue immediacy and resonance. This was particularly relevant for those members of faith groups, who were looking for ways of giving the millennium deeper spiritual significance. As one participant commented, this emphasis on the importance of the biblical meaning of the Jubilee stood in stark contrast with the somewhat less meaningful dome being planned for Greenwich to mark the year 2000 in London. Jubilee 2000 was described as 'an idea whose time had come'. As another commentator reflected, previous campaigns on the debt had seemed 'rather academic', whereas the Jubilee focus was seen as both 'simple and sensible' with its emphasis on 'what needed to be done and who needed to take decisions and action to make it happen'. 'We turned the debt into a non-technical issue. It's a justice issue.' The demands were given immediacy, and they were presented in a format specifically geared towards winning the broadest possible support.

There are two aspects of the campaign's success to be emphasized here. The first is the timing – the 'simple message' whose time had come. Some commentators reflected that the time was ripe in another sense, too: there were widening political opportunity structures in this period. The centre Left had gained power in a number of states in Europe. There was also a democratic President, Clinton, in the USA (although it was also recognized that there were significant limits to this apparent shift to the centre Left, including the fact that Congress was controlled by the Republicans in the latter period). Nevertheless, it was suggested, this wider political scenario offered windows of opportunity for campaigning that had not been present in the previous Thatcher/Reagan years.

In addition, it was suggested, the fact that a number of key 'third way' politicians (including the British Prime Minister, Tony Blair, and the Chancellor of the Exchequer, Gordon Brown) were Christian socialists reinforced the view that lobbying them on these issues might be effective. They might be persuaded to shift in relation to national policy agendas and they might also be persuaded to use their votes to support the case for debt relief in international forums. The interviews with participants provided specific examples to demonstrate the extent to which Gordon Brown, for instance, had been personally supportive (including references to his speech in St Paul's Cathedral, London, in 1999, broadly supporting Jubilee 2000's goals). Although the role of particular politicians was emphasized by a number of participants, however, it was also pointed out that the support of politicians was not entirely unprecedented. There had actually been some space for campaigning for debt relief, under the previous Conservative government. Nor were supportive speeches by politicians sufficient in themselves.

For a combination of reasons already summarized in Chapter 1, key international organizations like the World Bank and the IMF were also demonstrating their preparedness to consider policy adjustments at this time. In the post-Washington consensus era, this greater willingness to address issues of global poverty provided further encouragement to campaigners. By 1999, the World Bank had clearly recognized that the trickle-down effect supposed to bring the benefits of free-market policies to the poor and the poorest was not necessarily succeeding in alleviating poverty (World Bank 1999).

It was also becoming more widely argued that international organizations needed to work in partnership with civil society as well as the private sector and the state, to promote social as well as economic development. The World Bank had already recognized that the poor needed to be directly involved in the development of poverty reduction strategy papers – albeit within the continuing framework of neoliberal free-trade agendas (ibid.). Even the IMF had announced in 1999 that poverty reduction was a core objective. Whatever the limitations, this was a scenario seen as offering very particular opportunities – opportunities that Jubilee 2000 set out to seize.

The second aspect of Jubilee 2000's success that was emphasized more or less unanimously was the campaign's breadth, from faith-based groups to trade unions, business people, academics, artists and media stars. Commentators reflected upon the impact that the huge public events made, especially since participation in these was so obviously not confined to the 'usual suspects'. Many of those taking part in the major public demonstrations (75 per cent, according to one source) had never participated in anything remotely comparable before. The 'events' were intentionally not described as 'demonstrations', in fact, precisely because this was a term that might have deterred political neophytes. Jubilee 2000 supporters included many who might have been far more alarmed than inspired by being associated with the negative publicity that accompanied the demonstrations that took place in Seattle, for example. In this respect, Jubilee 2000 supporters were typical of the vast majority of demonstrators who were, of course, overwhelmingly non-violent, although this was not the message portrayed by many of the journalists who covered these events.

The fact that Jubilee 2000 activists were so evidently not the 'usual suspects' was believed to have surprised and impressed politicians. Similarly, hand-written letters from concerned individuals had particular impact, it was suggested, over and above the impact of e-mails (which could have been sent by a relatively small number of people). As one commentator (who had been a civil servant) reflected,

> ordinary people would ring up [politicians and government departments] and say, 'I'm Mrs So and So and I want to talk to you about the debt.' This had more impact than lots of standard letters (although these also made an impact. The Treasury was getting 300,000 different communications a year, letters, cards and emails on the debt issue). At this time a quarter of the Treasury's entire correspondence was on debt. Hand-written letters made the most impact.

This direct involvement of such a wide range of people was key, then, to the campaign's success. Although this breadth was identified as such a positive factor, spanning North and South, this breadth did also raise its own challenges in terms of developing effective forms of democratic accountability, as will be suggested below.

Before addressing these organizational issues, however, one further aspect of the campaign's history deserves mention: the use of history per se. Participants consciously drew upon the experiences of international campaigning in the past, both the recent past (including campaigns against apartheid in South Africa) and the less recent past. Campaigners had studied accounts of nineteenth-century mobilizations against slavery, and drew lessons – and the symbol of the chain – from these. These lessons were explored, for example, in the account published by Martin Dent and Bill Peters, two key figures in the development of Jubilee 2000 – with a strong interest in the campaign's historical antecedents (Dent and Peters 1999). 'We remember that a popular international movement in the 19th century, after a long struggle, brought about the end of the slave trade,' a Jubilee 2000 publication commented in 2000. 'The chains of debt are not yet broken, but they have been loosened; and as people continue to join hands against debt bondage, we will prise the chains of debt apart' (Jubilee 2000 Coalition 2000: 20).

Jubilee 2000 emphasized its links with the past, as well as the novelty of its particular approach in the present. In this respect, as already suggested, Jubilee 2000 did not fit that closely into new social movement categories. While the campaign was certainly aiming to empower those who had been defined as 'victims' to redefine themselves as actors, speaking effectively with their own voices, the objectives were also very specific and intentionally achievable, or at least partially achievable, within the allotted timespan, in the run-up to the millennium. The focus upon building alliances with existing organizations, including trade unions as well as churches (drawing upon experiences of anti-apartheid campaigning), was also less characteristic of new social movement theorists' approaches. On the contrary, in fact, Jubilee 2000 was a coalition of formal organizations and social movement organizations as well as looser groupings and individuals, with varying levels of commitment from signing the petition to participating in mass protest events.

Jubilee 2000 did, however, adopt an organizational structure that was deliberately distinct and intentionally flexible, relatively informal and temporary. In this respect there were perhaps more resonances with new social movement models. When and how precisely the Debt Crisis Network developed into Jubilee 2000 was not entirely clear to all the participants who commented on this, though. Nor was the particular format that did evolve unanimously agreed to have been the most appropriate. Differing views were expressed as to whether Jubilee 2000 should have been the secretariat of a coalition of campaigning organizations and groups, for example, or a campaign in its own right. In the event, Jubilee 2000 remained a coalition, but with increasing identity, effectively, as a campaign in its own right.

This had advantages, including advantages for the campaign's secretariat, enabling them to work with flexibility and speed. But there were also disadvantages from the perspectives of some of the constituent organizations, including some of the NGOs that had been involved in the earlier campaigns from the 1980s and early 1990s. Once Jubilee 2000 became identified as a campaign in its own right, there were some expressions of concern that there might be less space for the constituent organizations' campaigning roles.

As one commentator reflected, the fact was that since the 1990s a number of NGOs had increasingly come to recognize that 'campaigning is both essential (in order to tackle the causes of poverty, globally) and practically beneficial to the NGOs in question'. Getting a logo and 'brand name' more widely and positively known was contributing to fundraising, and some NGOs were beginning to recruit marketing expertise from the private sector to increase their effectiveness in this respect. As another participant commented, 'the tools of marketing are key here – how the public perceives you and your brand label'. 'If six campaigning organizations are working together in partnership,' he continued, 'there is bound to be pressure to get to be the spokesperson – to get your logo on television.'

Some of the possible implications of increasing competition between NGOs, as they have faced pressures to become more market-orientated, have already been raised in previous chapters (Jordan and Maloney 1997). The point to raise here is simply that the organizational form adopted by Jubilee 2000 was potentially contentious for these reasons. Meanwhile the reality was that Jubilee 2000 effectively became 'the brand' – with worldwide brand recognition. As one participant reflected, this development of the Jubilee 'brand' was key to such success as the campaign achieved.

There were also tensions about the balance to be struck between enabling decision-making to be rapid and ensuring democratic accountability, taking sufficient account of the decision-making structures of component organizations. The leadership style was characterized in terms of 'getting on with it', and this had enormous strengths. There was widespread and extremely enthusiastic appreciation of the dynamism and commitment of the staff and particularly of the director, who was singled out for special appreciation and praise. Her personal contribution was clearly immense. She was described as dynamic, articulate, high-profile and passionate. Inevitably, perhaps, being such a strong charismatic personality also provoked criticisms and disagreements.

On the other hand, democratic representation and accountability were inevitably going to be problematic, and especially so in such a broad coalition, spanning North and South. As has already been suggested in Chapter 5, representation and accountability have been and continue to be problematic in community participation, whether locally or globally. It would have been extraordinary if these issues had not also emerged as issues for Jubilee 2000.

Jubilee 2000 developed its own approaches to addressing these problems. As a paper by Ed Mayo of the New Economics Foundation (an organization that played a key role in supporting Jubilee 2000 and its successor Jubilee Research) argued, with Jubilee 2000 'the purpose, direction and vision of the campaign is the DNA of every component of the organisation' (Mayo 1999). In his view, the campaign had resolved organizational tensions creatively with a number of shifts in gear, as the momentum developed. As the campaign had grown, so the organizational structure had developed from a relatively loose network to a more clearly defined one. There had been a continuing process of reviewing progress and learning from mistakes, keeping up the momentum of engaging people in events and activities to maintain and further strengthen the campaign.

The team of staff and volunteers in the secretariat worked with initiative and because this was a new venture, it was suggested, there was no organizational baggage to contend with. The regular planning meetings showed 'no deference', participants commented. People were respected not because of their formal position in the organization but for what they were doing. As a number of participants also pointed out, there was continuing commitment to being as inclusive and genuinely accountable as possible, and especially to involve Southern partners fully and enable them to speak with their own voice. Jubilee 2000 was strongly committed to working towards this aim and the inclusion of Southern voices gave the campaign legitimacy, it was argued. While these views were strongly expressed, the difficulties of ensuring that these commitments were carried out, in practice, were also recognized, however. Similar questions were also raised by participants from constituent organizations.

One particular feature of Jubilee 2000's organizational approach was its commitment to being time-limited. As one participant explained, 'there was a strong ethical discourse about not setting up a long term poverty business'. As another person put this, 'values on human rights and justice – that was our brand'. Unlike other organizations, including large NGOs, it was argued, Jubilee 2000 was determined not to become focused upon its own organizational survival or the careers of its staff. This also related to Jubilee 2000's decision not to invest time and effort in developing complex formalized structures (for what would in any case be a time-limited campaign).

Being time-limited gave Jubilee 2000 particular strengths and added moral authority – because this was so evidently not a 'protest business'. The immediacy of the campaign was a key factor in maintaining such sharp focus, too. But the decision to be time-limited was also potentially contentious. As one participant commented, 'being time-bound can have both strengths and weaknesses'. The underlying issues were long-term problems with continuing effects, particularly in the world's poorer countries. There was a view that some damage was done by the decision to wind the campaign up in its current form at the end of the millennium year. Some Southern coalitions – with fewer resources at their disposal – had taken longer to develop. By the year 2000 these Southern groupings felt that they were just beginning really to get going. As a result of the decision to wind up at this point, some trust was broken in the South, it was suggested. This was a source of potential anxiety to development NGOs, among others, with long-term partnerships with Southern NGOs to sustain. 'Mistakes were made here,' according to one participant, suggesting that the campaign ended too abruptly with the result that some momentum was lost. This was evidently a contentious decision.

In the event, the campaign did not simply evaporate on 31 December 2000. In the UK 'Drop the Debt' took on the specific task of keeping up the momentum until the next G8 meeting, pressurizing to ensure that millennium commitments on debt relief were honoured. This campaign continued until the Genoa meeting of the G8 in 2001. Meanwhile, the Jubilee Debt Campaign, a network of regional and faith groups, NGOs, trade unions and others, continued to co-ordinate campaigning activity and policy work for Genoa and beyond. In addition, Jubilee Plus took on the role of providing analysis and research on international debt and finance. Subsequently, this became Jubilee Research, a 'think-and-do tank' housed in the New Economics Foundation, providing up-to-date research, analysis, news and data via its publications and website. The international links were taken forward by the Jubilee Movement International. So while Jubilee 2000 itself was time-limited as a campaign, this could be seen as a phase in a longer-term movement for global economic justice.

It was also suggested by some commentators that being time-limited did not completely solve the potential problems around individual or organizational self-interest. Jubilee 2000 was strongly committed to avoiding becoming a self-serving bureaucracy. But social movements are not immune from wider social pressures, any more than NGOs are (Edwards 2001). In a global context in which Northern NGOs have much greater access to resources and to politicians and the media than their Southern counterparts, becoming a partner in a Northern campaign can be seen as potentially highly advantageous. As one participant explained, 'every Southern partner depended on an outside funder and that affected the relationship'.

One commentator suggested, for instance, that in some countries, though certainly not all, Jubilee 2000, like other initiatives seen as coming from the North, could be perceived as a gravy train, offering valuable contacts with potential supporters. As another participant reflected, 'realistically being linked with a Northern NGO gives huge prestige and access to resources'. Given their relative lack of resources, compared with their Northern counterparts, Southern NGOs could hardly be criticized for being on the look-out for links of this type. How can Northern NGOs be sure, though, this commentator queried, that Southern NGOs are not seeking to link with them for self-interested reasons? And how can they ensure that Southern partners are themselves representative and democratically accountable, especially if other potential partners in the South approach them with the argument that 'you are supporting the wrong people here, so switch over and support us'?

Realistically, these are not questions that can easily be answered in the current context, characterized as it is by such inequalities, internationally. Efforts have been made (including, for example, the efforts of some Northern NGOs to draw up criteria to guide decisions on which Southern NGOs to support). But this is an ongoing problem and, as commentators pointed out, 'Northern NGOs affect the power balance' through the decisions they take. As several participants suggested, in the long term the development of civil society needs to be supported in the South. Northern NGOs could be supporting Southern NGOs to do their own advocacy, not leading it themselves, but focusing upon pressurizing their own governments in the North and, through them, applying pressure on international decision-making processes.

One particular aspect of these debates about who spoke for whom related to the use of celebrities to publicize the campaign. The involvement of big names such as pop stars has potential disadvantages as well as evident advantages. Pop stars attract media coverage, and this, in turn, engages the interest of politicians and decision-makers, nationally and internationally – being photographed with a pop star being an outcome to be relished in this age of spin. This all helps to build up a campaign's profile, as well as engaging the interest of potential supporters at the grass-roots. The involvement of Bono, for example, was cited as having brought the campaign to the attention of a generation of young people who would not have been reached easily in other ways. This applied to teenagers and street children in Latin America as well as to young people in the North. Bono was described as having been superb and his commitment continued subsequently. Bob Geldof's commitment similarly continued subsequently.

There were others who complained that the use of pop stars 'turned our stomachs', however. In particular, there were fears that media celebrities may turn out to be high risks, liable to go off on their own tack (possibly more concerned about putting across their own publicity than conveying the campaign's particular message). The use of celebrities can trivialize a campaign, it was suggested. And this may be particularly unacceptable in the South when the celebrities concerned are from the North. There were tributes to particular Northern celebrities, however, especially Bono and Bob Geldof – for their genuine and continuing commitment and for being so well-informed and so articulate on the campaign's behalf. Three years after Jubilee 2000 had wound itself up in its previously existing form, Bob Geldof was still arguing the case, pointing out that although much had been achieved, debt relief had been accompanied by conditions imposed by the rich world. The rich world had been demanding that markets be opened up, 'but don't expect us to do the same'. Although some global debt had been cancelled, most had not, 'while the rich world has slashed aid and rigged trade' (Geldof 2003: 21). Poor families in Third World countries might die before they saw the changes that needed to be made, he concluded; 'indeed I may die before I see it – but change it will because change it must' (ibid.).

Reflecting on the use of celebrities in general, a number of participants commented that Jubilee 2000 had become highly skilled in doing this without allowing them to run off with the campaign. Others reflected on the attributes of the particular celebrities concerned – it had been crucially important that these celebrities had been so articulate and so well-informed as well as being so committed. In summary, then, it had been very important to publicize results and celebrate successes. This had been achieved through the media work overall.

Despite being such a broad alliance, a 'big tent' with room for many different views and interests, Jubilee 2000 succeeded in keeping the coalition together effectively over its lifetime. Although the constituent organizations had varying structures and styles, this had not necessarily been a source of friction in practice. Without minimizing the inherent challenges in building such a broadly based campaign, even on a temporary basis, there were some very positive evaluations overall. Such differences as there were had been kept within the campaign, it was argued. No one 'ran off to the media with their side of any particular story', it was pointed out – a factor attributed to the strength of shared commitment to the common cause.

There were also very positive comments about the shared learning that had developed through working together over this period. Despite different organizational structures and styles, for example, it was suggested that the campaign had contributed to the fact that trade union organizations and NGOs were developing more effective ways of working together. That was, in itself, an aspect of Jubilee 2000 that increased its popular appeal. As a number of participants commented, people like to see organizations working together.

The process of involvement and dialogue had also been a radicalizing experience for some groups, it was suggested, including some faith-based groups. And there were powerful accounts of the learning that had been taking place for individuals as well as for organizations in the South as well as the North. This included different types of learning, in theory and in practice.

In India, for instance, for some people with limited literacy skills, the Jubilee 2000 petition was the first paper they had ever signed. Signing the petition became an educative experience too in the sense that this involved becoming informed about the debt issue itself. When a journalist challenged the basis of the 2 million signatures to the petition in Peru, doubting whether all 2 million really understood the issues involved, he went to a remote village to find out for himself. To his amazement, he was immediately treated to a cogent explanation of the global debt and how this was affecting people in the area, locally.

Exploring lessons and their potential implications

As the previous example illustrated, the learning associated with involvement in Jubilee 2000 represented a significant achievement in its own right. From signing the petition to participating in campaigning events, those involved had been engaged in what might be considered as a truly massive global process of adult and community education. Participants gained critical understanding of global development issues, itself a major achievement, especially given the anxieties so often associated with economics, popularly perceived as a complex subject, the domain of experts rather than 'lay' activists. And they gained knowledge and understanding of decision-making processes and how to organize to impact on these, globally as well as nationally and locally. Although the active engagement of grass-roots groups was inevitably problematic, this was at least partially achieved even in some rural contexts where grass-roots groups lacked access to basic communication tools such as newspapers, television and even radio (Collins et al. 2001). And Jubilee 2000 was educative in the wider ways in which the campaign impacted upon popular perceptions/misconceptions and self-perceptions, focusing as it did on the causes rather than the 'victims' of global poverty. This has been identified as one of the main reasons for Jubilee 2000's appeal.

There are resonances here with approaches to popular education, drawing upon Paulo Freire's concept of 'conscientization' (Freire 1972). Chapter 5 included examples, such as the popular education initiatives developed by the Landless People's Movement in Brazil. Jubilee 2000 similarly enhanced participants' critical consciousness, facilitating collective action as the basis for empowerment and social transformation.

The challenges faced by Jubilee 2000 have parallels, too, with the challenges and dilemmas identified in Chapter 5 in relation to community development theory and practice (Mayo 1994). How to build a broad coalition without losing focus, for example? How to maintain long-term support and build up momentum through winning immediate, achievable objectives – such as the objectives on debt cancellation for the poorest countries under existing initiatives – without losing sight of longer-term aims for more total debt cancellation and fairer trade? How to avoid becoming marginalized, on the one hand, or becoming co-opted, on the other, incorporated into the agendas of the decision-makers who were to be lobbied and challenged? How to campaign around key policy issues, engaging with political processes without becoming the creature of any particular political party or grouping? How to work effectively with professionals, media stars and politicians without allowing them to hi-jack the agenda?

Some of these dilemmas have taken on added significance, with increasing parallels between experiences in the South and in the North, in the context of globalization. Issues of democratic representation and accountability have become more evidently problematic, in particular, as civil society has become more central in international policy debates. As Chapter 2 suggested, civil society has been conceptualized as an arena containing conflicting interests and agendas (Edwards 2001). These include the tensions between neoliberal market-orientated agendas on the one hand and bureaucratic state agendas and solutions on the other. Civil society organizations are being subjected to pressures from both directions, pressures to become more 'businesslike' in their operations and pressures to become major service providers on the state's behalf. Rather than necessarily guaranteeing legitimacy, let alone consensus, civil society contains its own dilemmas and conflicts, including dilemmas and conflicts around democratic representation and accountability.

Increasing policy emphasis on community participation in the North has been accompanied by increased questioning as to who is actually speaking for whom and whose voices are – or are not – being effectively heard (Anastacio et al. 2000). In the global context, where access to power and resources (including media resources) is so unevenly distributed, the effective representation of less powerful Southern voices is potentially even more problematic. There was widespread agreement among those who reflected on the achievements and challenges of Jubilee 2000 that this had indeed been a key issue, if not the most central challenge for the development of global citizen action in the future. As one participant reflected, 'If people try to create movements *for* other people they implode.' The way forward, in the longer term, according to this participant, was for the North to be resourcing the South to do its own advocacy and campaigning. The North, meanwhile, should be concentrating its advocacy on pressurizing its own governments. As the experiences of Jubilee 2000 illustrated, Northern governments were potentially crucial, both in their own right and as members of key international organizations such as the World Bank and the IMF.

If campaigning is effectively focused on the causes rather than the victims of global poverty, then these approaches are absolutely complementary. It is not only that Northern campaigners need to pressurize their own governments to take action to support Southern campaigning. Challenging the processes of capitalist globalization is about solidarity rather than charity, with the potential for building a global social movement genuinely in the interests of campaigners in the North as well as in the interests of those in the South.

Jubilee 2000 and differing perspectives on social movements

New social movement theorists' concerns to differentiate the 'new' social movements from the 'old' have already been questioned. As Chapter 4 suggested, the 'new' may not be so 'new' nor the 'old' so 'old'. New social movements have grown from the networks developed by older movements. And they have worked within and through formal bureaucratic structures as well as experimenting with more fluid organizational forms. Meanwhile, older movements, including the trade union and labour movement, have been 'seeking ways out of the apparent impasse of the old tactics, organizational modes and even objectives' (Waterman 1999: 13), developing new approaches to organizing and building social movement unionism, globally as well as locally. This is absolutely not to deny that there is anything new in the current context, simply to point to particular areas of overlap and to highlight some of the ways in which different movements interact.

On the basis of their study of social movement organizations concerned with the environment and human rights, Jordan and Maloney concluded that the new social movement literature did not have very much to contribute overall (Jordan and Maloney 1997). This would seem somewhat harsh as a conclusion in relation to Jubilee 2000. Although Jubilee 2000 explicitly acknowledged the achievements of the past, the campaign was also concerned to develop new approaches, introducing more flexible organizational formats and campaigning styles. While Jubilee 2000 focused on the debt, an issue with vital implications for people's livelihoods in the poorest parts of the world, the campaign was not confined to the most immediate practical concerns, raising wider challenges to predominant ideologies of development. It was noteworthy, too, that Jubilee 2000's supporters campaigned with such altruism. For the 70,000-strong crowd around the centre of Birmingham in 1998, for example, there were no obvious personal benefits to be gained in the short term. Jubilee 2000's achievements in moblizing so many supporters cannot be understood without reference to this ideological commitment. Aspects of new social movement theorists' approaches have relevance here, rather than approaches emphasizing the importance of actors' self-interests.

On the other hand, Jubilee 2000 was not predominantly concerned with issues of identity, lifestyle or culture (although the campaign did challenge negative stereotypes of the poor as the passive 'victims' of globalization). Nor did Jubilee 2000's commitment to flexibility inhibit the campaign from building alliances with more formal organizational structures, including trade unions as well as faith groups and NGOs. Jubilee 2000 campaigned pragmatically as well as with principle, mobilizing resources and seizing political opportunities. The literatures on resource mobilization and political process approaches have relevance in these respects. Jordan and Maloney's conclusion – that both approaches could contribute to the understanding of global social movements, although neither, on its own, seemed entirely satisfactory – could be applied in the case of Jubilee 2000.

Challenging the negative effects of neoliberal agendas globally, Jubilee 2000 developed the campaign with the benefit of globalized communications technologies. Campaigners seized new global opportunities to mobilize for alternatives agendas, exploring ways of building a social movement that would be both effective and genuinely representative, locally as well as globally. While the campaign wound itself up in its existing form, there were supporters who recognized the need to keep the pressure up until all the promises were redeemed (Dent and Peters 1999) – a longer-term project for economic and social justice.

10 | Resisting imperialism: building social movements for peace and social justice

The novelty of contemporary challenges to capitalist globalization has been explored in previous chapters – the view that the world will never be the same again. But the relevance of particular legacies from the past has also been emphasized. Nineteenth-century imperialism and twenty-first-century capitalist globalization have points of comparison as well as of difference. And previous chapters have similarly explored comparisons as well as contrasts between the ways in which challenges to these have been developed over time – down to the organizational styles of the mobilizations concerned.

Reflecting on the experiences of the Campaign for Nuclear Disarmament (CND), Mattausch pointed to the significance of continuity as well as change. Postmodernists' – and following them, new social movement theorists' – emphasis on the need for new analytical tools and approaches was misplaced, he argued. Modernity had not been wholly superseded and 'cultural developments of the past do not just go away; past patterns of imperialism, nationalism and ethnic identifications do not have an expiry date' (Mattausch 2000: 194). While social movements such as CND have their ups and downs, the peace movement's significance 'has lain less in its specific achievements and more in its bequests to future campaigners. This bequest has included campaigning skills, experience, knowledge and inspiration' (ibid.: 195) – emphasizing the moral dimensions of the movement's appeal.

Ironically, this turned out to be something of an underestimation of CND's particular legacy. Three years after Mattausch's chapter was published, the largest peace demonstration ever, in Britain, was jointly organized by CND, the Stop the War Coalition and the Muslim Association of Britain. At least one and a half million people marched through London on 15 February 2003. And millions demonstrated for peace in more than 300 cities across the globe, from New Zealand through Asia and Africa, from Europe to North and South America.

This chapter starts by summarizing some of the ways in which these mobilizations have built upon previous movements, including anti-capitalist globalization movements as well as anti-war movements in particular countries. As the experiences of Jubilee 2000 illustrated, in the previous chapter, past campaigns have been built upon and developed in new ways, linking campaigning on the debt, for example, with campaigning on aid, trade and the particular challenge of HIV/AIDS. The Trade Justice Campaign similarly exemplifies these processes, building on previous campaigns to take forward the social justice agenda. This leads into the concluding discussion about possible implications for building sustainable challenges to capitalist globalization, challenges that make an impact in the here and now, while contributing to strategies for social transformation in the longer term.

Building on the links: the peace movement and the Stop the War Coalition

The history of CND, within the wider peace movement, exemplifies ways in which movements ebb and flow over time, building on previous experiences and networks as they re-emerge (Byrne 1988; Mattausch 1989; 2000). The first campaign against Britain's development of nuclear weapons was organized by the British Peace Committee in the 1950s, a mobilization that succeeded in obtaining a million signatures for a petition, despite criticisms for links with the World Peace Committee (labelled as 'communist' during this Cold War period) (Ruddock 1987). CND itself was formed in 1958, the year of the first march to Aldermaston (the site of nuclear weapons developments). These marches developed momentum with 100,000 attending the rally associated with the largest, in 1962. There was considerable focus upon trying to persuade the Labour Party to adopt the policy of unilateral nuclear disarmament – using lobbying tactics as well as encompassing non-violent direct action. In subsequent years, from the mid-1960s, however, support levelled off. This was for a number of reasons (including the focus shifting to opposition to the Vietnam War, from 1965).

The movement only really began to revive in the late 1970s, with membership growing by 200 per cent between 1982 and 1985 (Byrne 1988). This was at least in part in response to new threats from NATO deployments, including the threats posed by the deployment of cruise missiles at Greenham Common, the site of major mobilizations. (The Women's Peace Camp at Greenham Common started in 1981.) While new activists came forward, including women, activated via their involvement in second-wave feminism, there were activists with experiences dating back to the previous period, including faith-based groups (such as the Quakers and others involved in Christian CND) and some trade unionists. There was continuity then, as well as change, both in terms of organizations and individuals.

Then as previously, the majority of supporters were middle-class – many of them public sector professionals such as teachers and health workers (Mattausch 1989) – and many were also members of other organizations. A survey of members in 1985 identified that around a third were members of a trade union, around a quarter belonged to a political party (mostly Labour but others too, including other Left parties and the Green Party) and a fifth belonged to a church, pointing to the view that participation is a cumulative process (Byrne 1988). Being involved in one organization/campaign tends to lead to further involvement in others too. There are parallels here with the interconnected memberships of organizations such as Amnesty International, Friends of the Earth and Greenpeace (discussed in Chapter 3).

While CND was a broad organization, encompassing those engaged in direct action as well as those who joined marches and organized petitions, the focus was upon the nuclear issue per se. CND had developed links with other movements internationally, but not with anti-capitalist globalization movements more specifically. It was not immediately obvious, then, that CND would join with anti-globalization campaigners to stop the war threatened against Iraq, the war that did eventually break out in 2003.

In the event, CND took the view that nuclear weapons might be used as part of a first strike, by Britain, for instance. It was therefore appropriate to mobilize against this threat. Similar arguments had been used to justify CND's involvement in campaigning against the earlier war in Afghanistan. At this point, however, there had been other reservations about joining the Stop the War Coalition, too. This was partly because some elements within the coalition were not condemning the attacks on the World Trade Center (11 September 2001) and partly, perhaps, because of more general anxieties about getting involved in a coalition with Left political groupings. These anxieties evidently continued, and CND retained its separate identity as a campaigning organization. But CND did participate in joint events with the Stop the War Coalition and the Muslim Association of Britain. 'The CND banners were right up at the front' in fact, on 15 February 2003, 'behind the main joint banner of the three organizations who had worked so hard to make the day such a success, CND with the Muslim Association of Britain and the Stop the War Coalition' (Naughton 2003: 7).

Subsequently, activists reflected on the ways in which the events of 15 February themselves had changed the situation. This was the culmination of processes of change over time, as different organizations developed ways of working together, based on increasing trust and mutual understanding. There had been differences of opinion, including differences over the campaign's overall focus. Should this be broadened to include related issues in the region (such as Palestine, as the Muslim Association of Britain, among others, argued), or should it be kept tightly focused on Iraq? Either way, the campaign might lose supporters (although this fear was not actually realized when the campaign did decide to include demands on the Palestinian question). Without minimizing these differences, activists reflected on the ways in which trust had actually been developed, increasing the chances of keeping the links together to be in a position to campaign again in the face of future threats.

Meanwhile similar processes could be identified in building the Stop the War Coalition itself. Here too, the campaign against the threat of war against Iraq built upon previous mobilizations against interventions in the Balkans, Afghanistan and the Gulf. But this was much bigger and broader – partly because the issues were clearer to a wider range of potential supporters.

From the Stop the War Coalition's perspective, the key elements in the campaign were Left groupings (from the Socialist Workers Party, the Communist Party and the left of the Labour Party) and the Muslim Association of Britain, representing a broad section of the Muslim community, not just the Left within it. CND peace activists were also involved. The pattern of trade union involvement was rather similar, although this also developed over time, with more active involvement as the movement built up to the demonstration on 15 February 2003.

It was through the anti-globalization movement's networks, networks already developed through the World Social Forum and the European Social Forum, for example, that the Stop the War Coalition succeeded in linking with anti-war mobilizations internationally. Globalise Resistance had already made the connections between globalization, war and imperialism, with a particular focus on US imperialist interests in oil. There were, of course, a number of analyses that could be drawn on, to develop these arguments.

For example, Hardt and Negri's study *Empire* had pointed to the links between the emergence of the 'new world order' and the military interventions being undertaken to protect its interests – in the name of 'just wars'. 'The Gulf War', Hardt and Negri argued, 'gave us perhaps the first fully articulated example of this new epistemology of the concept' of the 'just war' (Hardt and Negri 2000: 13). Andrew Murray, chair of the Stop the War Coalition, had also previously published an analysis of the disturbing realities behind the rhetoric of the 'new world order'. His book pointed to similarly terrifying conclusions about the threats to world peace from globalization and the resurgence of inter-imperialist rivalry between the great powers (Murray 1997). Through the Stop the War Coalition these theoretical links could be brought together with campaigning networks, in practice, to build resistance on a global scale.

Like CND activists, Stop the War Coalition activists reflected on the importance of the processes of working together, building mutual understanding and trust. Mutual stereotypes were challenged as young women came forward to speak for the Muslim community, for example. And Leftists increasingly resisted the temptation to put the interests of their own organizations before the interests of the campaign as a whole. The movement itself transformed those involved in the process, it was argued.

Working with political parties poses particular challenges for social movements, however. Political parties can, of course, provide valuable support, both in terms of resources and in terms of access to decision-making processes. But being closely associated with any particular political party has its downside, potentially threatening the movement's independence and alienating supporters who do not share that particular political perspective. Opponents can and do use such political connections to smear social movements, attempting to discredit them by labelling them as tools of this or that particular political tendency. The chair of the Stop the War Coalition, for example, was labelled as 'an apologist for Stalin' in the context of an article that questioned the coalition's democratic credentials and potential sustainability (Cohen 2003: 24).

The World Social Forum and the European Social Forum dealt with these issues by limiting the participation of political parties. But political parties have also provided key support. Rifondazione Comunista and the left social democrats in Italy were credited with having played a major role in organizing the European Social Forum in Florence, for example. The Workers' Party (PT) – emanating, itself, from the trade unions and social movements in Brazil – played a similarly important role in organizing the meetings in Porto Alegre (although it was also criticized for using the second forum to publicize its own political messages). There were differences of view here about the desirability of such links with political parties, reflecting the breadth of views within the anti-globalization movement more generally, a breadth encapsulated in the slogan 'One no and many yeses' (Kingsnorth 2003). As Kingsnorth has commented, referring to anti-globalization movements more generally, 'this is an enormous and chaotically diverse movement, full of passionate and intensely argumentative people' (ibid.: 316).

Realistically, the difficulties of building and sustaining such a broad coalition are not to be underestimated. There have been continuing differences of focus and varying perspectives on the roles of the range of organizations and individuals involved as well as differences of organizational style. Previous chapters have explored some of the challenges inherent in building such alliances – as well as the crucial importance of developing strategies to address them.

Building on the links: campaigning on debt and trade

As the previous chapter also pointed out, global campaigning on the debt has similarly continued, if in differing organizational form. For instance, the campaign on Debt, AIDS and Trade in Africa (DATA) links the debt issue with the related issues of trade and aid as well as HIV/AIDS – with support from organizations and individuals previously involved in Jubilee 2000. After the millennium, they decided to continue, linking the issue of debt with trade justice and with AIDS – because AIDS has had such devastating effects, economically as well as socially. And the particular focus on Africa was agreed because the most serious problems were located there. Both Bono and Bob Geldof continued to play key roles, actively supporting DATA. If anything, it has been suggested, they even became more deeply committed, over time, doing a great deal of work behind the scenes as well as continuing with their more public roles. DATA has campaigned extensively in the USA, as well as in Britain and the European Union – and, of course, in Africa.

Summarizing the connections between debt, trade and aid, Bob Geldof explained,

> while the debts were being written off, aid has been run down. According- ing to Jubilee Research, total resource flows to the 53 countries identified as highly indebted have fallen sharply, from 6.2 billion dollars at the time of the Birmingham summit to 4.3 billion in 2000 [... debt relief] comes with conditions: G7 leaders (through the IMF) require countries to jump impossible economic hurdles they themselves decline. 'Open up your markets' is one condition, 'but don't expect us to do the same.' [...] 'Remove all protection for your producers – but don't ask us to reform the state-backed protection we give to pharmaceutical industries' (result- ing in unaffordable prices for life saving drugs including drugs for HIV/ Aids). How much harder can we make it? It's not just that we won't write off debts that cripple their economies – we won't let them earn their way out of poverty through trade either. (Geldof 2003: 21)

A number of the organizations previously involved in Jubilee 2000, including the Jubilee Debt Campaign, came together subsequently to form the Trade Justice Campaign (TJC) to pursue the issue of trade in particular. Like the issue of debt, the issue of trade justice had already been emerging on organizing agendas. This had a history of support from a number of NGOs, as well as from progressive organizations and individuals involved in developing fair trade initiatives – including the Greater London Council and the Greater London Enterprise Board in the 1980s.

The TJC was formed to take the debt campaign further, linking this not only with trade but also with TRIPs and GATS and with campaigning against privatization more generally. The specific focus, for 2003, centred on three international summits, the EU Heads of State Summit, the G8 Summit and the World Summit on Sustainable Development, with emphasis upon the need to change the policies of the WTO. But this was to be the prelude to the development of campaigning for the longer term, taking on neoliberal agendas more holistically.

The Trade Justice Movement (TJM) has represented a fast-growing coalition including NGOs, faith groups and trade union organizations, concerned abut the threats to public services and jobs (as a result of GATS, for instance) as well as sharing TJM's broader commitment to campaigning for a more equal world. One particular feature of the TJM has been the emphasis on building trade union involvement, as well as that of NGOs and other groupings within civil society. War on Want, one of the constituent NGOs, itself emerged from labour and progressive movement support, roots that have made War on Want particularly well placed to develop these links. At the time of writing the largest single trade union, UNISON, was signed up as a member in its own right and the campaign had been endorsed by a number of other trade unions and the British TUC. This represented a major shift over time, it was pointed out, as the trade unions had become more actively involved in campaigning alongside NGOs on international issues, increasingly defining these in terms of solidarity rather than charity, in the face of neoliberal attacks on jobs and public services, globally.

Possible implications for building sustainable challenges?

Capitalist globalization continues to impact on the North as well as the South, from economics to politics, from trade union struggles over pay and conditions to community struggles around programmes for participation and empowerment. Neoliberal policy agendas impact on the provision of health and education services, the environment and human rights, just as the development of electronic communications facilitates the development of global campaigning for alternatives. Capitalist globalization implies the *potential* as well as the *need* for citizen action on a global scale.

But this in no way guarantees that solidarity in the pursuit of social justice will actually be developed in practice. As participants at Globalise Resistance's annual conference in London in 2003 pointed out, socialism is only one of the possible options (even if there were general agreement in the movement about the desirability of socialism – *which there was not*). Barbarism remained a possible alternative.

While previous chapters have celebrated achievements, building citizen action globally, they have also highlighted some of the inherent difficulties. The case studies illustrated no more than a few examples, the scope of citizen action being wider by far. Rather than attempting to provide a comprehensive picture – which would have been way beyond the scope of this particular book – these experiences have been summarized in order to identify potential features, elements that could contribute to the development of sustainable challenges for the future, if these could be knitted into a broad movement for social justice, for the longer term.

The importance of continuity has already been emphasized in this chapter, as well as the importance of change. While the media focused on the novelty of the mobilizations at Seattle and Genoa, social justice agendas have also been developed globally with the support of long-established organizations and groups, from trade unions to NGOs, from faith-based groups to political parties. New social movement theorists' approaches have had contributions to make, in terms of their analysis, but to set 'new' social movements against the 'old' would be seriously misleading. And it would miss the dynamic processes of change that have been taking place as trade unions and political parties of the Left have been developing new ways of working with social movements, based, in the most encouraging cases, on increasing co-operation and trust.

This is in no way to underestimate the difficulties of building alliances between very different types of organizations and structures – and non-structures. The point is simply to emphasize the importance of trying to do so. Movements need to build upon existing – and continuing – structures if they are to be sure of a sustainable base. Trade union organizations, churches, mosques, synagogues and temples, for example, tend towards longevity, offering the potential for supporting campaigns and movements over time. Previous chapters illustrated the fact that there are examples of particular campaigns' achievements, working with existing organizations and structures while attracting new supporters through the novelty of their strategies and tactics.

Ironically, given the criticisms that have been levelled at trade unions, in the past, for being bureaucratic organizations, insufficiently flexible or responsive to their memberships, there has been increasing recognition among NGOs that trade union structures do also provide for democratic accountability. Even if it takes time to consult the membership, trade union organizations *can* claim that they genuinely represent their members' views. This is less easily demonstrated in less formally structured contexts.

While representation and democratic accountability have been central concerns for social movements, they have proved more problematic in practice, especially at the global level, where resources to facilitate effective participation are so unevenly distributed. As Fung and Wright pointed out in the concluding chapter of their collection of essays on empowering participatory governance, to ignore the asymmetry of power would be seriously mistaken. Only a naïve pluralist would suppose 'that interests are all sufficiently well resourced and organized to participate and that none will be systematically excluded' (Fung and Wright 2003: 286). Participants at the World Social Forums, for example, have recognized this, just as it was identified as an issue to be struggled with by the Jubilee 2000 Coalition. Previous chapters have explored these dilemmas, both in theory, and in practice, in other contexts.

Previous chapters have also highlighted the importance of combining theory and practice more generally. Successful movements and campaigns have been firmly rooted in people's experiences (as people-to-people exchanges illustrated, for example, in Chapter 6). Experiences of developing alternative approaches in practice have also been valuable, as the REFLECT programmes and Elimu campaign demonstrated through their contributions to the Global Campaign for Education. Through their experiences, networks were developed, networks with determination and confidence that different approaches could actually work.

In addition, successful movements and campaigns have been backed by critical analysis and research. The importance of critical theory, together with the importance of evidence-based research, has emerged from a number of chapters, including those discussing the contributions of DAWN, the Global Campaign for Education and the Jubilee 2000 Coalition. Research and policy analysis continues to be centrally important to these campaigns and their successors.

On the basis of people's experiences, backed by critical analyses, successful campaigners have been able to 'frame' the issues in question, identifying the focus that will mobilize maximum support, the simple idea whose time has come, in the case of Jubilee 2000's formulation of the debt issue. 'Framing' the issue was only the beginning, though. As the Global Campaign for Education also illustrated, short-term objectives need to be formulated as well as longer-term strategic aims, keeping up the momentum with imaginative tactics, 'repertoires of contention' that grab the enthusiasm of participants as well as the attention of the media. The case studies included in previous chapters provide examples that emphasize the importance of winning immediate gains, in the here and now, as well as developing strategies for the longer term.

The case studies, in addition, provide evidence of the importance of moving beyond traditional dichotomies between 'top-down' versus 'bottom-up'. Rather than seeing these as being in conflict, there were examples where these approaches had been mutually reinforcing. Grass-roots memberships can and do put pressure on their leaderships, just as leaderships can put forward the arguments to win support for progressive policies. Lobbyists' hands can be strengthened as a result of the publicity attached to mass demonstrations, just as grass-roots organizing can be strengthened by being resourced from the top (as in the case of social movement organizing, in US trade union organizations). The key issue was not whether to lobby or to demonstrate, but whether the move-ment was strengthened – or incorporated – as a result of the tactic in question, in those particular circumstances.

Far from being in competition with each other, local organizations can be strengthened via involvement in wider social movements, just as international mobilizations also depend upon the strength of their local roots. And far from being irrelevant, in the twenty-first century, nation-states continue to represent key arenas of struggle, especially in countries that have votes in key international organizations, votes that could be used to support more progressive policies. As participants concluded, on the basis of their experiences of campaigning in the Jubilee 2000 Coalition, the North needed to be resourcing the South to do its own campaigning, while focusing on pressurizing Northern governments to challenge the neoliberal agendas that were still so predominant globally. This would contribute to the development of global movements firmly rooted in solidarity, North as well as South.

The battle of ideas continues

Meanwhile, the backlash has also been gathering momentum, inter-nationally. As Mowbray has argued, on the basis of his study of free-market advocacy groups, 'because of their very effectiveness advocacy

NGOs are now faced with a resurgent and serious challenge' (Mowbray forthcoming). In Australia, for example, the Institute of Public Affairs (IPA) has been targeting bodies such as Oxfam Community Aid Abroad and the Australian Council of Social Service as well as Amnesty and Greenpeace.

Similar mobilizations have been taking place in the USA. As Saskia Sassen has pointed out, there too 'the counterattack has begun' (Sassen 2003: 21). Global protests had been making a difference, she argued – which was precisely why 'the warlords will not simply leave it at that' (ibid.). Their responses have included targeting 'progressive' NGOs and their growing influence. The American Enterprise Institute, for example, described as an influential think tank closely associated with the Bush administration, has been liaising with the Australian IPA, sharing ideas about ways of limiting the growing influence of NGOs. John Fonte of the Hudson Institute has similarly been warning of these dangers of transnational progressivism, as promoted by human rights activists who pose grave threats, in his view, to American concepts of citizenship, patriotism, assimilation, and the meaning of democracy (Fonte 2002).

Mowbray traces the growth of this alarmist backlash to the increasing effectiveness of global campaigning. The success of the 'stop the MAI' campaign – to resist the OECD's promotion of neoliberal trade policies via the Multilateral Agreement on Investment – was a key factor, he argued, that 'palpably energized the antagonism of free-market advocacy groups' (Mowbray forthcoming). Mowbray quoted Henderson (a former chief economist in the OECD), who analysed the lessons of the demise of the MAI initiative as follows: the moral was that to protect 'new moves toward freer international trade and investment' there must be more proactive defence. 'Hence the ground has to be prepared better, politically as well as technically' than was the case with the ill-fated MAI (Henderson 1999, quoted in ibid.).

These free-market advocacy groups have been attacking NGOs concerned with civil or human rights, industrial and labour issues and the environment. The IPA, for example, has been campaigning that NGOs that receive public money 'must fully support government values and objectives. There is no place for dissent. To control these NGOs the IPA urges that governments adopt stringent provisions for credentialing or certification' (ibid.) to control their activities.

The international business press has reinforced these messages when carrying articles that caricature global advocacy organizations and groups. NGOs have been described, for example, as 'Luddites, extremist and leftover left; unaccountable interest groups that undermine the authority of elected officials; armchair radicals from the rich world who have no right to speak for the developing world poor' (*Financial Times*, 19 June 2000, quoted in ibid.). As citizen mobilizations to promote social and environmental responsibility and human rights have become increasingly effective then, they are increasingly being attacked through 'a hostile, negative, and often emotional, public campaign' (ibid.).

There would seem to be lessons here for global citizens concerned to promote agendas for human rights and social justice – as well as for those determined to undermine them. The battle of ideas is being waged by the protagonists of neoliberalism. Global citizens need to respond to these challenges.

Select bibliography

Abbott, D. (1997) 'Who Else Will Support Us? How Poor Women Organise the Unorganisable in India', *Community Development Journal*, Vol. 32, No. 2, July, pp. 199–209.

ActionAid (2000) *Civil Society Perspectives on Education for All: Broken Promises, New Hopes*: Report by ActionAid on behalf of the Collective Consultation of NGOs (London: ActionAid).

— (2002a) *Global Education Review* (London: ActionAid).

— (2002b) *Review of the Elimu Campaign* (London: ActionAid).

Alinsky, S. (1971) *Rules for Radicals* (New York: Vintage Books).

— (1989) *Reveille for Radicals* (New York: Vintage Books).

AMA (Association of Metropolitan Authorities) (1989) *Local Authorities and Community Development* (London: Association of Metropolitan Authorities).

Amin, S. (2001) 'Capitalism's Global Strategy', in F. Houtart and F. Polet (eds), *The Other Davos* (London: Zed Books), pp. 17–24.

Amnesty International (2002) *Amnesty International Handbook* (London: Amnesty International).

Anastacio, J., B. Gidley, L. Hart, M. Keith, M. Mayo and U. Kowarzik (2000) *Reflecting Realities: Participants' Perspectives on Integrated Communities and Sustainable Development* (Bristol: Policy Press).

Aronowitz, S. (1992) *The Politics of Identity: Class, Culture and Social Movements* (London: Routledge).

— (2002) 'Seeds of a Movement', in E. Yuen, G. Katsiaficas and D. Burton Rose (eds), *The Battle of Seattle* (New York: Soft Skull Press), pp. 195–200.

Ashwin, S. (2000) 'International Labour Solidarity After the Cold War', in R. Cohen and S. Rai (eds), *Global Social Movements* (London: Athlone), pp. 101–16.

Bauman, Z. (2001) 'Quality and Inequality', *Guardian Saturday Review*, 29 December.

Beck, U. (2000) *The Brave New World of Work* (Cambridge: Polity Press).

Berry, J., K. Portney and K. Thompson (1993) *The Rebirth of Urban Democracy* (Washington, DC: Brookings Institute).

Blackburn, R. (ed.) (1991) *After the Fall: The Failure of Communism and the Future of Socialism* (London: Verso).

Blair, T. (1998) *The Third Way: New Politics for the New Century* (London: Fabian Society).

Blumer, H. (1969) 'Collective Behaviour', in A. McClung-Lee (ed.), *Principles of Sociology* (New York: Barnes and Noble).

Bourdieu, P. (1977) 'Cultural Reproduction and Social Reproduction', in

J. Karabel and A. Halsey (eds), *Power and Ideology in Education* (Oxford: Oxford University Press), pp. 487–511.

Bourdieu, P. and J.-C. Passeron (1977) *Reproduction in Education, Society and Culture* (London: Sage).

Bransford, S. and J. Rocha (2002) *Cutting the Wire: The Story of the Landless Movement in Brazil* (London: Latin America Bureau).

Brecher, J., T. Costello and B. Smith (2000) *Globalization from Below: The Power of Solidarity* (Cambridge, MA: South End Press).

Bronfenbrenner, K. et al. (eds) (1998) *Organizing to Win* (Ithaca, NY: ILR Press).

Brookfield, S. (2001) 'Repositioning Ideology Critique in a Critical Theory of Adult Learning', *Adult Education Quarterly*, Vol. 52, No. 1, November, pp. 7–22.

Budge, I. (1996) *The New Challenge of Direct Democracy* (Cambridge: Polity Press).

Bunch, C., P. Antrobus, S. Frost and N. Reilly (2001) 'International Networking for Women's Human Rights', in M. Edwards and J. Gaventa (eds), *Global Citizen Action* (London: Earthscan), pp. 217–29.

Bunting, M. (2000) '2000 Deadline Brought Sense of Urgency', *Guardian*, 28 December, p. 15.

Burbach, R. (2001) *Globalization and Postmodern Politics* (London: Pluto).

Byrne, P. (1988) *The Campaign for Nuclear Disarmament* (London: Routledge).

Callahan, M. (2001) 'Zapatismo and the Politics of Solidarity', in E. Yuen, G. Katsiaficas and D. Burton Rose (eds), *The Battle of Seattle* (New York: Soft Skull Press), pp. 37–40.

Canal, E. (1997) 'New Social Movement Theory and Resource Mobilization Theory: The Need for Integration', in M. Kaufman and H. Alfonso (eds), *Community Power and Grass Roots Democracy* (London: Zed Books), pp. 189–221.

Cary, L. (ed.) (1970) *Community Development as a Process* (Columbia, MN: University of Minnesota Press).

Castells, M. (1996) *The Information Age*, Vol. I (Oxford: Blackwell).

— (1997a) *The Information Age*, Vol. II (Oxford: Blackwell).

— (1997b) *The Power of Identity* (Oxford: Blackwell).

— (1998) *The Information Age*, Vol. III (Oxford: Blackwell).

Chant, S. and M. Gutmann (2000) *Mainstreaming Men into Gender and Development* (Oxford: Oxfam).

— (2002) '"Men-streaming Gender"? Questions for Gender and Development Policy in the Twenty-first Century', *Progress in Development Studies*, Vol. 2, No. 4, pp. 269–82.

Chatfield, C. (1997) 'Intergovernmental and Nongovernmental Associations to 1945', in J. Smith, C. Chatfield and R. Pugnacco (eds), *Transnational Social Movements and Global Politics* (Syracuse, NY: Syracuse University Press), pp. 19–41.

Chossudovsky, M. (1998) *The Globalisation of Poverty* (London: Zed Books).

Cleaver, H. (1998) 'The Zapatistas and the Electronic Fabric of Struggle', in J. Holloway and E. Pelaez (eds), *Zapatista! Reinventing Revolution in Mexico* (London: Pluto), pp. 81–103.

Coben, D. (1998) *Radical Heroes* (New York and London: Garland Institute).

Cockburn, C. (2000) 'The Women's Movement: Boundary-crossing on Terrains of Conflict', in R. Cohen and S. Rai (eds), *Global Social Movements* (London: Athlone Press), pp. 46–61.

Cohen, N. (2003) 'Strange Bedfellows', *New Statesman*, 7 April, pp. 24–5.

Cohen, R. and P. Kennedy (2000) *Global Sociology* (Basingstoke: Palgrave).

Cohen, R. and S. Rai (2000) *Global Social Movements* (London: Athlone Press).

Coleman, J. (1988) *Foundations of Social Theory* (Cambridge, MA: Harvard University Press).

Collins, C., Z. Gariyo and T. Burdon (2001) 'Jubilee 2000: Citizen Action Across the North–South Divide', in M. Edwards and J. Gaventa (eds), *Global Citizen Action* (London: Earthscan), pp. 135–48.

Cooke, B. and U. Kothari (2001) 'The Case for Participation as Tyranny', in B. Cooke and U. Kothari (eds), *Participation: The New Tyranny?* (London: Zed Books), pp. 1–15.

Cornia, G., R. Jolly and F. Stewart (eds) (1987) *Adjustment with a Human Face* (Oxford: Clarendon Press).

Craig, G. and M. Mayo (1995) *Community Empowerment: A Reader in Participation and Development* (London: Zed Books).

Cronin, T. (1989) *Direct Democracy: The Politics of Initiative, Referendum and Recall* (Cambridge, MA: Harvard University Press).

Crossley, N (2002) *Making Sense of Social Movements* (Buckingham: Open University Press).

Crow, G. and G. Allen (1994) *Community Life* (London: Harvester Wheatsheaf).

Crowther, J., I. Martin and M. Shaw (eds) (1999) *Popular Education and Social Movements in Scotland Today* (Leicester: NIACE).

Dahl, R. (1989) *Democracy and Its Critics* (New Haven, CT: Yale University Press).

Dalton, R. (1994) *The Green Rainbow: Environmental Groups in Western Europe* (New Haven, CT: Yale University Press).

Davis, J. (2002) 'This is What Bureaucracy Looks Like', in E. Yuen, G. Katsiaficas and D. Burton Rose (eds), *The Battle of Seattle* (New York: Soft Skull Press), pp. 175–82.

Davis, M. (1993) *Comrade or Brother* (London: Pluto).

DAWN (1985) *Development Crisis and Alternative Visions: Third World Women's Perspective* (Delhi: DAWN).

— (1990) *Interregional Meeting and General Report* (Rio de Janeiro: DAWN).

— (2002) DAWNInforms <www.dawn.org.fj/publications/DAWNInforms>.

Deakin, N. (2001) *In Search of Civil Society* (Basingstoke: Palgrave).

Della Porta, D. and M. Diani (1999) *Social Movements* (Oxford: Blackwell).

Denny, C. and L. Elliott (2003) 'G8 Has "Failed to Deliver on Debt"', *Guardian*, 16 May, p. 20.

Dent, M. and B. Peters (1999) *The Crisis of Poverty and Debt in the Third World* (Aldershot: Ashgate).

Dickenson, D. (1997) 'Counting Women in: Globalization, Democratization and the Women's Movement', in A. McGrew (ed.), *The Transformation of Democracy* (Cambridge: Polity Press), pp. 97–120.

Drachkovitch, M. (ed.) (1966) *The Revolutionary Internationals, 1864–1943* (Oxford: Oxford University Press).

Edwards, M. (2001) 'Introduction', in M. Edwards and J. Gaventa (eds), *Global Citizen Action* (London: Earthscan), pp. 1–14.

Edwards, M. and J. Gaventa (2001) *Global Citizen Action* (London: Earthscan), pp. 1–14.

Edwards, R. (1997) *Changing Places? Flexibility, Lifelong Learning and a Learning Society* (London: Routledge).

Elimu (2000) *Elimu Update: Newsletter of the Elimu Campaign*, July <www.elimu. org>.

Elson, D. (2002) 'Gender Justice, Human Rights, and Neo-liberal Economic Policies', in M. Molyneux and S. Razavi (eds), *Gender Justice, Development and Human Rights* (Oxford: Oxford University Press), pp. 78–114.

Elster, J. (1998) *Deliberative Democracy* (Cambridge: Cambridge University Press).

Ennew, J. (1998) 'Preface', in V. Johnson, E. Ivan-Smith, G. Gordon, P. Pridmore and P. Scott (eds), *Stepping Forward: Children and Young People's Participation in the Development Process* (London: Intermediate Technology Publications), pp. xviii–xx.

Epstein, B. (2002) 'Not Your Parents' Protest', in E. Yuen, G. Katsiaficas and D. Burton Rose (eds), *The Battle of Seattle* (New York: Soft Skull Press), pp. 53–7.

Escobar, A. and S. Alvarez (1992) 'Introduction: Theory and Protest in Latin America Today', in A. Escobar and S. Alvarez (eds), *The Making of Social Movements in Latin America* (Boulder, CO: Westview Press).

Etzioni, A. (1993) *The Spirit of Community* (New York: Crown Inc).

Eyerman, R. and A. Jamison (1991) *Social Movements: A Cognitive Approach* (Cambridge: Polity).

Face-to-face (2000) *Notes from the Network on Community Exchange* (Bangkok: Asian Coalition for Housing Rights).

Falk, R. (1995) *On Humane Governance: Towards a New Global Politics* (Cambridge: Polity).

Featherstone, L. (2002) *Students Against Sweatshops* (London: Verso).

Fine, B. (2001) *Social Capital versus Social Theory* (London: Routledge).

Fine, B. and P. Rose (2001) 'Education and the Post-Washington Consensus', in B. Fine, C. Lapavitsas and J. Pincus (eds), *Development Policy in the Twenty-first Century* (London: Routledge), pp. 151–81.

Fletcher, B. and R. Hurd (1998) 'Beyond the Organizing Model: The Transformation Process in Local Unions', in K. Bronfenbrenner et al. (eds), *Organizing to Win* (Ithaca, NY: ILR Press), pp. 37–53.

Foley, G. (1999) *Learning in Social Action* (London: Zed Books).

Fonte, J. (2002) 'Ideological War within the West', *IPA Review*, Vol. 54, No. 2, June, pp. 24–5.

Foweraker, J. (1995) *Theorizing Social Movements* (London: Pluto).

Francis, P. (2001) 'Participatory Development at the World Bank: The Primacy of Process', in B. Cooke and U. Kothari (eds), *Participation: The New Tyranny?* (London: Zed Books), pp. 72–87.

Francisco, G. (n.d.) 'Sighting Paradoxes for Gender in the Social Movements' <www.dawn.org.fj/publications/DAWNInforms>.

Fraser, N. (1997) *Justice Interrupted* (London: Routledge).

Freire, F. (1972) *Pedagogy of the Oppressed* (Harmondsworth: Penguin Books).

— (1990) Conversation with Myles Horton, in B. Bell, J. Gaventa and J. Peters (eds), *We Make the Road by Walking* (Philadelphia, PA: Temple University Press).

— (1995) *Paulo Freire at the Institute* (London: Institute of Education).

Freire, P. and I. Schor (1987) *A Pedagogy for Liberation* (London: Macmillan).

Fukuyama, F. (1992) *The End of History: The Last Man* (London: Hamish Hamilton).

— (1995) *Trust: The Social Virtues and the Creation of Prosperity* (London: Hamish Hamilton).

Fung, A. and E. O. Wright (2003) 'Countervailing Power in Empowered Participatory Governance', in A. Fung and E. O. Wright (eds), *Deepening Democracy* (London: Verso), pp. 259–89.

Gamarnikow, E. and A. Green (1999) 'The Third Way and Social Capital: Education Action Zones and a New Agenda for Education, Parents and the Community?', *International Studies in the Sociology of Education*, Vol. 9, No. 1, pp. 3–22.

Ganguli, D. (2000) *History of the World Federation of Trade Unions* (New Delhi: World Federation of Trade Unions).

Gaventa, J. (2001) 'Global Citizen Action: Lessons and Challenges', in M. Edwards and J. Gaventa (eds), *Global Citizen Action* (London: Earthscan), pp. 275–87.

GCE (Global Campaign for Education) (2001) *Quality Public Education for All*, report of the World Conference on Education, New Delhi (Brussels: Global Campaign for Education) <www.campaignforeducation.org>.

Geldof, B. (2003) 'Return to Ethiopia', *Guardian*, 17 May, p. 21.

George, S. (2001) 'A Short History of Neoliberalism', in F. Houtart and F. Polet (eds), *The Other Davos* (London: Zed Books), pp. 7–16.

Giddens, A. (1990) *The Consequences of Modernity* (Cambridge: Polity Press).

— (1998) *The Third Way: The Renewal of Social Democracy* (Cambridge: Polity Press).

Gilroy, P. (1987) *There ain't No Black in the Union Jack* (London: Hutchinson).

Giugni, M., D. McAdam and C. Tilly (eds) (1998) *From Contention to Democracy* (Oxford: Rowman and Littlefield).

Gopal, A. and D. Archer (2002) 'ActionAid Global Education Review', *Education Action*, Issue 16, October (London: ActionAid).

Gorz, A. (1982) *Farewell to the Working Class* (London: Pluto).

Gramsci, A. (1968) *The Modern Prince and Other Writings* (New York: International Publishers).

Groundswell (2001) *Groundswell Newsletter*, Issue 13 (London: Groundswell).

— (n.d.) *Don't Agonise, Organise!* (London: Groundswell).

Gujit, I. and M. Shah (eds) (1998) *The Myth of Community: Gender Issues in Participatory Development* (London: Intermediate Technology).

Habermas, J. (1987) *The Theory of Communicative Action* (Cambridge: Polity Press).

Hall, S. (1990) 'Cultural Identity and Diaspora', in J. Rutherford (ed.), *Changing Identities* (London: Lawrence and Wishart), pp. 222–37.

— (2003) 'New Labour Has Picked Up Where Thatcherism Left Off', *Guardian*, 6 August, p. 20.

Hardt, M. and A. Negri (2000) *Empire* (London and Cambridge, MA: Harvard University Press).

Harvey, D. (1990) *The Condition of Postmodernity* (Oxford: Blackwell).

— (1998) 'What's Green and Makes the Environment Go Around?', in F. Jameson and M. Miyoshi (eds), *The Cultures of Globalization* (Durham, NC and London: Duke University Press).

Held, D. (1989) 'The Decline of the Nation State', in S. Hall and M. Jacques (eds), *New Times* (London: Lawrence and Wishart), pp. 191–204.

— (1995) 'Democracy and the International Order', in D. Held (ed.), *Cosmopolitan Democracy: An Agenda for a New World Order* (Cambridge: Polity Press).

Hellman, J. (2000) 'Virtual Chiapas: A Reply to Paulson', in L. Panitch and C. Leys (eds), *Socialist Register 2001* (London: Merlin), pp. 289–92.

Henderson, D. (1999) *The MAI Affair: A Story and Its Lessons* (Melbourne: Melbourne Business School).

Henderson, P. and H. Salmon (1995) *Community Organising: The UK Context* (London: Community Development Foundation).

Henderson, P. and D. Thomas (2002) *Skills in Neighbourhood Work* (London: Routledge).

Hensman, R. (2000) 'Organizing Against the Odds: Women in India's Informal Sector', in L. Panitch and C. Leys (eds), *Working Classes: Global Realities* (London: Merlin), pp. 249–57.

Herman, E. (1999) 'The Threat of Globalization', *New Politics*, No. 7, pp. 40–6.

Hirst, P. (1990) *Representative Democracy* (Cambridge: Polity Press).

Hirst, P. and G. Thompson (1996) *Globalization in Question: The International Economy and the Possibilities of Governance* (Cambridge: Polity Press).

HMSO (1997) *Eliminating World Poverty: A Challenge for the 21st Century* (London: HMSO).

Hobsbawn, E. (1994) *Age of Extremes: The Short Twentieth Century* (London: Michael Joseph).

Holloway, J. and E. Pelaez (eds) (1998) *Zapatista! Reinventing Revolution in Mexico* (London: Pluto) .

Holst, J. (2002) *Social Movements, Civil Society, and Radical Adult Education* (London: Bergin and Garvey).

Houtart, F. (2001) 'Preface: From Davos to Porto Allegre', in F. Houtart and F. Polet (eds), *The Other Davos* (London: Zed Books), pp. vi–viii.

Houtart, F. and F. Polet (eds) (2001) *The Other Davos* (London: Zed Books).

Hurley, P. (1991) *The Greenpeace Effect* (London: Macmillan).

Hyman, R. (1999) 'Five Alternative Scenarios for West European Unions', in R. Munck and P. Waterman (eds), *Labour Worldwide in the Era of Globalization* (Basingstoke: Macmillan), pp. 121–30.

ICFIU (1997) Sixteenth World Congress – 'The Global Market: Trade Unionism's Greatest Challenge' (Brussels: ICFIU, p. 4).

Jackson, C. (1998) 'Rescuing Gender from the Poverty Trap', in R. Pearson and C. Jackson (eds), *Feminist Visions of Development* (London: Routledge), pp. 39–64.

Jeffries, F. (2001) 'Zapatismo and the Intergalactic Age', in R. Burbach (ed.), *Globalization and Postmodern Politics* (London: Pluto), pp. 129–44.

Johnson, V., E. Ivan-Smith, G. Gordon, P. Pridmore and P. Scott (eds) (1998) *Stepping Forward: Children and Young People's Participation in the Development Process* (London: Intermediate Technology Publications).

Jordan, G. and W. Maloney (1997) *The Protest Business* (Manchester: Manchester University Press).

Jubilee 2000 Coalition (2000) *The World Will Never be the Same Again* (London: Jubilee 2000 Coalition).

Jubilee South <www.jubileesouth.org>.

Kabeer, N. (1999) 'Targeting Women or Transforming Institutions? Policy from NGO Anti-poverty Efforts', in D. Rowan-Campbell (ed.), *Development with Women* (Oxford: Oxfam), pp. 32–45.

Kandiyoti, D. (1999) 'Gender, Power and Contestation', in R. Pearson and C. Jackson (eds), *Feminist Visions of Development* (London: Routledge), pp. 131–51.

Kane, L. (2001) *Popular Education and Social Change in Latin America* (London: Latin America Bureau).

Kauffman, L. (2002) 'Who are Those Masked Anarchists?', in E. Yuen, G. Katsiaficas and D. Burton Rose (eds), *The Battle of Seattle* (New York: Soft Skull Press), pp. 125–9.

Keck, M. and K. Sikkink (1998) *Activists Beyond Borders* (Ithaca, NY: Cornell University Press).

Kessi, A. (2001) 'Millennium Round of the WTO Under Fire from Both the Left and the Right', in E. Yuen, G. Katsiaficas and D. Burton Rose (eds), *The Battle of Seattle* (New York: Soft Skull Press), pp. 203–7.

Khor, M. (2001) *Rethinking Globalization* (London: Zed Books).

Kingsnorth, P. (2003) *One No, Many Yeses* (London and New York: Free Press).

Klandermans, B. (1991) 'European and American Approaches', in D. Rucht (ed.), *Research on Social Movements* (Boulder, CO: Westview Press), pp. 17–44.

Klein, N. (2001) 'Farewell to the "End of History": Organization and Vision in

Anti-corporate Movements', in L. Panitch and C. Leys (eds), *Socialist Register 2002* (London: Merlin), pp. 1–14.

— (2002) 'The Vision Thing: Were the DC and Seattle Protests Unfocused, or are Critics Missing the Point?', in B. Shepard and R. Hayduk (eds), *From ACT Up to the WTO* (London: Verso), pp. 265–73.

Korten, D. (1995) *When Corporations Rule the World* (London: Earthscan).

Kozak, M. (1997) *Greenpeace* (London: Heinemann).

Krebbers, E. and M. Schoenmaker (2001) 'Seattle '99: Wedding Party of the Left and Right?', in E. Yuen, G. Katsiaficas and D. Burton Rose (eds), *The Battle of Seattle* (New York: Soft Skull Press), pp. 209–13.

Laclau, E. and C. Mouffe (1985) *Hegemony and Socialist Strategy: Towards a Radical Socialist Strategy* (London: Verso).

Learning for Social Change: Sharing Information and Experience (n.d.) (London: National Lotteries Charity Board).

McAdam, D. (1982) *Political Protest and the Development of Black Insurgency* (Chicago, IL: University of Chicago Press).

— (1988) *Freedom Summer* (Oxford: Oxford University Press).

McAdam, D., J. McCarthy and M. Zald (eds) (1996) *Comparative Perspectives on Social Movements* (Cambridge: Cambridge University Press).

McAdam, D., S. Tarrow and C. Tilly (2001) *Dynamics of Contention* (Cambridge: Cambridge University Press).

McCarthy, J. and M. Zald (1977) 'Resource Mobilization and Social Movements', *American Journal of Sociology*, Vol. 82, No. 6, pp. 1212–41.

McGrew, A. (ed.) (1997) *The Transformation of Democracy* (Cambridge: Polity Press).

Martin, I. (1999) 'Introductory Essay: Popular Education and Social Movements in Scotland Today', in J. Crowther et al. (eds), *Popular Education and Social Movements in Scotland Today* (Leicester: NACE), pp. 1–25.

Marx, K. and F. Engels (1985 [1967]) *The Communist Manifesto* (London: Penguin).

Mattausch, J. (1989) *A Commitment to Campaign A a Sociological Study of CND* (Manchester: Manchester University Press).

— (2000) 'The Peace Movement: Retrospects and Prospect', in R. Cohen and S. Rai (eds), *Global Social Movements* (London: Athlone), pp. 184–95.

Mayo, E. (1999) *Life and Death? The End of Jubilee 2000* (London: Jubilee 2000).

Mayo, M. (1994) *Communities and Caring: The Mixed Economy of Welfare* (London: Macmillan).

— (1997) *Imagining Tomorrow: Adult Education for Transformation* (Leicester: National Institute for Adult Continuing Education).

— (2000) *Cultures, Communities, Identities* (Basingstoke: Palgrave).

— (2002) 'Community Work', in R. Adams, L. Dominelli and M. Payne (eds), *Social Work* (Basingstoke: Palgrave).

Melucci, A. (1988) *Nomads of the Present* (London: Hutchinson).

Melucci, A. and T. Lyyra (1998) 'Collective Action, Change and Democracy', in M. Giugni, D. McAdam and C. Tilly (eds), *From Contention to Democracy* (Oxford: Rowan and Littlefield).

Michels, R. (1949) *Political Parties* (Glencoe, IL: Free Press).

Miliband, R. (1991) 'Reflections on the Crisis of Communist Regimes', in R. Blackburn (ed.), *After the Fall: The Failure of Communism and the Future of Socialism* (London: Verso), pp. 6–17.

Mkandawire, T. (2002) 'Preface', in M. Molyneux and R. Razavi (eds), *Gender Justice, Development and Rights* (Oxford: Oxford University Press).

Molyneux, M. and S. Razavi (eds) (2002) *Gender Justice, Development and Rights* (Oxford: Oxford University Press).

Momsen, J. (2002) 'Myth or Math: The Waxing and Waning of the Female-headed Household', *Progress in Development Studies*, Vol. 2, No. 2, pp. 145–51.

Morris, A. and C. McClurg Mueller (eds) (1992) *Frontiers in Social Movement Theory* (New Haven, CT: Yale University Press).

Morris, B. (1996) *Ecology and Anarchism* (Worcestershire: Images Publishing).

Moser, C. (1989) 'Community Participation in Urban Projects in the Third World', in D. Diamond, J. McLoughlin and B. Massam (eds), *Progress in Planning*, Vol. 32, Part 2.

— (1993) *Gender Planning and Development* (London: Routledge).

Mosse, D. (2001) '"People's Knowledge", Participation and Patronage: Operations and Representations in Rural Development', in B. Cooke and U. Kothari (eds), *Participation: The New Tyranny?* (London: Zed Books), pp. 16–35.

Mouffe C. (ed.) (1992) *Dimensions of Radical Democracy* (London: Verso).

— (2000) *The Democratic Paradox* (London: Verso).

Mowbray, N. (forthcoming) 'Combating NGOs: The Backlash Against Community Advocacy'.

Munck, R. (2000) 'Labour in the Global', in R. Cohen and S. Rai (eds), *Global Social Movements* (London: Athlone), pp. 83–100.

— (2002) *Globalisation and Labour* (London: Zed Books).

Munck, R. and P. Waterman (eds) (1999) *Labour Worldwide in the Era of Globalization* (London: Macmillan).

Murray, A. (1997) *Flashpoint: World War III* (London: Pluto).

Naughton, C. (2003) 'The Demo that Made History', *Campaign*, No. 5 (London: CND), p. 5.

Needleman, R. (1998) 'Building Relationships for the Long Haul: Unions and Community-based Groups Working Together to Organize Low-wage Workers', in K. Bronfenbrenner et al. (eds), *Organizing to Win* (Ithaca, NY: ILR Press), pp. 71–86.

Newton, K. (1999) 'Social and Political Trust in Established Democracies', in P. Norris (ed.), *Critical Citizens: Global Support for Democratic Government* (Oxford: Oxford University Press), pp. 167–87.

Nussbaum, M. (2002) 'Women's Capabilities and Social Justice', in M. Molyneux and S. Razavi (eds), *Gender Justice, Development and Rights* (Oxford: Oxford University Press), pp. 45–77.

O'Connor, J. (2001) 'On Populism and the Antiglobalist Movement', in E. Yuen, G. Katsiaficas and D. Burton Rose (eds), *The Battle of Seattle* (New York: Soft Skull Press), pp. 359–70.

Olin Wright, E. (1985) *Classes* (London: Verso).

Oxfam (1995) *A Case for Reform: Fifty Years of the IMF and World Bank* (Oxford: Oxfam).

Panitch, L. and C. Leys (eds) (2000) *Working Classes: Global Realities: Socialist Register 2001* (London: Merlin).

Passerin d'Entrèves, M. (1992) 'Hannah Arendt and the Idea of Citizenship', in C. Mouffe (ed.), *Dimensions of Radical Democracy* (London: Verso), pp. 145–68.

Patel, S., J. Bolnick and D. Mitlin (2001) 'Squatting on the Global Highway: Community Exchange for Global Transformation', in M. Edwards and J. Gaventa (eds) *Global Citizen Action* (London: Earthscan), pp. 231–45.

Patel, S. and D. Mitlin (2002) 'Sharing Experiences and Changing Lives', *Community Development Journal*, Vol. 37, No. 2, April, pp. 125–36.

Paterson, L. (1999) 'Social Movements and the Politics of Educational Change', in J. Crowther, I. Martin and M. Shaw (eds), *Popular Education and Social Movements in Scotland Today* (Leicester: NIACE), pp. 41–54.

Paulson, J. (2000) 'Peasant Struggles and International Solidarity: The Case of Chiapas', *Socialist Register 2001* (London: Merlin), pp. 275–88.

Pearson, R. (1998) '"Nimble Fingers" Revisited: Reflections on Women and Third World Industrialisation in the Late Twentieth Century', in R. Pearson and C. Jackson (eds), *Feminist Visions of Development* (London: Routledge), pp. 171–87.

Pearson, R. and C. Jackson (eds) (1998) *Feminist Visions of Development* (London: Routledge).

Piven, F. and R. Cloward (1982) *The New Class War* (New York: Pantheon).

— (1992) 'Normalizing Collective Protest', in A. Morris and C. McClurg Mueller (eds), *Frontiers in Social Movement Theory* (New Haven, CT: Yale University Press), pp. 301–25 .

Potter, D. et al. (eds) (1997) *Democratization* (Cambridge: Polity Press).

Power, J. (1981) *Against Oblivion* (London: Fontana).

Psacharopoulos, G. and M. Woodhall (1985) *Education for Development: An Analysis of Investment Choices* (Oxford: Oxford University Press).

Putnam, R. (1995) 'Bowling Alone: America's Declining Social Capital', *Journal of Democracy*, Vol. 6, No. 1, pp. 65-78.

— (1996) 'The Strange Disappearance of Civic America', *American Prospect*, Winter, No. 24, pp. 34–48.

Ramdin, R. (1987) *The Making of the Black Working Class in Britain* (Aldershot: Gower).

Robertson, R. (1992) *Globalization: Social Theory and Global Culture* (London: Sage).

Rowbotham, S. and S. Linkogle (eds) (2001) *Women Resist Globalization* (London: Zed Books).

Ruddock, J. (1987) *CND Scrapbook* (London: Macdonald Optima).

Sassen, S. (2003) 'New Lords of Africa', *Guardian*, 9 July, p. 21.

Sassoon Showstack, A. (1991) 'Civil Society', in T. Bottomore et al. (eds), *A Dictionary of Marxist Thought* (2nd edn) (Oxford: Blackwell), pp. 82–4.

Savage, L. (1998) 'Geographies of Organizing: Justice for Janitors in Los Angeles', in A. Herod (ed.), *Organizing the Landscape* (Minneapolis, MN: University of Minnesota Press).

Save the Children UK (2002) *Globalisation and Children's Rights: What Role for the Private Sector?* (London: Save the Children UK).

(SCCD) Standing Conference for Community Development (1992) *A Working Statement on Community Development* (Sheffield: Standing Conference for Community Development).

Scott, A. (1990) *Ideology and the New Social Movements* (London: Allen and Unwin).

Sen, A. (1993) 'Capability and Well-being', in M. Nussbaum and A. Sen (eds), *The Quality of Life* (Oxford: Clarendon Press), pp. 30–53.

Sen, G. (1997) 'Subordination and Sexual Control: A Comparative View of the Control of Women', in N. Visvanathan, N. Duggan, L. Nisonoff and N. Wiegersma (eds), *The Women, Gender and Development Reader* (London: Zed Books), pp. 142–9 .

Sen, G. and C. Grown (1987) *Development, Crises, and Alternative Visions* (New York: Monthly Review Press).

Shepard, B. and R. Hayduk (eds) (2002) *From Act Up to the WTO* (London: Verso).

Shore, C. (1990) *Italian Communism: An Anthropological Perspective* (London: Pluto).

Shukra, K. (1998) *The Changing Pattern of Black Politics in Britain* (London: Pluto).

Singh, K. (2001) 'Handing Over the Stick: The Global Spread of Participatory Approaches to Development', in M. Edwards and J. Gaventa (eds), *Global Citizen Action* (London: Earthscan), pp. 175–87.

Sirianni, C. and L. Friedland (2001) *Civic Innovation in America* (Berkeley, CA: University of California Press).

Sklair, L. (2002) *Globalization: Capitalism and Its Alternatives* (3rd edn) (Oxford: Oxford University Press).

Smith, J. (1997) 'Characteristics of the Modern Transnational Social Movement Sector', in J. Smith, C. Chatfield and R. Pagnucco (eds), *Transnational Social Movements and Global Politics* (Syracuse, NY: Syracuse University Press), pp. 42–58.

Smith, J., C. Chatfield and R. Pagnucco (eds) (1997) *Transnational Social Movements and Global Politics* (Syracuse, NJ: Syracuse University Press).

Stacey, M. (1969) 'The Myth of Community Studies', *British Journal of Sociology*, Vol. 20, No. 2, pp. 134–47.

Starr, A. (2000) *Naming the Enemy* (London: Zed Books).

Stienstra, D (2000) 'Making Global Connections Among Women', in R. Cohen and S. Rai (eds), *Global Social Movements* (London: Athlone), pp. 62–82.

Tarrow, S. (1990) 'The Phantom at the Opera: Political Protest and Social Movements of the 1960s and 1970s in Italy', in R. Dalton and M. Kuechler (eds), *Challenging the Political Order* (Cambridge: Polity Press), pp. 251–73.

Tawney, R. H. (1926) 'Adult Education in the History of the Nation', paper read at the Fifth Annual Conference of the British Institute of Adult Education.

Taylor, V. (2000) *Marketisation of Governance* (Cape Town: SADEP, University of Cape Town).

Thorpe, V. (1999) 'Global Unionism: The Challenge', in R. Munck and P. Waterman (eds), *Labour Worldwide in the Era of Globalization* (Basingstoke: Macmillan), pp. 218–28.

Tomasevski, K. (2003) *Education Denied* (London: Zed Books).

Touraine, A. (1974) *The Post Industrial Society* (London: Wildwood House).

— (1981) *The Voice and the Eye: An Analysis of Social Movements* (Cambridge: Cambridge University Press).

Turner, B. (1992) 'Outline of a Theory of Citizenship', in C. Mouffe (ed.), *Dimensions of Radical Democracy* (London: Verso), pp. 33–62.

Turning Point (2002) *Report: 10th International Study Visit to Brazil* (London: Turning Point).

Twelvetrees, A. (2002) *Community Work* (Basingstoke: Palgrave).

UNDP (1999) *Human Development Report* (New York: UNDP).

UNESCO (2001) *Reason for Hope: The Support of NGOs in Education for All* (Paris: UNESCO).

UNESCO (2002) *Education for All – Is the World on Track?* (Paris: UNESCO).

Visvanathan, N., L. Duggan, L. Nisonoff and N. Wiegersma (eds) (1997) *The Women, Gender and Development Reader* (London: Zed Books).

Voss, K. and S. Sherman (2000) 'Breaking the Iron Law of Oligarchy: Union Revitalization in the American Labor Movement', *American Journal of Sociology*, Vol. 106, No. 2, September, pp. 303–49.

VSO (Voluntary Service Overseas) (2002) *The Live Aid Legacy: The Developing World Through British Eyes* (London: VSO).

Walldanger, R. et al. (1998) 'Helots No More: A Case Study of the Justice for Janitors Campaign in Los Angeles', in K. Bronfenbrenner et al. (eds), *Organizing to Win* (Ithaca, NY: ILR Press), pp. 102–19.

Walters, S. (ed.) (1997) *Globalization, Adult Education and Training* (London: Zed Books).

Walzer, M. (1992) 'The Civil Society Argument', in C. Mouffe (ed.), *Dimensions of Radical Democracy* (London: Verso), pp. 89–107.

Waterman, P. (1999) 'A New Union Model for a New World Order', in R. Munck and P. Waterman (eds), *Labour Worldwide in the Era of Globalization* (London: Macmillan), pp. 247–64.

— (2002) 'Trade Union Internationalism in the Age of Seattle', in P. Waterman and J. Willis (eds), *Place, Space and the New Labour Internationalism: Beyond the Fragments?* (Oxford: Blackwell), pp. 8–32.

Watkins, K. (2000) *The Oxfam Education Report* (Oxford: Oxfam).

Weeks, W., L. Hoatson and J. Dixon (eds) (1993) *Community Practices in Australia* (New South Wales: Pearson Education Australia).

Wichterich, C. (2000) *The Globalized Woman* (London: Zed Books).

Wills, J. (2002) *Union Futures: Building Networked Trade Unionism in the UK* (London: Fabian Society).

Woodroffe, J. (2002) *GATS: A Disservice to the Poor* (London: World Development Movement).

World Bank (1996) *The World Bank's Partnership with Nongovernmental Organisations* (Washington, DC: World Bank) .

— (2002) *Entering the 21st Century: World Development Report 1999/2000* (Oxford: World Bank) <www.globalworkplace.org>.

Wright, E. O. (1985) *Classes* (London: Verso).

Young, B. (2001) 'Globalization and Gender: A European Perspective', in R. Kelly, J. Bayes, M. Hawkesworth and B. Young (eds) *Gender, Globalization and Democratization* (Oxford: Bowman and Littlefield), pp. 27–48.

Young, K. (1993) *Planning Development with Women* (London: Macmillan).

Youngman, F. (1986) *Adult Education and Socialist Pedagogy* (London: Croom Helm).

Yuen, E., G. Katsiaficas and D. Burton Rose (eds) (2001) *The Battle of Seattle* (New York: Soft Skull Press).

Index

communications technology, globalization of, 191

Communist Internationals, 79

Communist Manifesto *see* Marx, Karl, *Communist Manifesto*

community, contested concept, 100

community-based organizations (CBOs), 5, 8, 9

community development, 100–11

community festivals, 103

community participation, 5

community unionism, 84, 97

conditionality, 198; in debt relief, 177

Congress of Industrial Organizations (CIO), 79

conscientization, 109; concept of, 189

Convention on the Rights of the Child (1989), 153

Crossley, N., 60, 64, 77–8

cyberspace, control of, 120

Dahl, R., 40–1

Dalton, R., 70, 71

Davis, M., 76

debt: British Treasury addressed on issue of, 181; campaigning on, 198–9; relief of, 25, 177, 179 (mobilization for, 172–92)

Debt, AIDS and Trade in Africa (DATA) campaign, 198

debt crisis, effect of, on women, 141

Debt Crisis Network, 178, 182

deficit model of learning, 107

Della Porta, D., 53, 55–6, 97, 175

democracy, 5, 90, 96, 147; alternative approaches to, 40–5; deliberative, 43; direct, 42, 43 (in US, 41); in ancient Athens, 40–1; in context of globalization, 39; in Students against Sweatshops, 100; liberal, 35, 37, 51; participatory, 42–3; representative, 40, 41, 44; teledemocracy, 43

democratization, 34–52; different approaches to, 36; problematic nature of, 96

Dent, Martin, 182

Department for International Development (DfID), 125

Development Alternatives for Women for a New Era (DAWN), 9–10, 133, 139–45, 165, 201; *Marketisation of Governance*, 145–50, 151; particular contribution of, 150–2

Diani, M., 53, 55–6, 97, 175

direct action, 79

Direct Action Network, 27

disability movements, 61

division of labour, gendered, 85

doing is knowing, 123

Dorchester Hotel, recruiting drive, 83

dowry, issue of, 86

Drop the Debt campaign, 185

e-mail, 113, 116–17, 151

Earth First, 59

Earth Summit (1992), 66

ecological movement, 118

education: access to, 155; as a right, 159; fees for, 160 (abolition of, 172); global campaign for, 153–71; of girls, 157, 168; of women, 132; popular, 96, 108–9; primary, 159 (universal, 156); privatization of, 160; suffers the curse of consensus, 168, 171

Education for All, 171; barriers to, 167

Education International, 163, 164, 168, 169

educator, role of, 115

Elimu campaign, Zimbabwe, 161–2, 164, 166, 167, 201

empowerment, 5, 9, 93–112; of communities, 45–51

Engels, Friedrich, 95

environmental issues, 8, 65–72

environmental movements, 54, 55

European Social Forum, 196, 197

European Union (EU), 38

exchange visits, organizing of, 116

experiential learning, 97

Eyerman, R., 106–7

Face-to-Face, 124

faith-based groups, 194, 195, 199

female foeticide, 86

female-headed households, 134

feminism, 118, 174; and globalization,